Paul-Henri Mallet, Thomas Percy, E. D. Keaton

Northern Antiquities

A description of the manners, customs, religion and laws of the ancient Danes, and

other northern nations - Vol. 2

Paul-Henri Mallet, Thomas Percy, E. D. Keaton

Northern Antiquities
A description of the manners, customs, religion and laws of the ancient Danes, and other northern nations - Vol. 2

ISBN/EAN: 9783337103828

Printed in Europe, USA, Canada, Australia, Japan

Cover: Foto ©Lupo / pixelio.de

More available books at **www.hansebooks.com**

Northern Antiquities:
OR,
A DESCRIPTION
OF THE
Manners, Cuſtoms, Religion and Laws
OF THE
ANCIENT DANES,
And other Northern Nations;
Including thoſe of
Our own SAXON ANCESTORS.
WITH
A Tranſlation of the EDDA, or
Syſtem of RUNIC MYTHOLOGY,
AND
OTHER PIECES,
From the Ancient ISLANDIC Tongue.
In TWO VOLUMES.

TRANSLATED
From Monſ. MALLET's *Introduction a l' Hiſtoire de Dannemarc*, &c.

With Additional NOTES
By the Engliſh Tranſlator,
AND
Goranſon's Latin Verſion of the EDDA.

VOLUME II.

LONDON:
Printed for T. CARNAN and Co. at No. 65. in St. Paul's Church-yard.   MDCCLXX.

CONTENTS OF VOLUME II.

The Author's Introduction.   Page i

THE EDDA, or ANCIENT ICELANDIC (OR RUNIC) MYTHOLOGY.   p. 1

VIZ.

The Vision of Gylfe: and Illusions of Har.   p. 1

1 FABLE. *Questions of Gangler.*   p. 7

2 FAB. *Of the Burning of the World, and of Surtur.*   p. 13

3 FAB. *Of the Cow Œdumla.*   p. 18

4 FAB. *How the sons of Bore made Heaven and Earth.*   p. 22

5 FAB. *Of the formation of Aske and Emla.*   p. 28

6 FAB. *Of the Giant Nor.*   p. 33

7 FAB. *Of the Way that leads to Heaven.*   p. 40

8 FAB.

CONTENTS.

8 FAB. Of the Holy City, or Residence of the Gods. p. 49

9 FAB. Of the Cities which are in Heaven. p. 57

10 FAB. Of the Gods to be believed in. p. 61

11 FAB. Of the God Thor, the son of Odin. p. 65

12 FAB. Of the God Balder. p. 70

13 FAB. Of the God Frey, and the Goddess Freya. p. 76

14 FAB. Of the God Tyr. p. 79

15 FAB. Of Heimdall, and some other Gods. p. 82

16 FAB. Of Loke. p. 85

17 FAB. Of the Wolf Fenris. p. 90

18 FAB. Of the Goddesses. p. 96

19 FAB. Of Frey and Girde. p. 102

20 FAB. Of the Food of the Gods. p. 105

21 FAB. Of the Horse Sleipner, and his origin. p. 112

22 FAB. Of the Ship of the Gods. p. 116

23 FAB. Of the God Thor. p. 117

24 FAB. Of Thialfe's art. p. 125

25 FAB. Of the Trials that Thor underwent. p. 126

26 FAB. The Illusions accounted for. p. 129

27 FAB.

CONTENTS.

27 FAB. *Of the voyage undertaken by Thor, to go to fish for the Great Serpent.* p. 134

28 FAB. *Of Balder the Good.* p. 138

29 FAB. *Hermode's journey to Hell.* p. 149

30 FAB. *The flight of Loke.* p. 154

31 FAB. *The punishment of Loke.* p. 157

32 FAB. *Of the Twilight of the Gods.* p. 159

33 FAB. *The sequel of the Conflagration of the world.* p. 164

AN IDEA *of the* SECOND PART *of the* EDDA. p. 183

AN IDEA OF THE MORE ANCIENT EDDA, Viz. *Of the Voluspa.* p. 201

Of the Havamaal, or Sublime Discourse of Odin. p. 205

Of the Runic Chapter, or Magic of Odin. p. 216

ODES *and other* ANCIENT POEMS. p. 225

Extracts from the Ode of king Regner Lodbrog. p. 228

The Ode of Harald the Valiant. p. 236, 237

The

CONTENTS.

The Elogium of Hacon. p. 239, 240

The History of Charles and Grymer, Swedish kings; and of Hialmer, the son of Harec, king of Biarmland, p. 245, 248

SUPPLEMENT. p. 269

Hyperboreorum Atlantiorum, seu Suiogotorum et Nordmannorum EDDA, *&c. Opera et studio* JOHANNIS GORANSON. p. 275

THE AUTHOR'S INTRODUCTION
TO VOLUME THE SECOND.

I KNOW not, whether among the multitude of interesting objects which history offers to our reflection, there are any more worthy to engage our thoughts, than t e different Religions which have appeared with splendour in the world.

It is on this stage, if I may be allowed the expression, that men are represented, as they really are; that their characters are distinctly marked and truly exhibited. Here they display all the foibles, the passions and wants of the heart; the resources, the powers and the imperfections of the mind.

It is only by studying the different Religions that we become sensible how far our natures are capable of being debased by prejudices, or elevated, even above themselves, by sound and solid principles. If the

the human heart is a profound abyſs, the Religions that have prevailed in the world have brought to light its moſt hidden ſecrets: They alone have imprinted on the heart all the forms it is capable of receiving. They triumph over every thing that has been deemed moſt eſſential to our nature. In ſhort it has been owing to them that man has been either a Brute or an Angel.

This is not all the advantage of this ſtudy: Without it our knowledge of mankind muſt be extremely ſuperficial. Who knows not the influence which Religion has on manners and laws? Intimately blended, as it were, with the original formation of different nations, it directs and governs all their thoughts and actions. In one place we ſee it enforcing and ſupporting deſpotiſm; in another reſtraining it: It has conſtituted the very ſoul and ſpirit of more than one republic. Conquerors have frequently been unable to depreſs it, 'even' by force; and it is generally either the ſoul to animate or the arm to execute the operations of politics.

Religion acts by ſuch preſſing motives, and ſpeaks ſo ſtrongly to mens moſt important and deareſt intereſts, that where it happens not to be analagous to the national character of the people who have adopted it;

it; it will soon give them a character analogous to its own: One of these two forces must unavoidably triumph over the other, and become both of them blended and combined together; as two rivers when united, form a common stream, which rapidly bears down all opposition.

But in this multitude of Religions, all are not equally worthy of our research. There are, among some barbarous nations, Creeds without ideas, and practices without any object; these have at first been dictated by fear, and afterward continued by mere mechanical habit. A single glance of the eye thrown upon such Religions as these, is sufficient to show us all their relations and dependencies.

The thinking part of mankind, must have objects more relative to themselves; they will never put themselves in the place of a Samoiede or an Algonquin: Nor bestow much attention upon the wild and unmeaning superstitions of barbarians, so little known and unconnected with themselves. But as for these parts of the world, which we ourselves inhabit, or have under our own immediate view; to know something of the Religions which once prevailed here and influenced the fate of these countries, cannot surely be deemed uninteresting or unimportant.

Two* principal Religions for many ages divided between them all these countries, which are now blessed with Christianity: Can we comprehend the obligations we owe to the Christian Religion, if we are ignorant from what principles and from what opinions it has delivered us?

I well know that men find employment enough in describing one of these two systems; viz. that of the Greeks and Romans. How many books on their ancient mythology hath not that Religion occasioned? There have been volumes written upon the little petty Divinities adored only in one single village; or accidentally named by some ancient author: The most trivial circumstances, the most inconsiderable monuments of the worship prescribed by that

---

* Our Author says Two Religions, meaning, 1. The Polytheism of Greece and Rome, and, 2. The Druidical Religion of the Celts: which last he erroneously supposes to be the same with the Polytheism of the Scandinavians of Gothic Race. The truth is, the ancient Pagan Religions of Europe may be classed more properly thus. 1. The Polytheism of Greece and Rome, &c. 2. The Druidical Religion of the Celtic nations. 3. The Polytheism of the Teutonic and Gothic nations. 4. The Pagan Religion of the Sclavonian nations. And, 5. The low wretched Superstitions of the more northern savages, viz. The Laplanders, Fins, Greenlanders, &c. T.

Religion have occasioned whole folios: And yet we may perhaps, with reason assert, that a work which should endeavour to unfold the spirit, and mark the influence of that Religion in a moral and political view, is yet wanted.

Nevertheless that Religion only extended itself in Europe over Greece and Italy. How indeed could it take root among the conquered nations, who hated the Gods of Rome both as foreign Deities, and as the Gods of their masters? That Religion then so well known among us, that even our children study its principal tenets, was confined within very narrow bounds, while the major part of Gaul, of Britain, Germany and Scandinavia *uniformly* cultivated another very different, from time immemorial.

The Europeans may reasonably call this CELTIC * worship, the Religion of their fathers;

---

* " It little imports that the learned stile this Religion in France, the GAULISH; in England, the BRITISH; in Germany, the GERMANIC, &c. It is now allowed to have been the same, at least with respect to the fundamental doctrines, in all these countries: As I here all along consider it in a general light, I use the word CELTIC as the most universal term, without entering into the disputes to which this word hath given rise, and which proceed,

fathers; Italy itself having received into her bosom more than one conquering nation who professed it. This is the Religion

"proceed, in my opinion, from men's not understanding one another."

[Thus far our ingenious Author, who having been led by Pelloutier and Keysler into that fundamental error (which has been the stumbling-block of modern antiquaries) viz. That the CELTS and GOTHS were the same people, supposes that the Druidical system of the CELTIC nations, was uniformly the same with the Polytheism of the nations of GOTHIC Race: Than which there cannot be a greater mistake in itself, nor a greater source of confusion in all our researches into the antiquities of the European nations. The first inhabitants of Gaul and Britain, being of CELTIC Race, followed the Druidical superstitions. The ancient Germans, Scandinavians, &c. being of GOTHIC Race, professed that system of Polytheism, afterwards delivered in the EDDA: And the Franks and Saxons, who afterwards settled in Gaul and Britain, being of GOTHIC Race, introduced the Polytheism of their own nation, which was in general the same with what prevailed among all the other GOTHIC or TEUTONIC people, viz. the Germans, Scandinavians, &c.

After all it is to be observed, in favour of our Author's general course of reasoning, that in Gaul and Britain, and in many other countries, innumerable reliques both of the CELTIC and GOTHIC superstitions, are still discernable among the common people; as the present inhabitants of those countries derive their descent equally from the GOTHS and CELTS, who at different times were masters of these kingdoms, and whose descendants are now so blended and mingled together.] T.

which

which they would probably ſtill have cultivated had they been left for ever to themſelves, and continued plunged in their original darkneſs : This is the Religion, which (if I may be allowed to ſay ſo) our climate, our conſtitutions, our very wants are adapted to and inſpire : For who can deny, but that in the falſe religions, there are a thouſand things relative to theſe different objects ? It is, in ſhort, this Religion, of which Chriſtianity (though after a long conflict, it triumphed over it) could never totally eradicate the veſtiges.

We may reaſonably inquire how it comes to paſs that the Paganiſm of Greece and Rome ingroſſes all our attention, while there are ſo few, even among the learned, who have any notion of the Religion I am ſpeaking of ? Hath this preference been owing to any natural ſuperiority either in the precepts or worſhip of theſe learned nations ? Or do they afford ſubjects for more ſatisfactory reſearches than thoſe of the northern nations ? What indeed are they, after all, but a chaos of indiſtinct and confuſed opinions, and of cuſtoms indiſcriminately borrowed and picked up from all other religions, void of all connection and coherence ; and where, amidſt eternal contradictions and obſcurities, one has ſome difficulty to trace out a few bright rays of

reaſon

reason and genius ? What was this Religion, but a rude and indigested system, wholly composed of superstitious ceremonies, directed by blind fear, without any fixed principles, without a single view for the good of humanity, without rational consolations, which, although in some circumstances it might arrest the hand, wholly abandoned the heart to all its weaknesses ? Who can be afraid of finding among the most savage nations ideas of Religion more disgraceful to human nature, than these ?

But perhaps the Grecian Mythology may have been studied, in order to discover the origin of many customs still existing in Europe ! It cannot indeed be denied, but that it is often necessary to recur thither, in order to explain some peculiarities of our manners, of which it is easier to discover the cause, than to ascertain the reason.

But doth not a knowledge of the Religions professed by the ancient Celtic ' and ' Gothic' nations lead to discoveries of the same kind, and perhaps to others still more interesting ? One generation imitates the preceding; the sons inherit their fathers sentiments, and whatever change time may effect, the manners of a nation always retain traces of the opinions professed by its first founders. Most of the present nations of Europe derive their origin ' either' from

the

the Celts ' or Goths,' and the sequel of this work will show, perhaps, that their opinions, however obsolete, still subsist in the effects which they have produced. May not we esteem of this kind (for example) that love and admiration for the profession of arms, which was carried among us even to fanaticism, and which for many ages incited the Europeans, mad by system and fierce through a point of honour, to fight, with no other view, but merely for the sake of fighting? May not we refer to this source, that remarkable attention and respect which the nations of Europe have paid to the fair sex, by which they have been so long the arbiters of glorious actions, the aim and the reward of great exploits, and that they yet enjoy a thousand advantages which every where else are reserved for the men? Can we not explain from these Celtic ' and Gothic' Religions, how, to the astonishment of posterity, judiciary combats and ordeal proofs were admitted by the legislature of all Europe; and how, even to the present time, the people are still infatuated with a belief of the power of Magicians, Witches, Spirits, and Genii, concealed under the earth or in the waters, &c.?

In fine, do we not discover in these religious opinions, that source of the marvellous

lous with which our anceſtors filled their Romances, a ſyſtem of wonders unknown to the ancient Claſſics, and but little inveſtigated even to this day; wherein we ſee Dwarfs and Giants, Fairies and Demons acting and directing all the machinery with the moſt regular conformity to certain characters which they always ſuſtain.

What reaſon then can be aſſigned, why the ſtudy of ' theſe ancient Celtic and Gothic ' Religions' hath been ſo much neglected? One may, I fancy, be immediately found in the idea conceived of the Celts ' and ' Goths' in general, and eſpecially of the Germans and Scandinavians. They are indiſcriminately mentioned under the title of Barbarians, and this word, once ſpoken, is believed to include the whole that can be ſaid on the ſubject. There cannot be a more commodious method of diſpenſing with a ſtudy, which is not only conſidered as not very agreeable, but alſo as affording but little ſatisfaction. Were this term to be admitted in its ſtricteſt ſenſe, it ſhould not even then excuſe our intire diſregard of a people, whoſe exploits and inſtitutions make ſo conſiderable a figure in our hiſtory. But ought they, after all, to be repreſented as a troop of ſavages, barely of a human form, ravaging and deſtroying by mere brutal inſtinct, and totally devoid of all notions of

religion,

religion, policy, virtue and decorum? Is this the idea Tacitus gives us of them, who, though born and educated in ancient Rome, professed that in many things ancient Germany was the object of his admiration and envy. I will not deny but that they were very far from possessing that politeness, knowledge and taste which excite us to search with an earnestness almost childish, amid the wrecks, of what by way of excellence, we call ANTIQUITY; but allowing this its full value, must we carry it so high, as to refuse to bestow the least attention on another kind of Antiquities; which may, if you please, be called Barbarous, but to which our manners, laws and governments perpetually refer?

The study of the antient Celtic ' and ' Gothic' Religions hath not only appeared devoid of blossoms and of fruits; it hath been supposed to be replete with difficulties of every kind. The Celtic Religion, it is well known, forbad its followers to divulge its mysteries in writing *, and this prohibition, dictated either by ignorance or by idleness, has but too well taken effect. The glimmering rays faintly scattered among

---

* So Cæsar relates of the British Druids, " Neque fas esse existimant ea " (Carmina sc.il.) Litteris " mandare."——De Bell. Gall. lib. 6. 13.

the

the writings of the Greeks and Romans, have been believed to be the sole guides in this enquiry, and from thence naturally arose a distaste towards it. Indeed, to say nothing of the difficulty of uniting, correcting and reconciling the different passages of ancient authors, it is well known that mankind are in no instance so little inclined to do justice to one another, as in what regards any difference of Religion. And what satisfaction can a lover of truth find in a course of reading wherein ignorance and partiality appear in every line? Readers who require solid information and exact ideas, will meet with little satisfaction from these Greek and Roman authors, however celebrated. Divers circumstances may create an allowed prejudice against them. We find that those nations who pique themselves most on their knowledge and politeness, are generally those, who entertain the falsest and most injurious notions of foreigners. Dazzled with their own splendor, and totally taken up with self-contemplation, they easily persuade themselves, that they are the only source of every thing good and great. To this we may attribute that habit of referring every thing to their own manners and customs which anciently characterized the Greeks and Romans, and caused them to find

find MERCURY, MARS and PLUTO, their own Deities and their own doctrines, among a people who frequently had never heard them mentioned.

But even if there were no cause to distrust the contemptuous and hasty relations, which the ancients have left us of their barbarous neighbours; and even if the little they have told us were exact, do their writings after all contain wherewith to interest us on the subject of the Celtic ' or Gothic' doctrines? Can a few words describing the exterior worship of a religion teach us its spirit? Will they discover the chain, often concealed, which unites and connects all its different tenets, precepts and forms? Can they convey to us an idea of the sentiments which such a religion implanted in the soul, or of the powerful ascendancy which it gained over the minds of its votaries. We can assuredly learn nothing of all this in Cæsar, Strabo or Tacitus, and how then can they interest or engage such readers, as only esteem in learning and erudition, what enlightens the mind with real knowledge?

It is only from the mouths of its own professors that we can acquire a just knowledge of any Religion. All other interpreters are here unfaithful; sometimes condemning and aspersing what they explain;

and

and often venturing to explain what they do not underftand. They may, it is true, give a clear account of fome fimple dogmas; but a religion is chiefly characterized and diftinguifhed by the fentiments it infpires; and can thefe fentiments be truly reprefented by a third perfon, who has never felt the force of them?

In order then to draw from their prefent obfcurity the ancient Celtic ' and Gothic' Religions, which are now as unknown, as they were formerly extenfively received, we muft endeavour (if we can) to raife up before us thofe ancient Poets who were the Theologues of our forefathers: We muft confult them in perfon, and hear them (as it were) in the coverts of their dark umbrageous forefts, chant forth thofe facred and myfterious hymns, in which they comprehended the whole fyftem of their Religion and Morality. Nothing of moment would then evade our fearch; fuch informations as thefe would diffufe real light over the mind: The warmth, the ftile and tone of their difcourfes, in fhort, every thing would then concur to explain their meaning, to put us in the place of the authors themfelves, and to make us enter into their own fentiments and notions.

But why do we form vain and idle wifhes? Inftead of meeting with thofe poems

poems themselves, we only find lamentations for their loss. Of all those verses of the ancient Druids, which their youths frequently employed twenty years to learn *, we cannot now recover a single fragment, or the slightest relique. The devastations of time, and a false zeal, have been equally fatal to them in Spain, France, Germany and England. This is granted, but should we not then rather look for their monuments in countries, later converted to Christianity? If the poems, of which we speak, have been ever committed to writing, shall we not more probably find them preserved in the north, than where they must have struggled for five or six centuries more against the attacks of time and superstition? This is no conjecture; it is what has really happened. We actually possess some of these Odes †, which

are

---

* Cæsar, mentioning the British Druids, says, " *Magnum ibi numerum verſuum ediſcere dicuntur; itaque nonnulli annos vicenos in diſciplinâ permanent.*" De Bell. Gall. 6. 13.

† Here again our author falls into the unfortunate mistake of confounding the CELTIC and GOTHIC Antiquities. The CELTIC Odes of the Druids are for ever lost; but we happily possess the RUNIC Songs of the Gothic Scalds: These however have nothing in common with the Druid Odes, nor contribute to throw the least

are so much regretted, and a very large work extracted from a multitude of others. This extract was compiled many centuries ago by an author well known, and who was near the fountain head; it is written in a language not unintelligible, and is preserved in a great number of manuscripts which carry incontestible characters of antiquity. This extract is the book called the EDDA; the only monument of its kind; singular in its contents, and so adapted to throw light on the history of our ancient opinions and manners, that it is amazing it should remain so long unknown beyond the confines of Scandinavia.

To confess the truth, this work is not devoid of much difficulty; but the obscurity of it is not absolutely impenetrable, and when examined by a proper degree of critical study, assisted by a due knowledge of the opinions and manners of the other 'Gothic *' nations, will receive so much light, as that nothing very material will escape our notice. The most requisite preparative for the well understanding this

least light on the Druidical Religion of the Celtic nations: But then they are full as valuable, for they unfold the whole Pagan system of our Gothic ancestors; in the discovery of which we are no less interested, than in that of the other. T.

* *Celtiques.* Fr.

work,

work, but which hath not always been observed, is to enter as much as possible into the views of its Author, and to transport ourselves, as it were, into the midst of the people for whom it was written.

It may be easily conceived, that the EDDA first written in Iceland, but a short time after the Pagan Religion was abolished there, must have had a different use from that of making known doctrines, then scarcely forgotten. I believe, that on an attentive perusal of this work, its true purpose cannot be mistaken. The EDDA then was neither more nor less than a Course of Poetical Lectures, drawn up for the use of such young Icelanders as devoted themselves to the profession of *Scald* or POET. In this art, as in others, they who had first distinguished themselves, in proportion as they became ancients, acquired the right to be imitated scrupulously by those who came after them, and sometimes even in things the most arbitrary. The inhabitants of the north, accustomed to see ODIN and FRIGGA, GENII and FAIRIES make a figure in their ancient poetry, expected still to find their names retained in succeeding Poems, to see them act, and to hear them speak agreeably to the ideas they had once formed of their characters and functions. From the same custom it arises, that in our Colleges

leges, such as write Latin poetry cannot to this day rob their verses of the ornamental assistance of ancient Fable: But at the expence of reason, taste, and even Religion, we see sacred and profane Mythology jumbled together; and false Gods and Angels, Nymphs and Apostles in friendly converse. If our Icelanders have not given into these abuses, they at least, for a long time, composed their poetry in the old taste, and I am even assured that, at this day, the verses that are composed in Iceland often preserve strong traces of it. A knowledge of the 'ancient Runic *' Mythology continuing thus necessary for the purposes of poetry, it would easily occur to a lover of that art, to compile a kind of Dictionary of the Figurative Expressions employed by the ancient SCALDS; with which the succeeding Bards were as fond of embellishing their works as our modern Latin Poets are of patching theirs with the shreds of Horace and Virgil. This dictionary could only become useful, by subjoining to the figurative expression, the Fable which gave rise to the figure. Thus, when they read in the dictionary, that the Earth was poetically stiled " the Body of the Giant " YMER;" the Last Day, " the Twilight of " the Gods;" Poetry, " the Beverage of " ODIN,"

* *Celtique.* Orig.

"ODIN," the Giants, " the Sons of the " Froſt," &c. they would naturally wiſh to know the origin of ſuch ſingular modes of ſpeech. It was then to render this knowledge eaſy, that the Author of the EDDA wrote; nor am I ſurprized, that this book hath appeared whimſical and unintelligible to thoſe who were ignorant of its deſign.

Hence likewiſe we learn why this work came to be divided into Two principal parts. The FIRST conſiſts of this brief Syſtem of Mythology, neceſſary for underſtanding the ancient Scalds, and for perceiving the force of the Figures, Epithets and Alluſions with which their poetry abounds. This is properly called the EDDA. The SECOND is a kind of Art of Poetry, which contains a Catalogue of the Words moſt commonly uſed by the Poets, together with Explanations and Remarks; it contains alſo a treatiſe on the ancient Language, and Orthography; and an explication of the Structure and Meaſure of their different ſorts of Verſe. Hence it is, that this part is called SCALDA or POETICS. It is very extenſive, and leads one to ſuppoſe that this people had among them a vaſt number of Bards, and that the Author poſſeſſed an uncommon depth of erudition on theſe ſubjects. The Reader will doubtleſs be ſurprized to find ſo compleat a Treatiſe of Poetry, amid the few monuments now remaining of ancient Scandinavia: Especially among thofe Goths and Normans, who contributed fo much to replunge Europe into ignorance, and whom many nations have had fo much reafon to accufe of ferocity and barbarifm. Could one have expected to find among fuch a people, fo decifive a tafte for an Art which feems peculiarly to require fenfibility of foul, a cultivation of mind, and a vivacity and fplendor of imagination? for an Art, I fay, which one would rather fuppofe muft be one of the laft refinements of luxury and politenefs.

I trufted we fhould find the caufes of this their love of poetry, in the ruling paffion of the ancient Scandinavians ' for war,' in the little ufe they made of writing, and efpecially in their peculiar fyftem of Religion. What was at firft only conjecture, a later refearch hath enabled me to difcover to have been the real cafe: And I flatter myfelf that the perufal of the EDDA will remove every doubt which may at firft have been entertained from the novelty and fingularity of the facts which I advanced.

IT now remains for me to relate in a few words the hiftory of this Book, and to give a fhort account of my own labours. I have already hinted that there have been two
EDDA'S.

EDDAS. The firft and moft ancient was compiled by SOEMUND SIGFUSSON, firnamed the LEARNED, born in Iceland about the year 1057. This Author had ftudied in Germany, and chiefly at Cologne, along with his countryman ARE, firnamed alfo FRODE, or the LEARNED; and who likewife diftinguifhed himfelf by his love for the Belle-Lettres *. Sœmund was one of the firft who ventured to commit to writing the ancient religious Poetry, which many people ftill retained by heart. He feems to have confined himfelf to the meer felecting into one body fuch of the ancient Poems as appeared moft proper to furnifh a fufficient number of poetical figures and phrafes. It is not determined whether this collection (which, it fhould feem, was very confiderable) is at prefent extant, or not: But without engaging in this difpute, it fuffices to fay, that Three of the Pieces of which it was compofed, and perhaps thofe three of the moft important, have come down to us. We fhall give a more particular account of thefe in the body of this work.

* *V. Arii Frode fchedæ, feu libellus de Iflandiâ, edita ab And. Buffæo. Havn. 1733. in Præfat.* This ARE FRODE is the oldeft of all the northern hiftorians whofe works have come down to us. He wrote many Hiftories which are loft; that which remains is on the eftablifhment of the Norwegians in Iceland.

The firſt collection being apparently too voluminous, and in many reſpects obſcure, and not ſufficiently adapted to common uſe, the young poets would naturally wiſh that ſome body would extract from the materials there collected, a courſe of Poetic Mythology, more eaſy and intelligible. Accordingly, about 120 years afterwards, another learned Icelander engaged in this taſk: This was the famous SNORRO STURLESON, born in the year 1179, of one of the moſt illuſtrious families in his country, where he twice held the dignity of firſt magiſtrate, having been the ſupreme judge of Iceland in the years 1215 and 1222. He was alſo employed in many important negotiations with the King of Norway, who inceſſantly ſtrove to ſubdue that iſland, as being the refuge of their malcontent ſubjects. SNORRO, whoſe genius was not merely confined to letters, met at laſt with a very violent end. He was aſſaſſinated in the night that he entered into his 62d year, anno 1241 [*],

by

---

[*] Vid. *Peringſkiold* in Præfat. ad *Hiemſkringla Saga*, &c. Since I firſt wrote this, it hath been obſerved to me, that the ſecond part of the EDDA mentions the Kings of Norway who have lived down to the year 1270, and conſequently who outlived SNORRO near thirty years; whence it is inferred, that this muſt have been the work of a later hand. Neverthelefs, as tradition and univerſal opinion

by a faction of which he was the avowed enemy. We owe all that is rational, certain and connected in the ancient hiſtory of theſe vaſt countries, to his writings, and eſpecially to his " Chronology of the Nor-" thern Kings." There runs through this whole work ſo much clearneſs and order, ſuch a ſimplicity of ſtile, ſuch an air of truth, and ſo much good ſenſe, as ought to rank its author among the beſt hiſtorians of that age of ignorance and bad taſte. He was alſo a poet, and his verſes were often the entertainment of the courts to which he was ſent. It was doubtleſs a love for this art which ſuggeſted to him the deſign of giving a new EDDA, more uſeful to the young poets than that of Sœmund. His deſign therefore was to ſelect whatever was moſt important in the old Mythology, and to compile a ſhort Syſtem, wherein ſhould, notwithſtanding, be found, all the Fables

opinion attribute it to Snorro, it may be ſufficient to ſay that ſome writer who lived a few years later than that celebrated ſage, may have added a Supplement, drawn up after the manner of Snorro, by way of continuation of that Author's work. Beſides, it is a matter of little importance which ever opinion we adopt. We are only intereſted in the firſt part of the EDDA; and it is ſufficient that the Author of that part, whoſoever he was, hath there faithfully preſerved the ancient religious traditions of the northern nations.

explanatory of the expreſſions contained in the Poetical Dictionary. He gave this abridgment the form of a Dialogue, whether in imitation of the ancient northern poets, who have ever choſen this moſt natural kind of compoſition, or whether from ſome ancient tradition of a converſation ſimilar to that which is the ſubject of the Edda.

This name of EDDA hath frequently exerciſed the penetration of the etymologiſts. The moſt probable conjectures are, that it is derived from an old Gothic word ſignifying GRANDMOTHER. In the figurative language of the old poets, this term was, doubtleſs, thought proper to expreſs an ancient doctrine. The Edda is preceded by a Preface *, of greater or leſs extent, according to the different Original Copies, but equally uſeleſs and ridiculous in all †. Some people have attributed it to Snorro, and he might perhaps have written that part which contains the ſame facts that are found in the beginning of his Chronicle; but the reſt has certainly been added by ſome ſcholar un-

---

* Vid. Verel. ad Hervar. Saga. p. 5.

† The Reader may ſee a literal tranſlation of this PREFACE prefixed to GoRANSON's Latin Verſion, at the end of this Volume: Vid. pag. 275—280. It is printed in Italics, to diſtinguiſh it from the EDDA itſelf.   T.

known

known to him; nor do we find it in the manuscript at Upsal, which is one of the most ancient.

I have not translated this absurd piece, and shall only say, that we are there carried back to the Creation and the Deluge, and thence passing on to the Assyrian Empire, we at length arrive at Troy; where, among other strange circumstances, we find in the heroes of that famous city, the ancestors of Odin, and of the other Princes of the north. We know it has ever been the folly of the western nations to endeavour to derive their origin from the Trojans *. The fame of the siege of Troy did not only spread itself over the neighbouring countries; it extended also to the ancient Celts ' and Goths.' The Germans and Franks had probably traditions of it handed down in their historical songs, since their earliest writers deduce from the Trojans the original of their own nations. We owe doubtless to the same cause, the invention of Antenor's voyage to the country of the Vineti †; and of Æneas's arrival in Italy, and the origin of Rome.

This conversation, (described by SNORRO) which a Swedish King is supposed to

* Timagines quoted by Ammianus Marcellinus, refers the origin of the Celts to the Trojans.
† Vid. Liv. i. 1.   T.

have

have held in the court of the Gods, is the firſt and moſt intereſting part of the EDDA. The leading tenets of the ancient 'Gothic*' Mythology are there delivered, not as maintained by their Philoſophers, but (which makes an important diſtinction) by their SCALDS or Poets. By reading it with care, we diſcover, through the rude and ſimple ſtile in which it is compoſed, more of art and method than could be expected; and ſuch a chain and connection, that I know not whether it can be equalled by any book of Greek or Roman Mythology. It is this part only of the EDDA that I have endeavoured to tranſlate with accuracy, and to elucidate with Remarks. The SECOND PART is likewiſe in the dialogue form, but carried on between other ſpeakers, and is only a detail of different events tranſacted among the Divinities. Amidſt theſe Fables, none of which contain any important point of the 'Gothic' Religion though they are all drawn from that ſource, I have only ſelected ſuch as appear to contain ſome ingenuity, or are expreſſive of manners. At the ſame time, I have only given a very general idea of them. Let me beg of ſuch as regret this omiſſion, to conſider, that what I ſuppreſs, would afford them no in-

* *Celtique.* Orig.

formation,

formation, and that pleasure alone can plead for a subject devoid of utility.

In regard to the Poetical Treatise at the end of the EDDA, what I can say of it is confined to some Remarks and Examples selected from among the few articles which are capable of being translated. The three pieces remaining of the more ancient EDDA of SOEMUND deserve our close attention, both on account of their antiquity and their contents. The first, stiled VOLUSPA, or "Oracles of the Prophetess," appears to be the Text, on which the EDDA is the Comment. In the second, called HAVA-MAAL*, or "the Sublime Discourse," are found lectures on morality, supposed to have been given by Odin himself. The third is the "Runic Chapter," which contains a short system of ancient Magic, and especially of the enchantments wrought by the operation of Runic characters. At the end of the EDDA will be found some account of these three Tracts; it would have been very difficult to have been more diffuse about them.

* *Maal* or *Mael*, signifies SPEECH in the old Icelandic; nor is the word unknown in the other dialects of the Gothic language. " MELL, *vet.* " *Ang. Loqui.* Mellynge, " *Collocutio. A. S.* Mæ-" lan. *Isl.* að mæla, " *quæ respondent Goth.* " MATHLJAN. *Huc* " *pertinent Lat. Barb.* " Mallus & Mallare." Lye apud Jun. Etym.

Some

Some people have maintained that all the Fables of the EDDA were nothing but the offspring of the Author's fancy. This even seems to have been the opinion of the famous HUET. We cannot pardon this learned man for the peremptory air he assumes in treating on a subject he so little understood as the antiquities of the north. All he has said upon this subject is full of inaccuracies *. To suppose that Snorro invented the Fables of the EDDA, plainly proves the maintainer of such an opinion, neither to have read that work, nor the ancient historians of the north, of Germany or of England. It shows him to be ignorant of this great truth, which all the ancient monuments and records of these countries; which all the Greek and Roman writers since the sixth century; which the Runic inscriptions, universal tradition, the popular superstitions, the names of the days, and many modes of speech still in

---

* See his book *De l'Origine des Romans*, p. 116. What is most astonishing is, that he pretends to have himself seen in Denmark, the ancient histories of that country, written in Runic characters on the rocks. Another author, Mr. DESLANDES, in his History of Philosophy, affirms, that one finds engraven on those stones the mysteries of the ancient Religion. This shows how little one can rely upon the accounts given of one country in another that lies remote from it.

use,

use, all unanimously depose, viz. That before the times of Christianity all these parts of Europe worshipped Odin and the Gods of the EDDA.

Nevertheless, if it were necessary to answer an objection, which the bare perusal of the EDDA alone, and the Remarks I have added, will sufficiently obviate; the reader need only cast his eyes over some Fragments of Poetry of the ancient northern SCALDS, which I have translated at the end of this book: He will there find, throughout, the same Mythology that is set forth in the EDDA; although the authors of these pieces lived in very different times and places from those in which Sœmund and Snorro flourished.

These doubts being removed, it only remains to clear up such as may arise concerning the fidelity of these different translations. I freely confess my imperfect knowledge of the language in which the EDDA is written. It is to the modern Danish or Swedish languages, what the dialect of *Ville-hardouin*, or the *Sire de Joinville* is to modern French [*]. I should have been frequently at a loss, if it had not been for

[*] i. e. As the language of CHAUCER or PIERCE PLOWMAN, compared to modern English.
T.

the affiftance of Danifh and Swedifh verfions of the EDDA, made by learned men fkilful in the old Icelandic tongue. I have not only confulted thefe tranflations, but by comparing the expreffions they employ with thofe of the original, I have generally afcertained the identity of the phrafe, and attained to a pretty ftrong affurance that the fenfe of my text hath not efcaped me. Where I fufpected my guides, I have carefully confulted thofe, who have long made the EDDA, and the language in which it is written, their peculiar ftudy. I ftood particularly in need of this affiftance, to render with exactnefs the two fragments of the more ancient EDDA, namely, the SUBLIME DISCOURSE OF ODIN, and the RUNIC CHAPTER; and here too my labours were more particularly affifted. This advantage I owe to Mr. ERICHSEN, a native of Iceland, who joins to a moft extenfive knowledge of the antiquities of his country, a judgment and a politenefs not always united with great erudition. He has enabled me to give a more faithful tranflation of thofe two pieces than is to be met with in the EDDA of RESENIUS.

I am however a good deal indebted to this laft. J. P. RESENIUS, profeffor and magiftrate of Copenhagen towards the end of the laft century, was a laborious and learned man,

man, who in many works manifested his zeal for the honour of letters and of his country. He published the first edition of the EDDA, and we may, in some respects, say it is hitherto the only one. This edition, which forms a large quarto volume, appeared at Copenhagen in the year 1665, dedicated to King Frederick III. It contains the text of the EDDA, a Latin translation done in part by a learned Icelandic priest, named MAGNUS OLSEN or OLAÏ, and continued by TORFAEUS; together with a Danish version, by the historiographer STEPHEN OLAÏ, and various readings from different MSS.

With regard to the text, Refenius hath taken the utmost care to give it correct and genuine. He collated many MSS. of which the major part are still preserved in the royal and university libraries; but what he chiefly made the greatest use of, was a MS. belonging to the King, which is judged to be the most ancient of all, being as old as the thirteenth, or at least the fourteenth century, and still extant. Exclusive of this, we do not find in the edition of Refenius any critical remarks, calculated to elucidate the contents of the EDDA. In truth, the Preface seems intended to make amends for this deficiency, since that alone would fill a volume of the size of this book; but, excepting

cepting a very few pages, the whole consists of learned excursions concerning Plato, the best editions of Aristotle, the Nine Sybils, Egyptian Hieroglyphics, &c.

From the manuscript copy of the EDDA preserved in the university library of Upsal, hath been published a few years since, a second edition of that work. This MS. which I have often had in my possession, seems to have been of the fourteenth century. It is well preserved, legible, and very entire. Although this copy contains no essential difference from that which Resenius has followed, it notwithstanding afforded me assistance in some obscure passages; for I have not scrupled to add a few words to supply the sense, or to suppress a few others that seemed devoid of it, when I could do it upon manuscript authority: and of this I must beg my readers to take notice, whenever they would compare my version with the original: for if they judge of it by the text of Resenius, they will frequently find me faulty, since I had always an eye to the Upsal MS. of which Mr. SOLBERG, a young learned Swede, well versed in these subjects, was so good as to furnish me with a correct copy. The text of this MS. being now printed, whoever will be at the trouble, may easily see, that I have never followed this new light, but when

when it appeared a furer guide than Refenius. M. GORANSON, a Swede, hath published it with a Swedish and Latin verfion, but he has only given us the firft part of the EDDA: Prefixed to which, is a long Differtation on the Hyperborean Antiquities; wherein the famous RUDBECK feems to revive in the perfon of the Author *.

Notwithftanding thefe helps, it muft be confeffed, that the EDDA hath been quoted by and known to a very fmall number of the learned. The edition of Refenius, which doubtlefs fuppofes much knowledge and application in the Editor, prefents itfelf under a very unengaging form; we there neither meet with obfervations on the parallel opinions of other Celtic ' or Gothic' people, nor any lights thrown on the cuftoms illuded to. Nothing but a patriotic zeal for the Antiquities of the North can carry one through it. Befides, that book is grown very fcarce; but few impreffions were

---

* The Latin Verfion of M. GORANSON is printed at the end of this Volume, by way of SUPPLEMENT to M. MALLET's Work. The curiofity of the fubject, and literal exactnefs of the Verfion, it is hoped will atone with the Reader of tafte, for the barbarous coarfenefs of the Latinity. In a piece of this kind, claffic elegance is lefs to be defired than fuch a ftrict minute (even barbarous) faithfulnefs, as may give one a very exact knowledge of all the peculiarities of the original.
T.

worked

worked off at firſt, and the greateſt part of them were conſumed in the fire which, in the year 1728, deſtroyed a part of Copenhagen. M. Goranſon's edition, as it is but little known out of Sweden, and is incompleat, hath not prevented the EDDA of Reſenius from being ſtill much ſought after; and this may juſtify the preſent undertaking.

Without doubt, this taſk ſhould have been aſſigned to other hands than mine. There are in Denmark many learned men, from whom the public might have expected it, and who would have acquitted themſelves much better than I can. I diſſemble not, when I avow, that it is not without fear and reluctance, that I have begun and finiſhed this work, under the attentive eyes of ſo many critical and obſerving judges: But I flatter myſelf that the motives which prompted me to the enterprize, will abate ſome part of their ſeverity. Whatever opinion may be formed of theſe Fables and of theſe Poems, it is evident they do honour to the nation that has produced them; they are not void of genius or imagination. Strangers who ſhall read them, will be obliged to ſoften ſome of thoſe dark colours in which they have uſually painted our Scandinavian anceſtors. Nothing does ſo much honour to a people as ſtrength of genius and

a

a love of the arts. The rays of Genius, which shone forth in the Northern Nations, amid the gloom of the dark ages, are more valuable in the eye of reason, and contribute more to their glory than all those bloody trophies, which they took so much pains to erect. But how can their Poetry produce this effect, if it continues unintelligible to those who wish to be acquainted with it; if no one will translate it into the other languages of Europe?

The professed design of this Work required, that the Version should be accompanied by a Commentary. It was necessary to explain some obscure passages, and to point out the use which might be made of others: I could easily have made a parade of much learning in these Notes, by laying under contribution the works of BARTHOLIN, WORMIUS, VERELIUS, AMKIEL, KEYSLER, SCHUTZE, &c. but I have only borrowed from them what appeared absolutely necessary; well knowing that in the present improved state of the republick of letters, good sense hath banished that vain ostentation of learning, brought together without judgment and without end, which heretofore procured a transitory honour to so many persons laboriously idle.

I am no longer afraid of any reproaches on that head: One is not now required to beg the Reader's pardon for prefenting him with a fmall book. But will not fome object, To what good purpofe can it ferve to revive a heap of puerile Fables and Opinions, which time hath fo juftly devoted to oblivion ? Why take fo much trouble to difpel the gloom which envelopes the infant ftate of nations ? What have we to do with any but our own cotemporaries ? much lefs with barbarous manners, which have no fort of connection with our own, and which we fhall happily never fee revive again? This is the language we now often hear. The major part of mankind, confined in their views, and averfe to labour, would fain perfuade themfelves that whatever they are ignorant of is ufelefs, and that no additions can be made to the ftock of knowledge already acquired. But this is a ftock which diminifhes whenever it ceafes to increafe. The fame reafon which prompts us to neglect the acquifition of new knowledge, leads us to forget what we have before attained. The lefs the mind is accuftomed to exercife its faculties, the lefs it compares objects, and difcovers the relation they bear to each other. Thus it lofes that ftrength and accuracy of difcernment which are its beft prefervatives from error. To think of confining our ftudies to what one may call meer neceffary truths, is to expofe one's felf

to

to the danger of being shortly ignorant of those truths themselves. An excess and luxury (as it were) of knowledge, cannot be too great, and is never a doubtful sign of the flourishing state of science. The more it occasions new researches, the more it confirms and matures the preceding ones. We see already, but too plainly, the bad effects of this spirit of œconomy, which, hurtful to itself, diminishes the present stock of knowledge, by imprudently refusing to extend it. By lopping off the branches, which hasty judgments deem unprofitable, they weaken and impair the trunk itself. But the truth is, it would cost some pains to discover new facts of a different kind from what we are used to; and therefore men chuse to spare themselves the trouble, by continually confining themselves to the old ones. Writers only show us what resembles our own manners. In vain hath nature varied her productions with such infinite diversity. Although a very small movement would procure us a new point of view, we have not, it seems, either leisure or courage to attempt it. We are content to paint the manners of that contracted society in which we live, or perhaps of only a small part of the inhabitants of one single city; and this passes without any opposition for a compleat

pleat portrait of the age, of the world, and of mankind. It is a wonder if we shall not soon bring ourselves to believe, that there is no other mode of exiſtence but that in which we ourſelves ſubſiſt.

And yet there never was a time, when the public was more greedy after novelty: But where do men for the moſt part ſeek for it? In new combinations of ancient thoughts. They examine words and phraſes through a microſcope: They turn their old ſtock of books over and over again: They reſemble an architect, who ſhould think of building a city by erecting ſucceſſively different houſes with the ſame materials. If we would ſeriouſly form new concluſions, and acquire new ideas, let us make new obſervations. In the moral and political world, as well as in the natural, there is no other way to arrive at truth. We muſt ſtudy the languages, the books, and the men of every age and country; and draw from theſe the only true ſources of the knowledge of mankind. This ſtudy, ſo pleaſant and ſo intereſting, is a mine as rich as it has been neglected. The ties and bands of connection, which unite together the different nations of Europe, grow every day ſtronger and cloſer. We live in the boſom of one great republic, (compoſed of the ſeveral European kingdoms)

doms) and we ought not to defpife any of the means which enable us to underftand it thoroughly: Nor can we properly judge of its prefent improved ftate, without looking back upon the rude beginnings from which it hath emerged *.

* The Tranflator hath concluded this Introduction in a manner fomewhat different from his Author, as he had taken occafion to give fome Remarks on the French Language, that would have been ufelefs in an Englifh Verfion, and had fpoke of his Work with a degree of diffidence, which could now be fpared, after it has received fuch full applaufe from the Public.
T.

N. B.

N. B. RESENNIUS's *Edition of the* EDDA, *&c. consists properly of Three distinct Publications: The* FIRST *contains the whole* EDDA: *Viz. not only the* XXXIII FABLES, *which are here translated; but also the other* FABLES, (XXIX *in number*) *which our Author calls in pag.* 183. *the Second Part of the* EDDA, *though in the original they follow without interruption; and also the Poetical Dictionary described below in pag.* xix. *and* 189, *which is most properly the* SECOND PART *of the* EDDA. (*vid. p.* xix.)

The Title Page of this whole Work is as follows,

" EDDA ISLANDORUM An. Chr. M.CC.XV Iſlandicé Conſcripta per SNORRONEM STURLÆ Iſlandiæ Nomophylacem, Nunc primum ISLANDICÉ, DANICE et LATINÉ ex Antiquis Codicibus MSS. Bibliothecæ Regis et Aliorum in lucem prodit, Opera et Studio PETRI RESENIJ. J. V. D. Juris ac Ethices Profeſſoris Publ. et Conſulis Havnienſis, &c. HAVNIÆ, M.DC.LX.V." 4to.

The SECOND *Work is thus intitled,*

" PHILOSOPHIA Antiquiſſima NORVEGO-DANICA dicta Uolufpa, quæ eſt pars EDDÆ SÆMUNDI, EDDA Snorronis non brevi antiquioris, ISLANDICÉ et LATINÉ publici juris primum facta à PETRO JOH. RESENIO. &c. HAVNIÆ M.DC.LXV." 4to.

The THIRD *Piece is intitled thus,*

" ETHICA ODINI pars EDDÆ SÆMUNDI vocata Haabamaal, una cum ejuſdem Appendice appellato Runa Capitule, a multis exoptata nunc tandem Iſlandicé et Latiné in lucem producta eſt per PETRUM JOH. RESENIUM, &c. HAVNIÆ 1665." 4to.

THE

THE
EDDA,
OR,
ANCIENT ICELANDIC
MYTHOLOGY.

The Vision of Gylfe: and Illusions of Har.

FORMERLY in Sweden reigned a king named GYLFE, who was famous for his wisdom and skill in magic. He beheld, with astonishment, the great respect which all his people shewed to the New-comers from Asia; and was at a loss whether to attribute the success of these strangers to the superiority of their natural abilities, or to any divine power resident in them. To be satisfied in this particular, he resolved to go to ASGARD (A), disguised under the appearance of an old man of ordinary rank. But the Asiatics * were too

* The original is *Æsirnir*, (*Asæ*) which signifies either *Gods* or *Asiatics*. T.

discerning not to see through his design, and therefore, as soon as he arrived, they fascinated his eyes by their inchantments (B). Immediately appeared to his sight a very lofty palace; the roof of which, as far as his eyes could reach, was covered with golden shields. The poet Diodolfe thus describes it, " The Gods had formed " the roof of brilliant gold, the walls of " stone, the foundations of the hall were " mountains (c)." At the entrance of this palace GYLFE saw a man playing with seven little swords, which he amused himself with tossing into the air and catching as they fell, one after another. This person asked his name; the disguised monarch told him, it was Gangler, and that he came from the rocks of Riphil. He asked, in his turn, to whom that palace belonged? The other told him it belonged to their king, and that he would introduce him to his presence. Gangler entering, saw many stately buildings, and innumerable halls crouded with people; some drinking, others engaged in various sports, others wrestling. Gangler seeing a multitude of things, the meaning of which he could not comprehend, softly pronounced the following verses. " Carefully ex-
" amine all the gates, before thou advancest
" further; for thou canst not tell where
" the foes may be sitting, who are placed
" in

" in ambush against thee." He afterwards beheld three thrones, raised one above another, and on each throne sat a man (D). Upon his asking which of these was their king, his guide answered, " He who sits on the lowest throne is the king, his name is HAR, or the lofty one: The second is JAFNHAR, i. e. equal to the lofty one: But he who sits on the highest throne is called THRIDI, or the third (E)." Har perceiving Gangler, desired to know what business had brought him to Asgard: Adding, that he should be welcome to eat and drink without cost, along with the other guests of his court. Gangler said, He desired first to know whether there was any person present who was famous for his wisdom and knowledge. Har answered, If thou art the more knowing, I fear thou wilt hardly return safe: But go, stand below, and propose thy questions; here sits one will be able to answer thee.

REMARKS.

In the edition of the EDDA, published by Refenius, there is a Chapter before this: But I have not translated it, because it has little or no relation to the rest, and contains nothing remarkable: It is also not found in the MS. at Upsal. That chapter seems to have been only prefixed by way of preamble, by SNORRO STURLESON, the compiler of the EDDA. As for GYLFE, Snorro informs us in the beginning of his larger Chronicle, that this prince, who governed Sweden before the arrival of Odin and his Asiatics, was obliged to yield to the supernatural power, which those intruders employed against him, and to resign his kingdom up to them. This gave rise to the supposition that Gylfe was willing to make trial himself of the skill and sagacity of these new-comers, by proposing to them a variety of captious questions. In the history of ancient Scandinavia, as well as that of all the eastern countries, we often see these contests or trials of skill between kings and princes, in which the victory is always assigned to him who could give an answer to every question, and assign a cause (true or false) for every phœnomenon. This was called Science or Wisdom; words originally synonimous in all languages, but at present so easily distinguished. It will be necessary here, to refer the reader to the account of Odin's arrival in the north, given in the former volume, (chap. II, III, &c.) for his more readily understanding this and the following chapters.

(A) " He resolved to go to Asgard."] Odin and his companions came from ASGARD: A word which signifies the "abode of Lords or Gods." Some words are difficult to be understood, because we cannot discover any meaning in them. Here on the contrary, the difficulty lies in the variety or multiplicity of significations. The word *As*, ' in the ancient languages ' of Europe *,' generally signified Lord or God, but in the EDDA, and other Icelandic writings, it signifies also Asiatics; and we know not in which of these senses the name is given to Odin and his companions. Eccard, in his treatise *De Origine Germanorum*, pag. 41. pretends that this word was never used in the last sense, and that the arrival of Odin from Asia was a meer fiction, founded on the resemblance of sounds;

* Fr. Dans toutes les Branches de la langue Celtique.

or that he certainly came from Vandalia, at prefent Pomerania. I refer the reader to the work itfelf, for the reafons on which this conjecture is founded; which would deferve the preference for its fimplicity, if a uniform and ancient tradition did not place the original country of the Scandinavians in the neighbourhood of the Tanais. See Vol. I. c. IV, &c.

(B) " By their inchant-" ments."] It fhould be remembered that the author of the EDDA was a Chriftian: On this account he is unwilling to allow Odin the honour of having performed real miracles. It was believed, indeed, in our author's time, that it was impoffible to do fupernatural things, but that yet there was an art of perfuading others that they faw them done. The fame opinion ftill prevails among many of our contemporaries. [*This note is only in the firft edit. of the orig.*]

(C) " Diodolfe thus " defcribes it."] Diodolfe, or Thiodolfe, was a celebrated ancient SCALD, who compofed a long poem, containing the hiftory of more than thirty princes of Norway. We fee in the text SNORRO's care to quote almoft always his authorities for whatever he relates: This will appear throughout his work. He has perfued the fame method in his great Chronicle, where we find every fact confirmed by a fragment of fome old hiftorical poem. This fhows, at the fame time, both the great erudition of this hiftorian, and the amazing quantity of fuch kind of verfes that fubfifted in his time. In like manner among the Gauls, their ancient poems were fo numerous, that the young people found fufficient employment for feveral years in committing them to memory.

(D) " Three thrones " . . . and on each fat " a man."] In the MS. copy of the EDDA preferved at Upfal, there is a reprefentation or drawing (very rudely done, as may be fuppofed) of thefe three thrones, and of the three perfons fitting on them.

them. They have crowns on their heads; and Gangler is drawn in a suppliant posture before them *.

' These figures bear so great a resemblance to the Roman Catholic pictures of the Trinity, that we are not to wonder if some have imagined them to be an allusion to that doctrine; particularly such as suppose it was already known to Plato, and some other of the ancient Pagans.' T.

(E) " He who sits on the highest throne."] Is it Odin, or some one of his court that fills this throne? This it is not easy to decide. It appears to me, however, that throughout this whole preamble, the ODIN here spoke of, is only the prince, the conqueror of the north, and not ODIN the father and ruler of the Gods §. Gangler had betaken himself to Odin's court, while that prince was subduing Sweden.

He found therefore at Asgard, only his vicegerents, that ruled in his absence. The names that are given them, perhaps allude to their rank and employments. Upon this supposition, there will be nothing in the relation but what is natural and easy. But I must here repeat it, that we must expect to see, throughout this Mythology, ODIN the conqueror of the north, every where confounded with ODIN the supreme Deity: Whose name was usurped by the other, at the same time that he came to establish his worship in Scandinavia. JUPITER, the king of Crete, and the sovereign lord of Heaven and Earth; ZOROASTER, the founder of the worship of the Magi, and the God to whom that worship was addressed; ZAMOLXIS, the high-priest of the Thracians, and the supreme God of that people, have not been more constantly confounded, than these two ODINS.

---

* The reader may find it engraven on a copper-plate in Bartholini *Causæ contemptæ à Danis mortis, &c.* pag. 473. 4to. T.
§ The reader will remember the distinction made in pag. 60, 88, 89, &c. of the preceding volume. T.

THE

THE FIRST FABLE.

Questions of Gangler.

GANGLER thus began his discourse. Who is the supreme or first of the Gods? Har answers: We call him here ALFADER, or the universal father; but in the ancient Asgard, he hath twelve names (A). Gangler asks; Who * is this God? What is his power? and what hath he done to display his glory (B)? Har replies; He lives for ever; he governs all his kingdom; and directs the great things as well as the small. Jafnhar adds: He hath formed the heaven, the earth, and the air. Thridi proceeds, He hath done more; he hath made man, and given him a spirit or soul, which shall live, even after the body shall have mouldered away. And then all the just shall dwell with him in a place

---

* Goranson translates this, *Ubi est hic deus?* HUAR ES SA GUD? *Where is this God?* Which is doubtless the true meaning. T.

named *Gimle* (or *Vingolf*, the palace of friendship:) But wicked men shall go to HELA, or death, and from thence to *Niflheim*, or the abode of the wicked; which is below in the ninth world. Gangler then asked, how this God was employed before he made the heaven and the earth? Har replied, He was then with the Giants (c). But, says Gangler, With what did he begin? or what was the beginning of things? Hear, replied Har, what is said in the poem of the VOLUSPA. " At the " beginning of time, when nothing was " yet formed, neither shore, nor sea, nor " foundations beneath; the earth was no " where to be found below, nor the hea- " ven above: All was one vast abyss (D), " without plant or verdure." Jafnhar added, Many winters before the earth was made, Nifleim (E) or Hell was formed; and in the middle of it is a fountain named *Hvergelmer*. From this fountain run the following rivers, Anguish, the Enemy of Joy, the Abode of Death, Perdition, the Gulph, the Tempest, the Whirlwind, the Bellowing and Howling, the Abyss. That which is called the Roaring runs near the grates of the Abode of Death.

R E-

REMARKS ON THE FIRST FABLE.

This fable is remarkable upon many accounts. It throws great light upon one of the principal doctrines of the 'ancient religion of Europe *;' and in particular, confirms what Tacitus tells us, concerning the idea which the Germans entertained of the Supreme God: *Regnator omnium deus, cætera subjecta atque parentia.* Germ. c. 39. The Germans and Scandinavians at first called this divinity, *Tis*, *Tuis* or *Teut*, a word to which the Gauls added that of *Tad*, or *Tat*, which signifies FATHER at this day in the British language. (v. Roſtrenen Diction. Celt. p. 712.) We see in the Edda that the name of Father was also given him by the Scandinavians. In future ages, and doubtless after the time of Tacitus, these people accustomed themselves to call him by an appellative name, *God*, or *Guodan*, i. e. THE GOOD: This, by degrees, they changed into ODIN, which the Anglo-Saxons pronounced WODAN.

Wodan (says Paulus Diaconus. Rer. Langobard. l. I. c. 3.) *quem, adjecta litera Guodan dixere, ab univerſis Germaniæ gentibus, ut Deus adoratur.* Consult, on this subject, Pelloutier Hist. des Celtes, tom. ii. p. 74. & seq.

(A) " He hath twelve " names."] These twelve names are enumerated in the Edda; but I did not chuse to interrupt the text with a list of such harsh and unusual sounds: I shall therefore give them here for the curious, together with some conjectures that have been made by the learned concerning their significations. 1. *Alfader* (the Father of all.) 2. *Herian* (the Lord, or rather, the Warrior.) 3. *Nikader* (the supercilious.) 4. *Nikuder* (the God of the sea.) 5. *Fiolner* (he who knoweth much.) 6. *Omi* (the sonorous.) 7. *Biflid* (the agile, or nimble.) 8. *Vidrer* (the munificent.) 9. *Suidrer* (the exterminator.) 10. *Suidur* (the destroyer by fire.)

* Fr. *La Religion Celtique.*

11. *Oſsi*

11. *Oski* (he who chuses such as are to die.) 12. *Salkir* (the happy, or blessed.) The name of *Alfader* is what occurs most frequently in the EDDA, I have translated it *Universal Father*.

(B) " To display his " glory."] These are important questions; but the answers are still more remarkable. From their conformity with the christian doctrines, one would be tempted to believe that Snorro had here embellished the religion of his Pagan ancestors, by bringing it as near as possible to the Gospel, if we did not find the same unfolded system literally expressed in the VOLUSPA, a poem of undoubted antiquity, and which was composed long before the name of Christianity was known in the north; and also if the same system were not continually referred to in every other place of the EDDA. But what ought to remove every remaining doubt, is that we know from other proofs, that the belief of the ' Gothic and ' Celtic nations upon most of these points, was much the same with what we have read in the text. I shall give many proofs of this below.

(c) " He was then " with the giants."] It is not easy to translate the original word. The ' Gothic *' nations had Giants and Spirits of many different orders, which we want terms to distinguish. Those mentioned in the text are called in the original Icelandic *Rymthusse*, from the word *Rym*, Frost, and *Thuss*, a Giant or Satyr. We shall see presently the origin of this denomination. With respect to the word *Thuss*, it may serve to show, by the bye, the conformity of thinking between the ' Gothic and ' Celtic nations, even upon the most trivial subjects. The Gauls, as well as the northern nations, believed the existence of the *Thusses*, and gave them the same names. Only the *Thusses*, or Satyrs of the Gauls, seem to have been somewhat more disposed to gallantry than those of the north; which

* *Les Celtes*, Fr. Orig.

we

we shall not be surprized at. Many of the fathers of the church speak of the strange liberties which these gentry took with women: They called them in Latin *Dusii*. St. Auguſtin, in particular, tells us, he had been aſſured by ſo many perſons that thoſe beings ſought a commerce with women, and ſeduced them; that none but an imprudent perſon could pretend to diſbelieve it. De Civit. Dei, l. 15. c. 23. If it were not for incurring this imputation, I ſhould have been tempted to look upon theſe ſtories as only ſo many excuſes, which love invents to cover the faults it induces frail females to commit.

(D) " All was one vaſt " abyſs."] It will not, I hope, be expected of me here, that I ſhould heap together all the paſſages of Greek and Latin authors, which are analogous to this in the text. Nobody is ignorant of them. Almoſt all the ancient ſects agree in the doctrine of the Primitive Chaos. To create Matter out of Nothing, appeared in ages ſo little metaphyſical as thoſe, a thing incomprehenſible or impoſſible. I ſhall only remark, that of all the ſyſtems we know, that of the ancient Perſians bears the greateſt reſemblance to this of the EDDA. I ſhall have occaſion more than once to repeat this obſervation, which confirms what has been advanced by ſome of the learned; That the ' Goths ' and' Celts were formerly the ſame people with the Perſians.

Is it not ſingular, that all thoſe who have treated of the religion of theſe people, ſhould have given themſelves ſo much trouble to gueſs at what they thought concerning the creation of the world, and ſhould at length conclude that they could know nothing about it, but what was very uncertain; when at the ſame time, they had at their elbow an authentic book, which offered them a detail of almoſt all the particulars they could deſire to know? I cannot help making this reflection, in its utmoſt extent, upon reading what the learned Abbé Banier hath

hath published concerning the religion of the Gauls, the Germans, and the nations of the north.

(E) "NIFLHEIM, or "Hell."] The original word "*Niflheim*," signifies in the Gothic language, the abode of the wicked, or more literally, *Evil-home*. We see, by this description of Hell, how much the genius of the ancient 'northern poets and' philosophers * inclined them to allegory; and it is very probable that almost all the fables that we shall meet with hereafter, contained in them some truth, the interpretation of which they reserved to themselves. This is confirmed by Cæsar and others, ' concerning the Gauls;' and needs no other proof 'here' than the mysterious and significant name which is given to every thing. So much for the HELL of the Celtic ' and Gothic' nations, on which I shall make no farther remarks at present, because they will occur more naturally on many occasions hereafter.

* *Des anciens Philosophes Celtes.* Fr. Orig.

THE SECOND FABLE

Of the burning World, and of Surtur.

THEN Thridi opened his mouth and said, Yet, before all things, there existed what we call *Muspelsheim* (A). It is a world luminous, glowing, not to be dwelt in by strangers, and situate at the extremity of the earth. *Surtur*, (the Black) holds his empire there. In his hands there shines a flaming sword. He shall come at the end of the world; he shall vanquish all the Gods, and give up the universe a prey to flames. Hear what the VOLUSPA says of him. " Surtur, filled " with deceitful stratagems, cometh from " the South. A rolling Sun beams from " his sword. The Gods are troubled; " men tread in crouds the paths of death; " the Heaven is split asunder." But, says Gangler, What was the state of the world, before there were families of men upon the earth, and before the nations were formed?

Har anfwered him. The rivers, called *Elivages*, flowed fo far from their fources, that the venom which they rolled along became hard, like the fcoria of a furnace when it grows cold. Hence was formed the ice; which ftopped and flowed no more. Then all the venom that was beginning to cover it, alfo became frozen: And thus many ftrata of congealed vapours were formed, one above another, in the vaft abyfs. Jafnhar added; By this means that part of the abyfs which lies towards the north, was filled with a mafs of gelid vapours and ice; whilft the interior parts of it were replete with whirlwinds and tempefts. Directly oppofite to it, rofe the fouth part of the abyfs, formed of the lightnings and fparks which flow from the world of fire. Then Thridi proceeded, and faid; By this means a dreadful freezing wind came from the quarter of Niflheim, whilft whatever lay oppofite to the burning world was heated and enlightened. And as to that part of the abyfs which lay between thefe two extremes; it was light and ferene like the air in a calm. A breath of heat then fpreading itfelf over the gelid vapours, they melted into drops; and of thefe drops were formed a man, by the power of him who governed (B). This man was named YMIR; the Giants call him

him *Aurgelmer*. From him are descended all the families of the Giants; according to that of the Voluspa; "The prophetes-ses are all come of *Vittolfe*, the spectres of *Vilmode*, and the Giants of YMIR." And in another place; "The rivers *Eli-vages* have run drops of poison; and there blew a wind, whence a Giant was formed: From him came all the families of the Giants." Then spake Gangler, and said, How did this family of YMIR spread itself? Or do ye believe that he was a God? Jafnhar replied, we are far from believing him to have been a God; for he was wicked, as were all his posterity. Whilst he slept, he fell into a sweat, and from the pit of his left arm were born a male and female. One of his feet begot upon the other a son, from whom is descended the race of the Giants, called from their original, the Giants of the Frost (c).

REMARKS on the SECOND FABLE.

(A) *Muspels-heim* signifies, the abode or residence of MUSPEL*. But who is this Muspel? Of this we are intirely ignorant. The ancient sages of the north were desirous to explain how the world had been framed, and to advance something probable for its being so cold towards the north, and warm towards the south. For this purpose they placed, towards the south, a huge mass of fire, which they supposed had been there for ever, and served as a residence to wicked Genii. This was the

* Literally, *Muspel's Home*. T.

matter

matter of which the Sun was made. This Ether, or Fire, so placed at one extremity of the world, enabled them also to assign a probable reason for its final conflagration; for they were absolutely persuaded, that it would at the last day be consumed by fire. And as to the north, it was continually cold there, because opposite to that quarter lay immense mountains of ice. But whence came that ice? Nothing could be more easily accounted for; for Hell, which had been prepared from the beginning of ages, was watered by those great rivers mentioned in the preceding fable; and those great rivers themselves, in flowing at so vast distance from the south, whilst the course of their streams carried them still farther from it, froze at last in their currents, and swelled into huge heaps of ice, which communicated a chilliness to the northern winds. Between that world of fire and this of ice, there lay a grand abyss, which contained nothing but air; and here was placed, in process of time, the earth which we inhabit. If we read the fragment of Sanchoniathon, preserved by Eusebius, De Prep. l. 2. c. 10. we shall find there a history of the formation of the world, very much resembling this.

(B) " By the power " of him who govern- " ed."] Here, we have the pleasure to observe, that our philosophers saw the necessity of having recourse to the intervention of a Deity in forming the world. The vivifying breath here mentioned, seems to carry in it a strong affinity to the " Breath of Life" which God breathed into the nostrils of the first man; according to the phrase of Scripture, Gen. chap. ii. ver. 7.—One cannot doubt that the Celtic and Gothic nations, as well as the Persians, and most of the Orientals, derived many of their traditions from Scripture.

(c) " Giants of the " Frost."] There would be no end of amassing all the ancient traditions
which

which some way or other relate to the subject of the text. It hath been a general opinion in the east, that God began with creating Genii, both good and bad, of very immense powers: who for a long time before we existed, inhabited a world prior to this of ours. One may see in Herbelot, what the Persians relate concerning the *Dives*, *Nerè*, *Peris*, and their king *Eblis.*——YMIR having been formed, as we see, out of the congealed drops, all the Giants descended from him are called, upon that account, THE GIANTS OF THE FROST. It must be observed, that these Giants are a species intirely distinct from the men of our race, the EDDA having not yet given any account of THEIR formation.

THE THIRD FABLE.

Of the Cow OEdumla.

GANGLER then desired to know where the Giant Ymir dwelt, and in what manner he was fed. Har answered, Immediately after this breath from the south had melted the gelid vapours, and resolved them into drops, there was formed out of them a Cow named *OEdumla*. Four rivers of milk flowed from her teats, and thus she nourished Ymir. The cow, in her turn, supported herself by licking the rocks that were covered with salt and hoar-frost. The first day that she licked these rocks, there sprung from her, towards evening, the hairs of a man; the second day, a head; on the third, an intire man, who was endowed with beauty, agility, and power. He was called *Bure*, and was the father of *Bore*, who married *Beyzla*, the daughter of the Giant *Baldorn*. Of that marriage were born three sons, *Odin*, *Vile*, and *Ve*; and 'tis our belief,

that

that this ODIN, with his brothers, ruleth both heaven and earth, that ODIN is his true name, and that he is the most powerful of all the Gods (A).

REMARKS ON THE THIRD FABLE.

In all likelihood this fable is only an allegory; but whatever right my privilege of commentator may give me to explain it, I shall decline the attempt.

There is, however, a very important remark to be made here. A powerful Being had with his breath animated the drops out of which the first Giant was formed. This Being, whom the EDDA affects not to name, was intirely distinct from Odin, who had his birth long after the formation of Ymir. One may conjecture, therefore, (since we know that the Druids never revealed their mysteries, but by degrees, and with great precaution) that the hidden philosophy of the Celts*, meant to inculcate that the supreme, eternal, invisible and incorruptible God, whom they durst not name out of fear and reverence, had appointed inferior divinities for the government of the world: and that it was those divinities who, at the last day, were to yield to the efforts of powerful enemies, and be involved in the ruins of the universe: and that then the supreme God, ever existing, and placed above the reach of all revolution and change, would arise from his repose, to make a new world out of the ruins of the old, and begin a new period, which should in its turn give place to another; and so on through all eternity. The same was the system of the Sto-

---

* It is sufficient just to hint to the reader, that our ingenious author goes here upon the hypothesis of M. Pelloutier, that the Goths and Celts were the same people, and that the doctrine of the Druids was also that of the Scandinavian Scalds: an hypothesis which I take to be extremely erroneous. T.

ics; who, as well as the philosophers of the north*, supposed that the world, after it had been consumed by flames, should be renewed; and that the inferior Deities should be destroyed at the same time. What confirms all this, is, that this God, superior to Odin himself, and of whom the vulgar among this people had scarce any idea, is represented in the Icelandic poems as making a second appearance, after the death of all the Gods, in order to distribute justice, and establish a new order of things. See the Icelandic odes, cited in the antiquities of Bartholin, l. 2. c. 14.

(A) "The most powerful of all the Gods."] 'Tis not undeserving of notice, that all the ancient nations of Europe † describe their origin with the same circumstances. Tacitus says, that the Germans, in their verses, celebrated a God born of the earth, named *Tuiston* (that is, the son of *Tis*, or *Tuis*, the supreme God.) This Tuiston had a son named *Mannus*, whose three sons were the original ancestors of the three principal nations of Germany. The Scythians, according to Herodotus, lib. 4. c. 6. & 10. said that *Targytaus* (i. e. the Good *Taus*) the founder of their nation, had three sons, *Leipoxain*, *Anpoxain* and *Kolaxain*. A tradition received by the Romans, imported (according to Appian, *Illyr. Lib.*) that the Cyclop POLYPHEME had by *Galatea* three sons, named *Celtus*, *Illyrius*, and *Gallus*. SATURN, the father of *Jupiter*, *Neptune*, and *Pluto*, might very well come from the same source; as well as the three sons whom Hesiod makes to spring from the marriage of HEAVEN and EARTH, *Coltus*, *Briareus*, and *Gyges*. A tradition so ancient and so general, must have certainly had its foundation in some real fact, though I pretend not to decide with Cluverius, that this fact is what the Scripture tells us of NOAH and his sons; yet one cannot deny, that there is some-

* Fr. *Les Celtes.* † Fr. *Tous les Peuples Celtes.*

thing

thing very probable in this; unless the reader is inclined to give the preference to the sons of GOMER, *Askenaz, Riphath,* and *Togarmah.* Gen. x. 3.

If I were not already too prolix, I might find here the traces of another tradition, not less ancient, very far spread over the east, and in some degree confirmed by the 6th chapter of Genesis *. I mean those two different races, the one good, the other evil, whom love at last united. But I leave the pleasure of making this research, to those who are fond of disquisitions of this kind. Let me only invite them to read, upon this subject, the pretended prophesy of Enoch, cited in Syncellus, p. 11, & seq. and Lactantius's Origin of Errors. They will find there many surprizing conformities with the above doctrines of the EDDA.

---

* The common versions of the passage referred to by our author, run as follows: " The sons of God " saw the daughters of men, that they were fair; and " they took them wives of all which they chose. ... " There were GIANTS in the earth in those days; " namely, after that the sons of God came in unto " the daughters of Men, and they bare children to " them: the same became mighty men; which were " of old men of renown, &c." Gen. vi. 2, 4.——— It is however but justice to the sacred writer, to observe, that it is only from a misinterpretation of the original words, that the wild traditions mentioned by our author could have any countenance from the above passage: For, by " the sons of God," the best commentators understand the virtuous race of Seth; and by " the daughters of men," the vicious offspring of Cain: and the fruits of this marriage were נכלים *Nephilim,* (not GIANTS, but) Men of Violence, from נפל, *ruit, irruit,* &c. T.

THE FOURTH FABLE.

How the sons of Bore made heaven and earth.

WAS there, proceeded Gangler, any kind of equality, or any degree of good understanding between those two different races? Har answers him; Far from it: the sons of Bore (A) slew the Giant Ymir, and there ran so much blood from his wounds, that all the families of the Giants of the Frost were drowned in it, except one single Giant, who saved himself, with all his houshold. He is called *Bergelmer*. He escaped by happening to be aboard his bark; and by him was preserved the race of the Giants of the Frost. This is confirmed by the following verses. " Many winters before the earth was fash-" ioned, was Bergelmer born; and well I " know that this sage Giant was saved and " preserved on board his bark (B)." Gangler demands, What then became of the sons of Bore, whom you look upon as Gods?

Gods? Har replied: To relate this is no trivial matter. They dragged the body of Ymir into the middle of the abyſs, and of it formed the earth. The water and the ſea were compoſed of his blood; the mountains of his bones; the rocks of his teeth; and of his hollow bones, mingled with the blood that ran from his wounds, they made the vaſt ocean; in the midſt of which they infixed the earth (c). Then having formed the heavens of his ſcull, they made them reſt on all ſides upon the earth: they divided them into four quarters, and placed a dwarf at each corner to ſuſtain it. Theſe dwarfs are called East, West, South, and North. After this they went and ſeized upon fires in Muſpelſhcim, (that flaming world in the ſouth,) and placed them in the abyſs, in the upper and lower parts of the ſky, to enlighten the earth. Every fire had its aſſigned reſidence. Hence the days were diſtinguiſhed, and the years reduced to calculation. For this reaſon it is ſaid in the poem of Voluspa, " Formerly the ſun knew not its palace, the " moon was ignorant of its powers, and " the ſtars knew not the ſtations they were " to occupy (d)." Theſe, cried out Gangler, were grand performances indeed! moſt ſtupendous undertakings! Har goes on, and ſays, The earth is round, and

about it is placed the deep sea; the shores of which were given for a dwelling to the Giants. But higher up, in a place equally distant on all sides from the sea, the Gods built upon earth a fortress against the Giants (E), the circumference of which surrounds the world. The materials they employed for this work, were the eye-brows of Ymir; and they called the place *Midgard*, or the Middle Mansion. They afterwards tossed his brains into the air, and they became the clouds: for thus it is described in the following verses. " Of
" the flesh of Ymir was formed the earth;
" of his sweat, the seas; of his bones, the
" mountains; of his hair, the herbs of
" the field; and of his head, the heavens:
" but the merciful Gods built of his eye-
" brows the city of Midgard, for the chil-
" dren of men; and of his brains were
" formed the noxious clouds."

REMARKS on the FOURTH FABLE.

I beg leave here, once for all, to observe, that my divisions do not always agree with those of the EDDA of Resenius, or those of the EDDA of Upsal. For as they differ in the several manuscripts, I thought I might regard them all as arbitrary, and form other divisions when they appeared more commodious.

(A) " The sons of " Bore" are the Gods, and particularly ODIN: for as to his brothers, *Vile* and *Ve*, they are scarcely mentioned elsewhere.

where. The ancient priests of the 'north *' affirmed themselves to be descended of the family of *Bore*; and in this, they might the more easily obtain credit, because among the Celts, as among the Jews, the priesthood descended from father to son.

(B) " This .. Giant " was saved .. on board " his bark."] We discover here evident traces of the history of the deluge. That all the nations of Asia, and even those of America, had preserved some remembrance of it, was generally known: but that the same prevailed among our northern ancestors, the 'Goths and' Celts, has never I believe been remarked before.

(c) " They infixed the " earth."] The reader will remember that nothing existed as yet, but the Flaming World towards the south, wherein resided evil Genii; and those masses of Ice towards the north, which were formed by the rivers of hell. Between these was a void space, called the ABYSS. This is the place into which the Gods threw the body of the Giant. This monstrous fiction probably at first contained some important doctrine: but as at present little regard is paid to profound and learned conjectures, I shall not give myself the trouble to fathom the meaning of so strange an allegory. Whatever was couched under it, it hath been a fruitful source of poetic figures and expressions; of which the ancient SCALDS incessantly availed themselves. Poets have in all ages been fond of appearing to speak the language of the Gods, by using these sorts of phrases; as by this means they could conceal their own want of invention, and poverty of genius.

Of all the ancient Theogonies, I find only that of the Chaldees, which has any resemblance to this of the EDDA. Berosus, cited by Syncellus, informs us that that peo-

* Fi. *Des Celtes.*

ple,

ple, one of the moſt ancient in the world, believed that in the beginning there was only Water and Darkneſs; that this Water and Darkneſs contained in them divers monſtrous animals, different in form and ſize, which were all repreſented in the temple of *Bel*; that a female, named *Omorca*, was the miſtreſs of the Univerſe; that the God *Bel* put to death all the monſters, deſtroyed *Omorca* herſelf, and dividing her in two, formed of the one half of her the Earth, and of the other the Heavens: to which another tradition adds, that men were formed out of her head; whence Beroſus concludes, that this occaſioned man to be endowed with intellectual powers. I do not pretend to aver, that the Chaldeans and northern nations borrowed all theſe chimæras of each other, although this is not impoſſible. Theſe ancient nations had as yet but a few ideas, and their imaginations, however fruitful, being confined within narrow limits, could not at firſt give their inventions that prodigious variety, which was diſplayed in ſucceeding ages.

(D) " The ſtars knew " not, &c."] The matter of the ſun and ſtars exiſted long before the formation of thoſe bodies: this matter was the Æther, the Luminous World. One cannot but remark in this Fable, the remains of the Moſaic doctrine; according to which the creation of a luminous ſubſtance, in like manner, preceeded that of the ſun and moon. And what indicates one common origin of both accounts, is what Moſes adds in the ſame place. " And God ſaid, Let " there be lights in the " firmament of heaven, " to divide the day from " the night; and let " them be for ſigns of " ſeaſons, and of days " and of years, &c." Gen. c. i. ver. 14.

(E) " A fortreſs againſt " the Giants, &c."] The Perſian mythology abounds with circumſtances analogous to this. There are always Giants, or miſchievous Genii, who

wiſh

wish ill to men, and hurt them whenever it is in their power. The Heroes have no employment so dear and so glorious as that of making war upon those Genii. At this very day they are supposed to be banished among the rocks of Caucasus, or Imaus, ever since *Tahmuras*, sur-named *Divbend* (he who subdued the *Dives*) vanquished and put them to flight. Mahometism has not been so severe as Christianity, in eradicating these ancient superstitions, and therefore the inhabitants of Persia are still very much infatuated with them.

THE

THE FIFTH FABLE.

Of the formation of Aſke and Emla.

THESE were indeed important labours, said Gangler; but whence came the men, who at preſent inhabit the world? Har anſwered, The ſons of Bore, as they were walking one day upon the ſhore, found two pieces of wood floating on the waves. They took them, and made a man of the one, and a woman of the other (A). The firſt gave them life and ſoul; the ſecond reaſon and motion; the third, hearing, ſight, ſpeech, garments, and a name. They called the man *Aſke*, and the woman *Emla*. From theſe two, are deſcended the human race; to whom the Gods have aſſigned a habitation near MIDGARD. Then the ſons of Bore built, in the middle of the world, the fortreſs of ASGARD; where dwell the Gods, and their families (B). There it is, that ſo many wonderful works are wrought on the earth, and in the air. Har added, And there it is that the palace of Odin is situated, called *Lidſkialf*, or the Terror of the Nations. When ODIN is there seated on his lofty throne, he thence discovers every country, he sees all the actions of men, and comprehends whatever he beholds. This wife is FRIGGA, the daughter of *Fiorgun*. The issue of that marriage is what we call the family of the ASES, that is, of the Gods; a race intirely divine, and which hath built the ancient ASGARD. Wherefore Odin is justly called the UNIVERSAL FATHER; for he is the parent of Gods, and men; and all things have been produced by his power. The Earth is his daughter and wife (c). On her hath he begotten *Aſa-Thor* (or the God THOR) his first-born. Strength and Valour are the attendants on this God, and therefore he triumphs over every thing that hath life.

REMARKS on the FIFTH FABLE.

(A) "They made a "man, &c."] We are come at last to the creation of our species. The circumstances of this fable, shew that it was invented among a people addicted to navigation, and settled in a country surrounded with seas and lakes. Bartholin conjectures, that the philosophers of the north, in making men spring from the sea, intended to fortify the Scandinavians against the fear, that annihilation was the consequence of being drowned; and to make them regard the sea, as their

proper

proper and natural element. We shall see, by the sequel, that the great aim of these warlike Theologians was to inspire courage, and to remove all pretences and grounds for fear. *Aske*, in the Gothic language, signifies an ASH-TREE, and *Emla*, an ELM. I shall leave to others to find out the reason why the preference hath been given to these two trees; and what relation there could be between the two sexes, and these two different sorts of wood.

(B) " Where dwell " the Gods and their fa- " milies."] ASGARD is literally the Court of the Gods. Some manuscripts add, that ASGARD is Troy; but this can be no other than the marginal note of some copyist, crept by mistake into the text. The Gods, being continually threatned with attacks by the Giants, built in the middle a large inclosure, named MIDGARD, or the Middle-Abode, one of the strongest of citadels. This is the Olympus of Homer; as the Giants are his Titans. I shall once for all observe, that the ' Go- ' thic and' Celtic nations, as well as the Greeks, derived all these fables from the inexhaustible source of eastern traditions. But the people of the north preserved them nearly the same as they received them, for above two thousand years; whereas the same fables found in Greece so favourable a soil, that in a short time they multiplied a hundred fold.

(c) " The EARTH is " his daughter and wife, " &c."] This fable proves that the ancient Scalds understood by the name *Frigga*, the spouse of the Supreme God; and that, at the same time, this Frigga was the Earth. This doctrine is of very great antiquity, and hath been in general received by all the ' Gothic and' Celtic nations. Their philosophers taught, that the Supreme God, *Teut*, or *Wodan*, was the active principle, the soul of the world, which uniting itself with matter, had thereby put it into a condition to produce the Intelligences, or Inferior Gods,

Gods, and Men, and all other creatures. This is what the poets express figuratively, when they say that *Odin* espoused *Frigga*, or *Frea*, that is, the LADY, by way of eminence. One cannot doubt, after having read this passage of the EDDA, but it was this same Goddess, to whom the Germans, according to Tacitus, consecrated one of the Danish islands, worshipping her under the name of *Herthus*, or the Earth: (the English word *Earth*, as well as the German *Erde*, being evidently the same with that, to which Tacitus has only given a Latin termination.) As to the worship that was paid her, see it described by Pelloutier, in his *Hist. des Celtes*, Vol. II. c. 8.

Though it was by the concurrence of the Supreme God and Matter, that this Universe was produced; yet the 'ancient philosophers of the north*' allowed a great difference between these two principles: the Supreme God was eternal, whereas Matter was his work, and of course had a beginning: all this, in the language of the ancients, was expressed by this phrase; " Earth is " the daughter and wife " of the Universal Fa- " ther."

Lastly, from this mystical marriage, was born the God THOR. *Asa-Thor* means THE LORD THOR. He was the first-born of the Supreme God, and the greatest and most powerful of all the inferior divinities, or intelligences that were born from the union of the two principles. One cannot doubt but it was he, who had the charge of launching the thunder. In the languages of the north, the name given to this God is still that of the Thunder. When they adopted the Roman Calendar, that day which was consecrated to *Jupiter*, or the Master of the Thunder, was assigned to *Thor*; and is called at this day *Thorsday*, THURSDAY, or the day of THOR. (See Vol. I. pag. 96.) To conclude, Adam of Bremen, an au-

* Tr. *Les Celtes*.

thor of the eleventh century, and a miſſionary in thoſe countries, inſinuates that this was the idea which the Scandinavians had formed of him. " *Thor cum ſceptro Jovem* " *exprimere videtur*, &c." Hiſt. Eccleſ. c. 223. There is not the leaſt doubt, but it was the Jupiter of the Gauls who had, according to Cæſar, " the " empire of things ce- " leſtial ;" as alſo the *Taran*, whom Lucan repreſents as having been adored by the ſame people, Pharſal. l. I. v. 444. *Taran*, ſignifies " Thun- " der," in the Welſh language at this day.

THE

THE SIXTH FABLE.

Of the Giant Nor.

THE Giant *Nor* was the first who inhabited the country of *Jotunheim* (A), 'or Giants-Land.' He had a daughter, named NIGHT; who is of a dark complexion, as are all her family. She was at first married to a man called *Naglefara*, and had by him a son, named *Auder*. Then she espoused *Onar*; and the daughter of this marriage was the Earth. At last she was wedded to *Daglingar*, who is of the family of the Gods. Between them they produced DAY, a child beautiful and shining, as are all his father's family (B).

Then the Universal Father took NIGHT and DAY, and placed them in heaven; and gave them two horses and two cars, that they might travel successively, one after the other, round the world. NIGHT goes first, upon her horse, named *Rimfaxe* (or Frosty-mane) who, every morning when he begins his courſe, bedews the earth with the foam that drops from his bit; this is the Dew. The horſe made uſe of by Day, is named *Skinfaxa* (or Shining-mane;) and by his radiant mane, he illuminates the air and the earth (c). Then Gangler aſked, How the Day regulates the courſe of the Sun and the Moon. Har anſwers, There was formerly a man, named *Mundilfara*, who had two children ſo beautiful and well-ſhaped, that he called the male *Mane*, or the Moon; and the female *Sunna*, or the Sun (d). She married a man called *Glener*. But the Gods, angry at their preſumption in taking upon them ſuch ſublime names, carried them up to heaven, and obliged the daughter to guide the car of the Sun, which the Gods, to illuminate the earth, had compoſed of the fires that iſſued from *Muſpelſheim*, or the flaming world. At the ſame time, the Gods placed under each horſe two ſkins filled with air, to cool and refreſh them; and hence, according to the moſt ancient accounts, comes the Freſhneſs of the morning. As for *Mane*, he was ſet to regulate the courſe of the Moon, and its different quarters. One day he carried off two children, named *Bil* and *Hiuke*, as they were returning from a fountain, carrying between them a pitcher ſuſpended on a ſtick. Theſe two children always accompany the Moon, as

one

one may obferve eafily even from the earth. But, interrupted Gangler, The Sun runs very fwiftly, as if fhe were afraid fome one fhould overtake her. So fhe well may, replied Har; for there are very near her two Wolves, ready to devour her. One of them clofely perfues the Sun, who is afraid of him, becaufe he fhall one day fwallow her up. The other as eagerly follows the Moon, and will make him one day or other undergo the fame fate. Gangler faid, Whence come thefe Wolves? Har replied, There was at the eaft of MIDGARD a Giantefs, who dwelt in the foreft of *Jarnvid* (or IRON-WOOD) all the trees of which are of iron. The Gianteffes of that place, derive their names from her. This old forcerefs is the mother of many Giants, who are all of them fhaped like favage beafts. From her alfo fprung thefe two Wolves. One in particular of that race is faid to be the moft formidable of all; he is called *Managarmer*; a monfter that fattens himfelf with the fubftances of men who draw near to their end. Sometimes he fwallows up the Moon, and ftains the heaven and the air with blood (E). Then the Sun is alfo darkened, as it is faid in thefe verfes of VOLUSPA: " Near the rifing
" of the Sun, dwelleth the old witch of
" the foreft of *Jarnvid*. There fhe brings
" forth

" forth the sons she hath by *Fenris*. One
" of these is become the most powerful of
" all. He feeds himself with the lives of
" those who approach to their end. Cloath-
" ed with the spoils of the other Giants,
" he will one day stain with blood the
" army of the Gods: the following Sum-
" mer the light of the Sun shall be extin-
" guished. Noxious winds shall blow
" from all quarters. Do not you compre-
" hend this saying?"

REMARKS on the SIXTH FABLE.

(A) " The country of the Giants, &c."] There are great contests among the learned about this country of *Jotunheim*, or of the Giants; which so constantly occurs in all the ancient Chronicles of the north. I needed only have given a sketch of their principal conjectures, to have produced a note of great erudition; which would certainly have tired my readers, but could have taught them nothing they wanted to know.

(B) " All his father's " family."] One may remark, that according to this allegoric genealogy, it is Night that brings forth the Day. All the Celtic, ' as well as Go- ' thic' nations, were of this persuasion. The ancient reasoners, more often even than the modern, were reduced to the necessity of explaining what was obscure, by what was still more obscure. That was a method very well suited, and intirely analogous to the turn of the human mind, whose curiosity is very voracious, but yet is easily satisfied, and often as well with words as ideas. Night being thus the mother of Day, they thought themselves felves obliged, in their computation of time, to prefer the name of the Mother to that of the Son. Besides, as they reckoned by months purely lunar, it was natural for them to compute the civil day from sun-set, and from the time when the Moon appears above the horizon. It will not be amiss here briefly to take notice of the universality of this custom: it was observed by the Gauls, even in the time of Cæsar, who positively affirms this of them; and that the Germans did the same, we have the testimony of Tacitus. The same modes of speech occur in the Salique-law, and in the constitutions of Charlemaigne. (Vid. Keysl. Antiq. p. 197.) The sentences pronounced in the Tribunals of France not long ago, often ordered the parties *(comparoir dedans* 14 *nuits)* " to " appear within 14 " nights *;" and as the DAY was thought to bring the NIGHT along with it, they afterwards expressed themselves *(dans* 15 *jours)* " within 15 " days," a manner of speaking no less familiar to the ' Goths and' Celts, than to the Romans. The English even at this day, say *senight* for *seven-night,* or seven nights, that is, a week; and *fortnight,* (i. e. fourteen nights) for two weeks, or 14 days. (See Vol. I. p. 358.) In the ancient histories of the north, frequent mention is made of " Children of " two or three nights," and " of two winters and " two nights."

(c) " He illuminates " the air, &c."] We have here a specimen of the natural philosophy of the first ages. In attempting to explain things the causes of which are obscure, men of all countries have gone in the same track; and have represented what was unknown by the image of something they were well acquainted with. This is doubtless the true ori-

---

* It may deserve inquiry, whether the French had not those modes of expression from the Frank, rather than the Gauls; i. e. rather from their Gothic, than their Celtic ancestors.   T.

gin of fable. We perceive, at first sight, that it cannot be men, who dispense rain and fine weather, who lanch the lightning, &c. There was therefore a necessity for imagining there were beings of much superior powers, to produce these wonderful operations; but none at all for assigning to them forms different from those of men and other animals. These solutions at once satisfied the curiosity and the imagination; they were easy to be comprehended; they interested the heart a thousand ways; and must therefore succeed, and become lasting. In fact, they have every where prevailed throughout the world. And those who have so far opened their eyes, as to see into the falsity of these explications, have not been able to renounce them without regret, and can still amuse themselves with what they believe no longer. We shall find in this Mythology more than one proof, that the people of the north have yielded, no less than others, to this natural propensity; and shall be forced to agree with M. de Fontenelle, that although a lively and burning Sun may inspire some nations with a greater warmth of imagination, and may give to their spirits that concoction, if I may so say, which compleats their relish and digestion of fables; yet all men have talents of this kind, independent of physical causes.

(D) " The female " *Sunna*, or the SUN."] The word for *Sun* is still of the feminine gender in the German tongue, and that for the *Moon* in the masculine. This obtained formerly in almost all the dialects of the Gothic language. The EDDA here gives an explication after the ancient manner, of all the celestial appearances. The poets were willing to give a reason for all the various phases of the Moon, for the freshness of the Morning, for the course of the Sun, &c. I shall leave some other commentator, more conversant in astronomy than myself, to examine whether the spots in the

Moon

Moon bear any resemblance to the image which the Edda gives of them in this Chapter.

(E) " Sometimes he " swallows up the " Moon."] Here we have the cause of Eclipses; and it is upon this very ancient opinion, that the general practice is founded, of making noises at that time, to fright away the monster, who would otherwise devour the two great luminaries. Threatened as they so often were with being swallowed up, could they hope always to escape the danger? The ' ancient Scandinavians*,' who never lost sight of the future ruin of this universe, did not flatter themselves so far. The monster was to prevail at the last day; as we shall see in the sequel. I say nothing here as to the idea of the other monster's sucking out the substances of men who die away insensibly. If it were worth while, one might find still traces of this notion among the popular prejudices of our own times. It is of more consequence to remark here, the great obligations we owe to the progress of science, and in particular to the study of nature, for our present security and exemption from such groundless terrors.

* *Les Celtes.* Orig.

D 4 THE

THE SEVENTH FABLE.

Of the Way that leads to Heaven.

GANGLER afks; Which way do they go from earth to heaven? Har anfwered, with a fmile of derifion, That is a fenfelefs queftion; have you never been told, that the Gods have erected a Bridge, which extends from earth to heaven, and that the name of it is *Bifrofl?* You have furely feen it; but, perhaps, you call it the RAINBOW. It is of three colours, is extremely folid, and conftructed with more art than any work in the world. But altho' it be fo very ftrong, it will neverthelefs be broke in pieces, when the fons of *Mufpell*, thofe mifchievous Genii, after having traverfed the great Rivers of Hell, fhall pafs over this Bridge on horfeback. Then, fays Gangler, It appears to me that the Gods have not executed their work truly and faithfully, in erecting a Bridge fo liable to be broken down, fince it is in their power er to perform whatever they pleafe. The Gods, replied Har, are not to be blamed on that account. Bifroſt is of itſelf a good bridge; but there is nothing in nature that can hope to make refiſtance, when thoſe Genii of Fire ſally forth to war (A).

But, ſays Gangler, What did the Univerſal Father do, after he had built Aſgard? Har anſwered, He in the beginning eſtabliſhed Governors (B); and ordered them to decide whatever differences ſhould ariſe among men, and to regulate the government of the celeſtial city. The aſſembly of theſe judges was held in the plain called *Ida,* which is in the middle of the divine abode. Their firſt work was to build a Hall, wherein are Twelve Seats for themſelves (C), beſides the throne which is occupied by the Univerſal Father. This Hall is the largeſt and moſt magnificent in the world. One ſees nothing there but gold, either within or without. Its name is *Gladheim* *, or the Manſion of Joy. They alſo erected another Hall, for the uſe of the Goddeſſes. It is a moſt delightful and delicate ſtructure: they call it *Vinglod,* or the Manſion of Love and Friendſhip. Laſtly, they built a houſe, wherein they placed furnaces, hammers, an anvil, and

---

* *Glad-heim,* is literally in Engliſh GLAD-HOME. T.

all the other instruments of a forge; then they worked in metal, stone, and wood; and composed so large a quantity of the metal called Gold, that they made all their moveables, and even the very harness of their horses of pure Gold: hence that age was named the Golden Age (D). This was that age which lasted till the arrival of those women, who came from the country of the Giants, and corrupted it. Then the Gods seating themselves upon their thrones, distributed justice, and took under consideration the affairs of the DWARFS; a species of beings bred in the dust of the earth; just as worms are in a dead carcase. It was indeed in the body of the Giant YMIR, that they were engendered, and first began to move and live. At first they were only worms; but by order of the Gods, they at length partook of both human shape and reason; nevertheless, they always dwell in subterraneous caverns, and among the rocks (E).

Here follow some verses of the Voluspa, accompanied with a long list of the principal Dwarfs. Some of which are said to dwell in the rocks, and others in the dust, &c.

REMARKS ON THE SEVENTH FABLE.

(A) " When those Genii of Fire sally forth " to war."] It is very remarkable that this menace

nace should so often occur. But the 'Gothic and' Celtic nations were in general persuaded, that nature was in continual danger; and that its secret and public enemies, after having for a long time undermined and shaken it, would at last bring on the great day of its general ruin. This melancholy idea must, I think, have had its rise from some of those disorders, to which our world is often exposed; at which times one would almost believe that the powers who govern it, were engaged in war with each other. And although this idea must have prevailed more extensively, and been more easily impressed in those climates where the seasons, subject to sudden and violent revolutions, often present nature under a languishing, or convulsed appearance: yet it is well known that there is scarcely any people, but what have had expectations of the end of the world; and have accordingly represented it some way or other; either as effected by a deluge, or a conflagration: or, lastly, under the veil of some allegory; as by a battle between good and evil Genii. The EDDA employs all these three means at the same time: such deep root had this doctrine taken in the minds of the poets, the theologians of the north.

(B) " He established " governors."] The legislators of the Scythians represented God himself, as author of the Laws which they gave to their fellow citizens. Neither ought we to esteem this pretence of theirs as altogether a political imposture. When men had brought themselves to look upon their Gods as the protectors of Justice and integrity; the Laws, which gave a public sanction to those virtues, being regarded as the expression of the divine will, might naturally enough be called the Work of the Gods. This manner of speaking, though misunderstood afterwards, would be sufficiently authorized by that respect and gratitude, which so great a benefit would inspire. It is well known

known that among all nations, the administration of justice was at first an office of the priest-hood. The ' Teutonic and' Celtic tribes retained this custom longer than most other people. All the ancients assure us, that the priests among the Gauls were arbiters, not only of private differences, but even of national disputes: that they disposed of controverted goods, excommunicated the contumacious, and inflicted death upon the guilty. Who could help trembling before governors, who, to speak in the language of the Edda, distributed justice in the name of the Supreme God? In effect, both Cæsar and Tacitus inform us, that among the Germans, none but the Priests had a right to inflict penalties; and this, not in the name of the Prince or People, but in the name of the God of Armies, in the name of that God, who had appointed them Governors. (V. Tacit. Germ. c. 7. Cæsar. l. 6.) Hence it was that these nations, when they embraced christianity, were beforehand so disposed to attribute to the Christian Priests and Bishops that unlimited and supernatural power; and to have for their decisions that implicit submission, as well as that blind reverence for their persons, which have been so long the misfortune and disgrace of humanity.

(c) " Wherein are " Twelve Seats for them- " selves."] These Judges were Twelve in number. Was this owing to there being Twelve primary Deities among the ' Gothic ' nations *', as there were among the Greeks and Romans? This I shall not take upon me to decide: but I think one may plainly observe here the first traces of a custom, which hath extended itself to a great many other things. Odin, the conqueror of the north, established a supreme court in Sweden, composed of Twelve Members, to assist him in the functions of the priesthood and civil

* *Les Celtes.* Orig.

govern-

government. This doubtlefs gave rife to what was afterwards called the Senate. And the fame eftablifhment in like manner took place in Denmark, Norway, and other northern ftates. Thefe Senators decided in the laft appeal all differences of importance; they were, if I may fay fo, the Affeffors of the Prince; and were in number Twelve, as we are exprefsly informed by Saxo, in his life of king Regner Lodbrog. Nor are other monuments wanting, which abundantly confirm this truth. We find in Zealand, in Sweden near Upfal, and, if I am not miftaken, in the county of Cornwal alfo, large ftones, to the amount of Twelve, ranged in the form of a circle, and, in the midft of them, one of fuperior heighth. Such, in thofe rude ages, was the Hall of Audience; the ftones that formed the circumference, were the feats of the fenators, that in the middle the throne of the king. The like monuments are found alfo in Perfia, near Tauris. Travellers frequently meet there with large circles of hewen ftones; and the tradition of the country reports, that thefe are the places where the *Caous*, or Giants, formerly held their councils. (Vid. Chardin's Travels into Perfia, Vol. III. p. .) I think one may difcover veftiges of this ancient cuftom, in the fable of the Twelve Peers of France, and in the eftablifhment of Twelve Jurymen in England, ' who are the proper ' Judges, according to ' the ancient laws of that ' country. T.'

(D) " Named the " Golden Age."] This Golden Age of the EDDA is not worthy to be compared with that of the Greek poets; but in return, it may perhaps have this advantage over the other, that it is not altogether without real exiftence. There is no doubt but this Mythology, like all others, perpetually confounds the natural Deities, with thofe perfons who were only deified by men, and to whom were afcribed the names of the former. Men, who rendered

rendered themselves illustrious by some noble invention, or by their attachment to the worship of the Gods, received the names of those Gods after their decease; and it was a long time before the following ages thought of distinguishing the one from the other. Among our Scythian ancestors, the first men who found out a mine of gold, or any other metal; and knew how to work that metal, and make something ornamental out of it, were doubtless regarded as divine persons. A mine discovered by chance, would easily afford and furnish out that slight magnificence; of which the EDDA has here preserved a faint remembrance.

(E) " Dwell ... among the rocks."] This passage deserves attention. We may discover here one of the effects of that ignorant prejudice, which hath made us for so many years regard all arts and handicrafts, as the occupation of mean people and slaves. Our Celtic ' and Gothic' ancestors, whether Germans, Scandinavians or Gauls, imagining there was something magical, and beyond the reach of man in ' mechanic' skill and industry, could scarcely believe that an able artist was one of their own species, or descended from the same common origin. This, it must be granted, was a very foolish conceit; but let us consider what might possibly facilitate the entrance of it into their minds. There was perhaps some neighbouring people, which bordered upon one of the Celtic ' or Gothic' tribes; and which, although less warlike than themselves, and much inferior in strength and stature, might yet excel them in dexterity; and addicting themselves to manual arts, might carry on a commerce with them sufficiently extensive, to have the fame of it spread pretty far. All these circumstances will agree well enough with the Laplanders: who are still as famous for their magic, as remarkable for the lowness of their stature; pacific, even to a degree of cowardice; but

of

of a mechanic induſtry, which formerly muſt have appeared very conſiderable. The ſtories that were invented concerning this people, paſſing thro' the mouths of ſo many ignorant relaters, would ſoon acquire all the degrees of the marvellous, of which they were ſuſceptible. Thus the Dwarfs ſoon became, (as all know, who have dipt but a little into the ancient romances) the forgers of enchanted armour, upon which neither ſwords, nor conjurations, could make any impreſſion. They were poſſeſſed of caverns, full of treaſure, intirely at their own diſpoſal. This, to obſerve by the bye, hath given birth to one of the Cabaliſtic doctrines, which is perhaps only one of the branches of the ancient northern theology*. As the Dwarfs were feeble, and but of ſmall courage; they were ſuppoſed to be crafty, full of artifice and deceit. This, which in the old romances is called Disloyalty, is the character always given them in thoſe fabulous narratives. All theſe fancies having received the ſeal of time and univerſal conſent, could be no longer conteſted; and it was the buſineſs of the poets to aſſign a fit origin for ſuch ungracious beings. This was done, in their pretended riſe from the dead carcaſe of a great Giant. The Dwarfs at firſt were only the maggots, engendered there by its putrifaction: afterwards the Gods beſtowed upon them underſtanding and cunning. By this fiction the northern warriors juſtified their contempt of them; and at the ſame time accounted for their ſmall ſtature, their induſtry, and their ſuppoſed propenſity for inhabiting caves and clefts of the rocks. After all, the notion is not every where exploded that there are in the bowels of the earth ' Fairies §', or a kind of dwarfiſh and tiny beings,

---

* *La Theologie Celtique.* Fr. Orig.

§ I have, in this one place of the tranſlation, applied the word Fairies, in our common Engliſh notion of it:—But our author has generally,

ings; of human shape, remarkable for their riches, their activity and malevolence. In many countries of the north, the people are still firmly persuaded of their existence. In Iceland, at this day, the good folks shew the very rocks and hills, in which they maintain that there are swarms of these small subterraneous men, of the most tiny size, but most delicate figures.

rally, throughout this work, used the French word *Fees*, (i. e. FAIRIES) to signify, not the little imaginary dwarfish beings, to which we appropriate the word; but to express the Fates or Destinies; or those inferior female Divinities that are assigned to watch over the lives and fortunes of individuals.—In this he seems rather to have had an eye to the Oriental fables, than to those of genuine Gothic origin: however, the duty of a translator requiring me to follow him, I beg leave here to apprize the reader of this our author's application of the word. T.

THE EIGHTH FABLE.

Of the Holy City, or Refidence of the Gods.

GANGLER demanded: Which is the capital of the Gods, or the facred city? Har anfwers, It is under the Afh *Ydrafil*; where the Gods affemble every day, and adminifter juftice (A). But, fays Gangler, What is there remarkable with regard to that place? That Afh, fays Jafnhar, is the greateft and beft of all trees. Its branches extend themfelves over the whole world, and reach above the heavens. It hath three roots, extremely diftant from each other: the one of them is among the Gods; the other among the Giants, in that very place where the abyfs was formerly; the third covers *Niflheim*, or Hell; and under this root is the fountain *Vergelmer*, whence flow the infernal rivers: this root is gnawed upon below by the monftrous ferpent *Nidhoger*. Under that root, which ftretches out towards the land of the Giants, is also a celebrated spring, in which are concealed Wisdom and Prudence. He who has possession of it is named *Mimis*; he is full of wisdom, because he drinks thereof every morning. One day the Universal Father came and begged to drink a cup of this water; but he was obliged to leave in pledge for it one of his eyes, according as it is said in the Voluspa: " Where hast thou concealed " thine eye, Odin? I know where; " even in the limpid fountain of Mimis. " Every morning does Mimis pour Hy- " dromel (or Mead) upon the pledge he " received from the Universal Father. Do " you, or do you not, understand this? " (B)." The third root of the Ash is in heaven, and under it lies the holy fountain of Time-past. 'Tis here that the Gods sit in judgment. Every day they ride hither on horseback, passing over the Rainbow, which is the bridge of the Gods. These are the names of the horses of the Gods: *Sleipner* is the best of them; he hath eight feet, and he belongs to Odin. The others are *Glader*, *Gyller*, &c. The horse of the God *Balder*, was burnt along with his master. As for Thor, he goes on foot to the tribunal of the Gods, and fords the rivers *Kormt*, *Gormt*, &c. All these is he obliged to cross every day on foot,

foot, in his way to the Ash *Ydrafil*; for the Bridge of the Gods is all on fire. How comes it to pass, interrupted Gangler, that the Bridge *Bifrost* is on fire? That, says Har, which you see red in the Rainbow, is the fire which burns in heaven: for the Giants of the mountains would climb up to heaven by that Bridge, if it were easy for every one to walk over it.

There are in heaven a great many pleasant cities, and none without a divine garrison. Near the fountain, which is under the Ash, stands a very beautiful city, wherein dwell three virgins, named *Urda*, or the PAST; *Verdandi*, or the PRESENT; and *Sskulda*, or the FUTURE. These are they who dispense the ages of men; they are called *Nornies*, that is, Fairies*, or Destinies. But there are indeed a great many others, besides these, who assist at the birth of every child, to determine his fate. Some are of celestial origin; others descend from the Genii; and others from the Dwarfs: as it is said in these verses,
" There are *Nornies* of different originals:
" some proceed from the Gods, some from
" the Genii, and others from the Dwarfs."
—Then, says Gangler, if these *Nornies* dis-

---

* *Nornir*, Isl. is rather Fates, or Destinies, *Parcæ*. I have therefore chose to retain the original word in some of the following passages rather than render it FAIRIES, after M. Mallet. T.

pense the destinies of men, they are very unequal in their distribution; for some are fortunate and wealthy, others acquire neither riches nor honours; some come to a good old age, while others die in their prime of life. Har answers, The *Nornies*, who are sprung of a good origin, are good themselves, and dispense good destinies: but those men to whom misfortunes happen, ought to ascribe them to the evil *Nornies* or Fairies (c). Gangler proceeds, and desires to know something more concerning the Ash. Har replied, What I have farther to add concerning it is, that there is an eagle perched upon its branches, who knows a multitude of things: but he hath between his eyes a sparrow-hawk. A squirrel runs up and down the Ash, sowing misunderstanding between the eagle and the serpent, which lies concealed at its root. Four stags run across the branches of the tree, and devour its rind. There are so many serpents in the fountain whence spring the rivers of hell, that no tongue can recount them, as it is said in these verses. " The " large Ash suffers more than man would " believe. A stag eats and spoils it above; " it rots on the sides; while a serpent " gnaws and corrodes it below." And also in these, " Under the great Ash are many " serpents, &c." They relate besides, that the Fairies or Destinies who reside near the

foun-

fountain of the PAST, draw up water thence, with which they bedew the Aſh, to prevent its branches from growing withered and decayed. Of ſo purifying a nature is that water, that whatever it touches becomes as white as the film withinſide an egg. There are upon this ſubject very ancient verſes, to this effect, " The great " and ſacred Aſh is beſprinkled with a " white water, whence comes the dew " which falls into the valleys, and which " ſprings from the fountain of PAST-" TIME." Men call this the Honey-dew, and it is the food of bees. There are alſo in this fountain two ſwans, which have produced all the birds of that ſpecies.

REMARKS ON THE EIGHTH FABLE.

(A) " Adminiſter juſtice."] We ſee in the preceeding fable, that the Gods aſſemble together in the open air, in a valley: Here is their principal reſidence, under an Aſh-Tree. In this, as in other things, the Gods are made to conform themſelves to the manners of men. The ancient ' Gothic and' Celtic nations for a long time had no other place of rendezvous, than ſome tree remarkable for its ſize and age. The ſtates of Eaſt Frieze1and, even ſo late as the thirteenth century, aſſembled under three large oaks which grew near Aurich; and it is not more than three centuries ago, that moſt of the German princes held their conferences under trees †. The averſion theſe people had for incloſed places; the fear of putting themſelves into the power of a perfidious

† Vid. Keyſl. Antiq. Sept. p. 78, 79, 8°. T.

chief-

chieftain, who, fortified in his castle, was stronger than the laws and magistrates: and lastly, that ancient impression, not even yet worn entirely out, with which their religion had inspired them in favour of trees; these are probably the causes of the singular custom here alluded to in the EDDA.

(B) " Do you, or do you not, understand this?"] To this I can only answer in the negative. This whole description is most certainly allegorical. We meet in it indeed with some glimmering rays of light, but they are so transient and so broken, that one may fairly own, the whole is unintelligible. One of the translators of the EDDA will have *Minis* to be *Minos*; I am no more warranted by reason to oppose him in this, than he was to entertain such a conceit.

(c) " The evil Fairies."] Here we have a compleat theory of Fairyism. In this passage of the EDDA we have the bud and germ (as it were) of what the ancient romances * and popular superstitions have so widely branched, and applied to such a variety of things. All the Celtic ' and Gothic' tribes have had a great veneration for the Fairies, or Destinies; and not without reason, since every man's fate or fortune was in their hands. The romances inform us, that there were two kinds of them, the Good and Bad; but they distinguish them no farther. The three principal, according to the Edda, are the PRESENT, the PAST, and the FUTURE; a circumstance which is wanting in the Greek fable of the

---

* The romances in which the FAIRIES and DESTINIES are used as synonymous, are not those of Gothic origin, but rather the Oriental tales and fables. The FAIRIE's of our own northern ancestors, are properly what are called throughout this work the DWARFS: whereas our author applies the word *Fees* (FAIRIES) in nearly the same sense as the Latin *Nymphæ* and *Parcæ*; and perhaps this may be the sense in which it is generally used by his countrymen. The *Nornæ*, however, of the Edda, seem to be evidently the same with the *Weird Sisters*, so famous in Gothic History and Romance. See Bartholin. Causæ Contempt. Mort. p. 630. Junii Etymol. Ang. (Verb. WERDE.) T.

Parcæ,

Parcæ, and which is in itself not badly imagined. The Romans, who enlarged their heaven, and increased the number of their Gods, in proportion as they extended their empire; having adopted these ' northern *' divinities, consecrated to them divers monuments, some of which have been recovered. These monuments agree very well with the EDDA §. They almost always present to view three females: the oracles these pronounced had rendered them famous. They were especially resorted to at the birth of a child. In many places there were caverns, where the people fancied they might enjoy the pleasure of their presence, and hear them speak. Some places in France retain still the name of the FAIRIES OVEN, the FAIRIES WELL, &c. Saxo, the Grammarian, speaks of a chapel, where king Fridleif went to consult them about the fate of his son Olaus, and he adds, that he saw three young women sitting there. Sax. l. 6. This superstition, so general throughout Europe, hath prevailed almost as long as that relating to witches and sorcerers. We see, in the process or trial of the famous MAID OF ORLEANS, that she was accused of going often to a certain oak in a solitary place, to consult the FAIRIES (Fr. *Fees.*) These Fairies were, I believe, as to their origin, deified prophetesses. The Celtic ' and Teutonic' women had a peculiar talent for improving all sorts of superstition; and turning every thing into omens. Those who had most distinguished themselves in this art, were deified, and became Goddesses after their decease; and as they had predicted the fate of men on earth, were believed still to do it in heaven.

This error is very ancient. In the time of Vespasian, there was, according to Tacitus, a female named *Velleda*, half a Prophetess, and half a Fairy, who, from the top

---

* Fr. *Cehiques*. § Vid. Keysl. Ant. p. 33. 270. 396. 446.

of a tower where she lived recluse, exercised far and near, a power equal to that of kings. *Late imperitabat* are the words of the historian. The most illustrious warriors undertook nothing without her advice, and always consecrated to her a part of the booty. V. Tacit. Hist. l. 4 & 5. In general, one may observe, that the worship paid to women, hath always had here in Europe great advantage over that which was directed to men. The religious respect which was here paid to the Fairies or Destinies, is of all the doctrines of the ancient religion *, that which hath longest prevailed. These fabulous divinities have survived all the Gods and Genii, both of the Celts and Romans, and though at last banished every where else, have found a kind of asylum in our romances.

* Fr. *La Religion Celtique*.

*** To the instances given by our Author (in Note A) of the Gothic nations assembling under Trees, may be added the following in our own country, viz.

The Wapentake of SKIRE-AKE in the West-riding of Yorkshire, is thought to have taken its name from a remarkable Oak, to which the inhabitants repaired upon public occasions, as at a general Convention of the District, &c. See Thoresby's Ducat. Leod. p. 84. 150.——So Berkshire is thought to have been denominated from BEROKE, a bare, or disbarked Oak, to which, upon particular emergencies, the inhabitants were wont, in ancient times to resort and consult about public matters. Camd. Brit. (by Gibson, 1 Ed. p. 137.)——The Translator of this Book knows a Manor in Shropshire, where the Manor-Court is held to this day under a very aged Ash-tree: there the Steward calls over the Copy-holders, and forms a Jury; and then adjourns the Court to a neighbouring inn, for the dispatch of business.   T.

THE NINTH FABLE.

Of the Cities which are in Heaven.

GANGLER says to Har, You tell me very wonderful things; but what are the other holy cities to be seen in heaven? Har replies, There are many other very fine cities to be seen there. In one of them, called *Alfheim* (A), dwell the luminous Genii, but the black Genii live under the earth, and differ from the others still more in their actions than in their appearance. The luminous Genii are more splendid than the Sun; but the black Genii are darker than pitch. In these parts there is also a city called *Breidablik*, which is not inferior to any other in beauty; and another named *Glitner*, the walls, columns and inside of which are gold, and the roof of silver *. There also is to be seen the city *Himinborg*, or the Celestial Mount, situated upon the frontiers, at the place

---

* The Edda of Goranson says *Asgulli*, of gold. T.

where the bridge of the Gods touches heaven. The great city of *Valafcialf*, which belongs to Odin, is all built of pure filver. There is the royal Throne, called *Lidfcialf*, or the Terror of the Nations. When the Univerfal Father is feated upon it, he can view the whole earth. On the utmoft limit of heaven, towards the fouth, is the moft beautiful city of all: it is called *Gimle*. It is more brilliant and fhining than the Sun itfelf, and will fubfift even after the deftruction of heaven and earth. Men of real goodnefs and integrity fhall abide there for everlafting ages. The poem VOLUSPA fpeaks thus of it; " I know that there is " a place brighter than the Sun, and in- " tirely covered with gold, in the city of " *Gimle:* there the virtuous are to refide; " there they fhall live happy throughout " all ages (B)." Then Gangler demands, What will preferve that city when the black flame comes to confume heaven and earth? Har replied, We have been told, that there is towards the fouth, another heaven, more elevated than this, called the Clear Blue; and above that, a third heaven, ftill more elevated, called the Boundlefs. In this laft we think the city of *Gimle* muft be feated, but it is at prefent inhabited only by the luminous Genii.

REMARKS on the NINTH FABLE.

(A) "In a city named Alfheim."] *Alfheim* signifies, in Gothic, the Abode of the Genii, that is, of the Fairies of the male sex. We may observe, that they are of different characters, Good and Bad; for there is no probability, that any one good quality could be ascribed to creatures blacker than pitch. It is needless to observe, that all the 'Gothic and' Celtic nations have had these Genii. The romances of Chivalry are full of allusions to this imaginary system. The same opinions prevailed among the Persians. In many places of High Germany, the people have still a notion, that these Genii come by night, and lay themselves on those they find sleeping on their backs; and thus produce that kind of suffocation which we call the Night Mare. (See Keysler. Antiq. Sept. p. 500.) In the same manner they accounted for those luxurious and immodest illusions, so common in dreams; hence are derived the fables of Incubuses and Sucubuses; and that general opinion that there were Genii or Sylphs of both sexes, who did not disdain the embraces of mortals. With one single fiction, so fruitful as this, they might have run through the whole world of nature, and not have left a single phænomenon unaccounted for. To do this there was only occasion for Good and Bad Genii, as we have seen above. With regard to the Bad, they were particularly dreaded at the hour of noon; and in some places they still make it a point of duty to keep company at that hour with women in childbed, for fear the Demon of Noon should attack them, if left alone. This superstition hath prevailed no less in France, than elsewhere; though it came from the east. St. Basil recommends us to pray to God some time before noon, to avert this danger. The Celtes with the same view, offered sacrifices,

crifices. One says pleasantly, the true Demon of no n is hunger, when one has nothing to satisfy it †. If one looks back upon so many chimerical terrors, and so many painful and absurd observances, from which we are at this day delivered; who but must applaud the progress of literature and the sciences? See, upon this subject, a dissertation of the learned Mr. Schutze, in his Exerc. ad German. Gentil. fac. Exercit. V. p. 221.

(B) " Live happy " throughout all ages."] We shall see this subject treated in a more extensive manner in another place of the EDDA, for which (to avoid repetitions) I shall reserve many remarks I have to make on this important passage.

† Vid. Keysler. Antiq. Sept. p. 500.—The same author gives a very curious passage from an ancient SCALD, concerning the ELFS. See p. 501, 502.
T.

THE TENTH FABLE.

Of the Gods to be believed in.

GANGLER goes on, and afks, Who are the Gods, whom men ought to acknowledge? Har anfwers, There are twelve Gods, whom you ought to ferve. Jafnhar adds, Nor are the Goddeffes lefs facred. Thridi proceeds, The firft and moft ancient of the Gods is ODIN. He governs all things. And although the Gods are powerful, yet they all ferve him, as children do their father (A). His fpoufe FRIGGA forefees the deftinies of men, but fhe never reveals what is to come, as appears from that converfation in verfe which Odin one day held with *Loke*. " Senfelefs " *Loke*, why wilt thou pry into the fates? " Frigga alone knoweth what is to come, " but fhe never difclofeth it to any perfon." Odin is called the Univerfal Father, becaufe he is the Father of all the Gods. He is alfo called the Father of Battles, becaufe
he

he adopts for his children all those who are slain with their swords in their hands. He assigns them for their place of residence, the palaces of *Valhall* and *Vingolf*, and bestows upon them the title of *Heroes* (B). He has a great many other names, as *Hanga-Gud*, &c. [*Here forty-six names are enumerated.*]

A great many names indeed! says Gangler: surely that man must be very learned who knows them all distinctly, and can tell upon what occasions they were given. Har replies, It requires, no doubt, a tolerable memory, to recollect readily all these names. But I will intimate to you however, in a few words, what principally contributed to confer them upon him: it was the great variety of languages (B): for each people being desirous to adore him, and address their vows to him, they have been obliged to translate his name each into his own language. Some of his other names have been owing to adventures, which have happened to him in his travels, and which are related in the ancient histories. Nor can you ever pass for a man of learning, if you are not able to give an account of all these wonderful adventures.

REMARKS on the TENTH FABLE.

(A) "As children do their father."] I am obliged to return again to Odin. There is nothing in all Pagan antiquity more exprefs than this paffage, with regard to the fupremacy of ONE GOD. The name of *As*, or LORD, is again afcribed to him in this place. The Gauls, in like manner, called him alfo *Æs*, or with a Latin termination *Efus*: for feveral manufcript copies of Lucan, who fpeak of this God, give the word *Efus*, without the afpirate †. I have faid elfewhere, that Suetonius pofitively afferts the fame thing of the Etrufcans. The Roman authors have often called him the *Mars* of the Celtic people; becaufe, as the EDDA clearly fhows here, he was the fame with the God of War. Wherefore, (although the learned Abbé Banier has maintained the contrary) this *Efus*, whofe name occurs in the monuments of the cathedral of Paris, is, at one and the fame time, the Supreme God, and, to fpeak with the EDDA, the Father of Battles; as P. Pezron had advanced. (See La Mythol. & les Fables expliq. T. II. p. 650, &c. Ed. Quarto.) Monf. Pelloutier, in my opinion, hath proved, beyond all doubt, that the Supreme God of the Celtes, *Efus*, *Teut* or *Odin*, was the God of War. (See Hift. des Celtes, T. II. c. 7.) It is to no purpofe to object, that the Father of Gods and Men could not at the fame time be called the Father of Combats, without manifeft contradiction; for the EDDA eftablifhes this to be the fact too ftrongly to be difputed. Befides, contradictions do not always hinder an opinion from being received. Various

† Vid. Keyfl. Antiq. p. 139, &c. 187.—The paffage referred to in Lucan, is this.

Et quibus immitis placatur fanguine cæfo
Teutates; horrenfque feris altaribus HESUS.
       Pharfal. L. 1. T.

modi-

modifications and diſtinctions are found out to clear up the difficulty. But there was no great need of any here; for the 'Goths and' Celtes regarded war as a very ſacred occupation. It furniſhed, according to them, opportunities for diſplaying courage; and of fulfilling the views of providence; which was to place us here as in a field of battle; and only to grant its favours as the peculiar rewards of fortitude and valour.

(B) " It was the great " variety of languages."] This reaſoning upon the names of Odin, may contain ſomething of truth in it. The text recounts a great number of theſe names, which I have ſuppreſſed, out of regard to thoſe ears which are not accuſtomed to Gothic ſounds. 'Tis certain that almoſt all the names aſcribed to the Supreme Deity, are either epithets taken from the qualities attributed to him, or the places where he was worſhiped, or from the actions he had performed, &c. This diverſity of names hath often miſled thoſe of the learned, who have applied themſelves to the ſtudy of the Celtic religion, juſt in the ſame manner as hath happened to thoſe, who applied themſelves to the Greek or Roman mythology. In the ancient Icelandic poetry, we find the Supreme God denominated in more than a hundred and twenty-ſix different phraſes. They are all enumerated in the *Scalda*, or Poetic Dictionary. It would therefore (as Gangler obſerves) require ſome application, to give the reaſons of all theſe different denominations, many of which allude to particular events.

THE

THE ELEVENTH FABLE;

Of the God Thor, the Son of Odin.

HEREUPON Gangler demanded, What are the names of the other Gods? What are their functions, and what have they done for the advancement of their glory? Har says to him, The most illustrious among them is THOR. He is called *Afa-Thor*, or the Lord Thor; and *Ake-Thor*, or the Active Thor. He is the strongest and bravest of Gods and Men (A). His kingdom is named *Thrudwanger*. He possesses there a palace, in which are five hundred and forty Halls. It is the largest house that is known; according as we find mentioned in the poem of *Grimnis*. " There " are five hundred and forty Halls in the " Winding Palace of the God Thor; and " I believe there is no where a greater fa- " bric, than this of the eldest of sons." The Chariot of Thor is drawn by two He-Goats. It is in that Chariot that he goes into the country of the Giants; and thence.

thence they call him the rapid Thor. He likewife poffeffes three very precious things. The firft is a Mace, or Club, called *Miolner*, which the Giants of the Froft, and thofe of the Mountains, know to their coft, when they fee it hurled againft them in the air: and no wonder; for with that Mace has this God often bruifed the heads of their fathers and kindred. The fecond jewel he poffeffes, is called the Belt of Prowefs; when he puts it on, he becomes as ftrong again as he was before. The third, which is alfo very precious, are his Gauntlets, or Gloves of Iron, which he always wears when he would lay hold of the handle of his Mace. There is no perfon of fo much learning, as to be able to relate all his marvellous exploits; I myfelf could tell you fo many, that day would end much fooner, than the recital of what immediately occur to me. Then fays Gangler to him, I would rather hear fomething about the other Sons of Odin. To this Har anfwered in thefe words:

T H E fecond

REMARKS on the ELEVENTH FABLE.

(A) " Thor is the ftrongeft of Gods and Men."] The reader will recollect here, what I have faid a little higher concerning this divinity

of

of the northern nations *. The function ascribed to him of launching the thunder, made him pass for the most warlike and formidable of all the Gods. It was also Thor who reigned in the air, distributed the seasons, and raised or allayed tempests. " Thor, says " Adam of Bremen, is " the God who, according to these people, " governs the thunder, " the winds, the rains, " the fair weather, and " harvest." (See Hist. Eccles.) This Mace or Club, which he hurled against the Giants, and with which he crushed their heads, is doubtless the Thunder, which most frequently falls upon elevated places. He was in general regarded as a divinity favourable to mankind; as he who guarded them from the attacks of Giants and wicked Genii; whom he never ceased to encounter and pursue. The name of his palace signifies, in Gothic, " The place of re-" fuge from Terrour." As he was the first-born of the Supreme God; or to speak in the language of the EDDA, " The " Eldest of Sons;" the first and principal intelligence proceeding from the union of the Deity with Matter; they have made him a middle divinity, a mediator between God and Men. It is probable that a great many people venerated him also, as the intelligence who animated the Sun and Fire. The worship of the Persians had in this respect, as in a great many others, the most exact resemblance to that of this people. The Persians held, that the most illustrious of all created intelligences was what they paid homage to under the symbol of Fire or the Sun, wherein the intelligence resided. They called it *Mithr-as*, or the Mediator Lord. (The word *As* still signifies Lord, in Persian.) They, as well as the Scandinavians, kept a perpetual and sacred fire, in consequence of this persuasion. The Scythians, according to Herodotus and He-

* Fr. De Cillet.

sychius, adored this divinity under the title of *Goeto-Syrus*, which signifies The Good Star. This word *Syr*, or *Scir*, which the Persians employed to denominate the Sun, seems to be the same with *Thor*, only in a different dialect. The ancient people of the north pronounced the *th* in the same manner as the English do at present; not very different from *ss*. They had a particular character for that letter, which was afterwards lost in the other dialects of the Saxon language. All the Celtic nations have 'in like manner,' been accustomed to the worship of the Sun; either as distinguished from Thor, or considered as his symbol. It was a custom that every where prevailed in ancient times, to celebrate a feast at the winter solstice, by which men testified their joy at seeing this great luminary return again to this part of the heavens. They sacrificed horses to him, as an emblem, says Herodotus, of the rapidity of this planet. This was the greatest solemnity in the year. They called it in many places, *Yole*, or *Yuul*, from the word *Hiaul*, or *Houl*, which even at this day signifies the SUN, in the languages of Bass Britagne, and Cornwal *. When the ancient Pagan religion gave place to the Christian, the rejoicings, feasts and nocturnal assemblies which that festival authorised, indecent as they were, were not suppressed, lest, by endeavouring to gain all, all should be lost.

* This is giving a Celtic derivation of a Gothic word, (two languages extremely different.)—The learned Dr. Hickes thus derives the term in question. " Jol, *Cimbricum*, *Anglo-Saxonicè scriptum*, Geol; et " *Dan. Sax.* Iul, o in u *facile mutato, ope intensivi præfixi* ꝺ *et* ᵹe, *faciunt* ꝺl, ol, *Commissatio, compotatio, convivium, symposium.*"— " *(Isl.* Ol. *cerevisiam denotat*, & *metonymicè Convivium.)* " Junii Etym. Ang. V. YEOL.

Our ingenious author, however, is certainly right as to the origin and design of the YULE-FEAST: the Greenlanders at this day keep a SUN-FEAST at the winter solstice, about Dec. 22. to rejoice at the return of the Sun, and the expected renewal of the Hunting season, &c. Which custom they may possibly have learnt of the Norvegian Colony formerly settled in Greenland. See an account of this festival in Dav. Crantz's Hist. of Greenland, 2 Vols. 8vo. 1767. Vol. I. p. 176. T.

The church was content to sanctify the end of this feasting, by applying it to the nativity of our Lord; the anniversary of which happened to be much about the same time. In the languages of the north, *Juul*, or *Yule*, still signifies Christmas; and the manner in which this festival is celebrated in many places, as well as the old name itself, reminds us of many circumstances of its first original. (See Scheffer. Upsal. Antiq. c. 7. Pellout. Hist. des Celt. T. II. c. 12 †.) I have already observed, that in all the languages of the north, the day consecrated to the *Jupiter tonans* of the Romans, was transferred to the God THOR, and was named *Thorsdag*, &c. that is, THURSDAY. See Vol. I. pag. 96.

† See also Kejſl. Antiq. p. 159, &c. 349, 367. T.

THE TWELFTH FABLE.

Of the God Balder.

THE second son of Odin is named BALDER. He is of an excellent natural temper; and hath the universal praise of mankind: so handsome in his person, and of so dazling a look, that he seems to dart forth rays of light (A). To make you comprehend the beauty of his hair, you should be informed that the whitest of all vegetables is called, the " Eye-brow of Balder." This God, so radiant and graceful, is also the most eloquent and benign; yet such is his nature, that the judgments he has pronounced can never be altered. He dwells in the city of *Breidablik*, before-mentioned. This place is in heaven, and nothing impure can have admittance there: this is confirmed by the following verses: " Balder hath his pala-
" ces in Briedablik, and there I know are
" columns, upon which are engraven verses,
" capable of recalling the dead to life."

The third God is he, whom we call KIORD. He dwelleth in a place named *Noatun.* He is ruler of the winds: he checks the fury of the sea, storms and fire (B). Whoever would succeed in navigation, hunting or fishing, ought to pray to this God. He is so rich, that he can give to his votaries kingdoms and treasures: and upon this account also he deserves to be invoked. Yet Niord is not of the lineage of the Gods. He was reared at *Vanheim,* that is, in the country of the VANES; but the Vanes delivered him up an hostage to the Gods, and received in his place *Haner.* By this means a peace was re-established between the Gods and the Vanes. Niord took to wife *Skada,* the daughter of the Giant *Thiaffe.* She prefers dwelling on the spot where her father inhabits, that is, in the land of the mountains; but Niord loves to reside near the sea: yet they came at length to this agreement between themselves, that they should pass together nine nights among the mountains, and three on the shore of the sea. One day Niord, returning from the mountains, composed this song; "How
" do I hate the abode of the mountains?
" I have only passed nine nights there;
" but how long and tedious did they seem!
" There one hears nothing but the howl-
" ing of wolves, instead of the sweet sing-
" ing

"ing of the swans *, who dwell on the sea-shores." In answer to this, Skada composed the following verses: "How is it possible for me to enjoy my rest on the couch of the God of the Ocean; whilst birds in flocks returning each morning from the forest, awake me with their screamings?" Then Skada returned to the mountains, where her father dwells; there snatching up her bow, and fastening on her snow-skates, she often employed herself in the chace of savage beasts †.

* It is very remarkable, that the ancient Icelandic bards should have got hold of that fabulous opinion of the SWAN's being a singing bird; which so generally prevailed among the Greek and Roman poets. It would be a curious subject of disquisition, to inquire what could have given rise to so arbitrary and groundless a notion. ——There can be no mistake about the bird here; for the Icelandic words are the same with our English: *Saungui Suana*, "The song, or singing of SWANS." *Cantus Cygnorum*.   T.

† The reader will find an additional passage here in the Latin version of Goranson; as also some parts of the preceding paragraph differently rendered.

REMARKS on the TWELFTH FABLE.

(A) " He seems to dart forth rays of light."] Of all the nations who have formerly adhered to the 'Gothic' religion †, none have given us such a particular description of it as the Icelanders. If we are not therefore always able to prove, that some of the points contained in the doctrine of the EDDA have been universally received by other ancient nations of Europe; must it be thence concluded, that these doctrines were unknown to them? Analogy authorises us to judge the contrary. The conformities, we discover in that part which we know, may serve to answer for what remains unknown. But this reasoning, which I think well founded, shall not hinder me from seeking more positive proofs of that resemblance and conformity, as far as one can discover any traces of it amid the ruins of antiquity. There is in this place matter for the exercise of investigation. Who is this God Balder? Was he known to the other nations of Europe? It seems to me probable, that Balder is the same God, whom the Noricians and Gauls worshiped under the name of *Belenus*. This was a celebrated God among the Celtes. Many inscriptions make mention of him. We even find monuments, where he is exhibited according to his attributes. That which hath been long preserved at the castle of Polignac, represents him with a radiated head, and a large open mouth; which exactly agrees with the picture here given of him in the EDDA; as a God resplendent and eloquent. We easily see, that Belen and Balder came from the same origin, that is, from the Phrygian word *Bal*, or *Balen*, which signifies King, and which they formerly applied to the Sun. Selden (de Diis Syris. Synt. II. c. 1.)

† Fr. *La Religion Celtique*.

thinks

thinks that the ancient Britons called him *Belertucades*. This was the Apollo of the Greeks and Romans, the Sun considered as a benign and salutary conftellation, who chaced away maladies, animated the fpirits, and warmed the imagination, that fruitful mother of poetry and all the other arts.

(B) " He checks the " fury of the fea, ftorms " and fire."] This God, ' or at leaft a God with ' thefe attributes,' hath been adored by all the ancient ' nations of Eu-' rope, as well Goths as' Celtes: as alfo by the Perfians, and the people who dwell around the Euxine and Cafpian feas. They all of them affigned a Genius or God to the waters, whether of the fea, or of rivers, or fountains. This God would not fail to be adored, and loaded with prefents. In many places among the Gauls, they every year confecrated to him animals, precious ftuffs, fruits, and gold and filver. Such was that fmall piece of water near Toulouſe, into which great riches were thrown in honour of this Deity. They looked upon him as eafily provoked, and upon his goodnefs as not a little precarious; but fuch as was not ill adapted to the temper of him who was the mafter and director of fo deceitful an element. Thus the EDDA fcruples to admit him into the family of the Gods. The common people, in divers places of Germany and the north, are ftill perfuaded that men owe him a yearly tribute; and that when any body is drowned, this God hath carried him away. They call him, in Germany, *Der Nix*; and formerly in the north, *Nocken*. They had no other phrafe to exprefs a perfon's dying in the water, but " Nocken hath taken " him;" and hence without doubt is derived the French word *Noyer*, to drown. The Gauls called this divinity *Neith*. They believed that he refided in the fea, and in pools. There was near Geneva, in the lake which goes by the name of that town, a rock confecrated

to

to him, which still retains the name of *Neiton*; a word approaching very near to that of *Noatun*, which, according to the EDDA, is the residence of the God of Waters. The Romans retained both the worship and name of this God, who was adored by the ancient Celtic nations of Italy. In general, all the several people of Europe have had a great veneration for this Divinity, and nothing was more difficult than to bring them off from the worship they paid him; this furnished subject for the prohibitions of many a council. Even within the bosom of the Christian Church, the people long continued to repair in crouds to certain fountains, in order to adore the beneficent Genius, who, by an incomprehensible power, made the waters flow in equal and uninterrupted abundance; they covered them with flowers and presents; and poured out libations.

O fons Bandusiæ, splendidior vitro;
Dulci digne mero; non sine floribus,
Cras donaberis hœdo . . .

THE THIRTEENTH FABLE.

Of the God Frey, and the Goddess Freya.

NIORD had afterwards, at his residence of Noatun, two children, named FREY, and FREYA; both of them beautiful and vigorous. Frey is the mildest of all the Gods. He presides over the rain, and the sun, and all the productions of the earth. He is to be invoked in order to obtain either fine seasons, or plenty, or peace; for it is he who dispenses peace and riches. Freya is the most propitious of the Goddesses. The place which she inhabits in heaven, is called " The Union of the " People." She goes on horseback to every place where battles are fought, and asserts her right to one half of the slain; the other half belongs to ODIN. Her palace is large and magnificent; thence she sallies forth in a chariot, drawn by two cats. She lends a very favourable ear to the vows of those who sue for her assistance.

ance. It is from her that the Ladies have received the name, which we give them in our language. She is very much delighted with the songs of lovers; and such as would be happy in their amours ought to worship this Goddess.

Then says Gangler, All these Gods appear to me to have great power: and I am not at all surprized (A) that you are able to perform so many great atchievements, since you are so well acquainted with the attributes and functions of each God, and know what it is proper to ask of each in order to succeed. But are there still any more of them, besides those you have already named?

REMARKS on the THIRTEENTH FABLE.

FREY is some inferior intelligence or divinity, who resided in the air. FREYA, who has often been taken for FRIGGA, is the Goddess of Love, the Venus of the Scandinavians. The ladies are called, in Danish, *Fruer*; and, in ancient Gothic, the word Freya appears to have signified the same thing. This name has a remarkable analogy to the following words in the French language, viz. *Frayer*, to engender or spawn as fishes do; and *Friand*, which anciently signified "full of desire:" as also to *Frija*, which in Swedish signifies to be amorous, and to seek in marriage; and *Friar*, a gallant. The name *Aphroditis*, which was given to Venus by the people of Greece, seems also to bear some affinity to this. Gallantry being one of the principal virtues of every

every brave warrior, it was but right that the Goddess of Love should have the charge of rewarding one half, at least, of those who had died with their swords in their hands.

(A) " I am not at all " surprized, &c."] The people settled in Scandinavia, before the arrival of Odin, were a very simple race, and easily astonished. This conqueror subdued them as much by imposing on their minds, as by vanquishing their arms. Amazed at those successes, which their own ignorance had occasioned, and was not able to account for; they very wisely sent to Odin himself, to inquire the cause. We have seen that this was the end, which GANGLER, or the king who assumed that name, proposed to himself. Here he learned so many new circumstances concerning the functions of the several Gods, and the worship to be paid them in order to secure their favour, that he thought he had discovered the mystery, and was now in a condition to cope with his rival.

THE

THE FOURTEENTH FABLE.

Of the God Tyr.

HAR anfwered, There is the God Tyr, who is the moſt bold and intrepid of all the Gods. 'Tis he who difpenfes victories in war; and therefore warriors do well to pay their addreffes to him. It hath become proverbial to fay, of a man who furpaffes others in valour, that he is as BRAVE AS TYR. Let me give you a proof of his intrepidity. The Gods one day would fain have perfuaded the wolf FENRIS, their enemy, to permit himfelf to be chained up; but he, fearing leſt they ſhould never afterwards unloofe him, perfiſted in his refufal, till Tyr put his hand, by way of pledge, into the mouth of this monſter. The Gods not judging it proper to redeem the pledge by unchaining the wolf, he bit off the God's hand, fevering it at that part, which has been ever fince called ‘ *Uſlithr*, ‘ or' THE WOLF'S JOINT. From that time this God hath had but one hand. His remarkable prudence has given occasion to this form of expression, such a one is "sagacious as Tyr:" but it is believed, that he does not love to see men live in peace.

There is another God, named BRAGE, who is celebrated for his wisdom, eloquence and majestic air. He is not only eminently skilled in poetry, but the art itself is called from his name *Brager*, and the most distinguished poets receive their names from him. His wife is called *Iduna*. She keeps in a box certain apples, which the Gods taste of, whenever they feel old age approaching; for these apples have the virtue of restoring youth to all who eat them: it is by this means that the Gods will subsist till the darkness of the last times. Hereupon Gangler cried out, Certainly the Gods have committed a great treasure to the guardianship and good faith of Iduna. Har smiling, says to him, And hence it happened, that they once ran the greatest risk in the world; as I shall have occasion to tell you, when you have learnt the names of the other Gods.

REMARKS ON THE FOURTEENTH FABLE.

TYR was some inferior divinity, who presided particularly over battles. I do not believe that mention is made of him any where else, except in the EDDA

EDDA and other Icelandic monuments. And yet it is certain that this God hath been adored by all the northern nations; since in all the different dialects of this people, the name of the third day of the week, which the Romans confecrated to Mars *(Dies Martis)* hath been formed from the name of *Tyr*. This day is called *Tyrſdag* in Daniſh and Swediſh: and in the other dialects by a somewhat softer modulation, *Thiſdag*, *Diſtag*, *Tuſdag*, TUESDAY. (See Vol. I. pag. 99.) Tacitus, here, as almoſt every where elſe, perfectly agrees with our monuments. He renders the name TYR, by that of Mars, and makes him a ſubaltern, and inferior divinity to the God ODIN, whom he deſcribes under the name of Mercury.

As to the God BRAGE, we know nothing more of him than what we learn from the EDDA; and yet the Gauls had likewiſe a God of eloquence, named by the Romans *Herculus Ogmius*; but whether he was the ſame with Brage does not appear. The apples of Iduna are a very agreeable fiction. In this part of the ſtory we again diſcover the favourite ſyſtem of the Celtes, reſpecting the inſenſible and continual decay of nature, and of the Gods, who were united to it, and depended upon it.

THE FIFTEENTH FABLE.

Of Heimdall, and some other Gods.

THERE is another very sacred and powerful Deity, who is called HEIMDALL. He is the son of nine Virgins, who are sisters. He is likewise called the "God with the Golden Teeth," because his teeth are of that metal. He dwells at the end of the bridge *Bifrost*, or the RAINBOW, in a castle called "the Celestial "Fort." He is the sentinel or watchman of the Gods. The post assigned him is to abide at the entry into heaven, to prevent the Giants from forcing their way over the bridge. He sleeps less than a bird; and sees by night, as well as by day, more than a hundred leagues around him. So acute is his ear, that he hears the grass growing on the earth, and the wool on the sheep's back; nor doth the smallest sound escape him. Besides all this, he hath a trumpet, which is heard through all the worlds.

worlds. This God is celebrated in the following verses: " The CELESTIAL FORT is the castle where Heimdall resideth, that sacred guardian of heaven, who drinketh divine hydromel in the secure and tranquil palaces of the Gods."

Among the Gods we reckon also HODER, who is blind, but extremely strong. Both Gods and Men would be very glad if they never had occasion to pronounce his name*; yet Gods and Men will long preserve the remembrance of the deeds performed by his hands. The ninth God is the silent VIDAR, who wears very thick shoes, but of so wonderful a contexture, that by means of them he can walk in air, and tread upon water. He is almost as strong as the God THOR himself; and in all critical conjunctures, affords the Gods great consolation. The tenth God, VILE, or VALI, is one of the sons of ODIN and RINDA. He is bold in war, and an excellent archer. The eleventh is ULLER, the offspring of *Sifia*, and son-in-law of THOR. He is so quick in shooting his arrows, and so nimble in the use of his skates, that nobody can stand before him. He is also very handsome in his person, and possesses every quality of a hero; wherefore it is very

---

* This, I presume, alludes to FABLE XXVIII.

proper to invoke him in duels, or single combats. FORSETE is the name of the twelfth God: he is the son of Balder. He hath a palace in heaven, named *Glitner*. All who refer to him the decision of their controversies, return from his tribunal mutually satisfied. It is the most excellent tribunal that is found among Gods or Men, according to these verses. " Glitner is the
" name of a palace, which is upheld by
" pillars of gold, and covered with a roof
" of silver. There it is that Forsete re-
" sides the greatest part of his time, who
" reconciles and appeases all sorts of quar-
" rels."

REMARKS ON THE FIFTEENTH FABLE.

I have no remark to offer upon this fable, but what every reader may make as well as myself. Most of the divinities, mentioned here, are only known to us by the EDDA. Perhaps some of them were unknown to the other 'Gothic and' Celtic nations, and are only to be considered as companions of the great northern conqueror, who were deified in subsequent ages.

THE SIXTEENTH FABLE.

Of Loke.

SOME reckon LOKE in the number of the Gods; others call him, "The calumniator of the Gods," "The artificer of fraud," "The disgrace of Gods and Men." His name is Loke. He is the son of the Giant *Farbautes* and of *Laufeya*. His two brothers are *Bileipter* and *Helblinde*, or Blind Death. As to his body, Loke is handsome and very well made; but his soul is evil, light, and inconstant. He surpasses all 'beings' in that science which is called Cunning and Perfidy. Many a time hath he exposed the Gods to very great perils (A), and hath often extricated them again by his artifices. His wife is called *Siguna*. He hath had by her *Nare*, and some other children. By the Giantess *Angerbode*, or Messenger of Ill, he hath likewise had three children. One is the wolf *Fenris*, the second is the great Serpent of Midgard, and the third is *Hela*, or Death.

The Gods were not ignorant, that those children were breeding up in the country of the Giants; they were apprized by many oracles, of all the evils they muſt ſuffer from them; their being ſprung from ſuch a mother was but a bad preſage; and from ſuch a Sire was ſtill worſe. Wherefore the Univerſal Father diſpatched ' certain of' the Gods to bring thoſe children to him. When they were come, he threw the Serpent down into the bottom of the ocean. But there the monſter waxed ſo large, that he wound himſelf around the whole globe of the earth; and that ſo intirely, that at pleaſure he can with his mouth lay hold of the end of his tail. Hela was precipitated into *Niflheim*, or hell; there ſhe had the government of nine worlds given her, into which ſhe diſtributes thoſe who are ſent her; that is, all who die through ſickneſs or old age (B). Here ſhe poſſeſſes vaſt apartments, ſtrongly built, and fenced with large grates. Her hall is GRIEF; FAMINE is her table; HUNGER, her knife; DELAY, her valet; SLACKNESS, her maid; PRECIPICE, her gate; FAINTNESS, her porch; SICKNESS and PAIN, her bed; and her tent *, CURSING and HOWLING. The one half of her body is blue; the other half covered with ſkin, and of the colour

---

* Or perhaps, her curtains, &c.

of

of human flesh. She hath a dreadful terrifying look, and by this alone it were easy to know her.

REMARKS on the SIXTEENTH FABLE.

(A) " He hath exposed the Gods to very great perils."] I should be inclined to call LOKE, the Momus of the northern Deities; did not the tricks he plays them often exceed the bounds of raillery. Besides, the monsters he hath engendered, and who are along with their father, in the latter ages, to make rude assaults upon the Gods, plainly indicates a system little different from that of the Evil Principle. Notwithstanding what hath been advanced by some learned men, this opinion was not unknown either to the Persians, ' Goths,' or Celtes: perhaps indeed we ought thus far only to agree with them, that it did not belong to the ancient religion of either of these people. But the hazardous and labouring condition in which they believed all nature to be, and the assaults which it was to sustain at the last day, led them insensibly to imagine that there was a power who was at enmity with Gods and Men, and who wrought all the evils which desolate the universe. This was the occupation of *Arimanes* among the Persians, and of *Loke* among the Scandinavians. Loke produces the great serpent, which intirely encircles the world. This serpent, by some of the characteristics of it in this same Mythology, seems to have been intended as an emblem of corruption or sin. He also gives birth to *Hela*, or Death, that queen of the infernal regions, of whom the EDDA gives us here so remarkable a portrait: And lastly, to the wolf *Fenris*, that monster who is to encounter the Gods, and destroy the world. How could the Evil Principle have been more strongly characterized?

(B) " All

(B) "All who die through sickness or old age."] *Cimbri & Celtiberi in acie exultabant, tanquam gloriosè & feliciter vitâ excessuri. Lamentabantur in morbo, quasi turpiter & miserabiliter perituri.* Val. Max. c. 6. "The Cimbri and Celtiberi leaped with joy in marching to battle, as being to quit this life in a manner equally happy and glorious; but bewailed themselves when confined by distempers, alarmed at the thought of dying a shameful and miserable death." Here we have a proof, that this doctrine of the EDDA was that 'also' of all the Celtic nations; and here we see what an impression it made upon their minds. I could accumulate ancient authorities still further in confirmation of it, but refer the reader to the preceding volume. (See Vol. I. p. 206, &c.) Let us observe, however, that the infernal region here described, where a punishment, rather disagreeable than cruel, is reserved for those who have died without their arms in their hands, is not an eternal Hell, but only an intermediate abode, or, if you will, a Prison, whence those who are confined, will come forth at the last day, to be judged upon other principles; and to be condemned or absolved for more real virtues and vices. To this intermediate Hell was opposed an Elysium of the same duration; viz. *Valhalla*, or *Valhall*, of which we shall presently have ample mention. One sees with surprize, in attentively reading this Mythology, that the whole is better connected and the parts more dependant on one another, than in any other work of the same kind, that hath come to our knowledge. The inferior Gods, created along with this world, and united to it by their nature, and the conformity of their destiny, had every thing to fear at the last day from the enemies of nature. In order therefore to be the better able to resist them, they called home to them all the warriors, who had given proof of their valour by shedding their blood in battle.

battle. These, thus received into the residence of the Gods, were still exercised in all the operations of war, in order to keep them in breath, ready against the last great conflict. This was the great end to which all their pleasures and employments were directed. As to cowardly or inactive persons, what could the Gods have done with them, when they were thus threatened with an attack as sudden, as dangerous? They gave them up to the custody of Death, who was to punish their weakness with languor and pain. All this hath nothing to do with that Eternal Hell and Elysium, which we shall see sketched out in the EDDA with much more force and dignity; and where nothing will be regarded but fidelity, chastity, integrity and justice.

THE

THE SEVENTEENTH FABLE.

Of the Wolf Fenris.

AS to the Wolf FENRIS, the Gods bred him up among themselves; Tyr being the only one among them who durst give him his food. Nevertheless, when they perceived that he every day increased prodigiously in size, and that the oracles warned them that he would one day become fatal to them; they determined to make very strong iron fetters for him, and presenting them to the Wolf, desired him to put them on to shew his strength, in endeavouring to break them. The Monster perceiving that this enterprize would not be very difficult to him, permitted the Gods to do what they pleased; and then violently stretching his nerves, burst the chains, and set himself at liberty. The Gods having seen this, made a new set of iron chains, half as strong again as the former, and prevailed on the Wolf to put

them

them on, assuring him that in breaking these he would give an undeniable proof of his vigour. The Wolf saw well enough that these second chains would not be very easy to break; but finding himself increase in strength, and that he could never become famous without running some risk, he voluntarily submitted to be chained. As soon as this was done, he shakes himself, rolls upon the ground, dashes his chains against the earth, violently stretches his limbs, and at last bursts his fetters, which he made to fly in pieces all about him. By these means he freed himself from his chains; and gave rise to the proverb which we still apply, when any one makes strong efforts *. After this, the Gods despaired of ever being able to bind the wolf: wherefore the Universal Father sent Skyrner, the messenger of the God Frey, into the country of the black Genii, to a dwarf; to engage him to make a new bandage to confine Fenris †. That bandage was perfectly smooth,

---

* In the *Icelandic*, *Leyfa or Læthingi edr drepi or Droma*, i. e. according to Goranson's Latin verfion, *Solvi ex Lædingo, et excutti ex Droma*. DROMA is the name given in the EDDA, to this chain of the Gods.
T.

† Goranson's Edition adds, " This nerve or string " was made of six things, viz. of the noise made by " cats feet; of a woman's beard; of the roots of
" moun-

smooth, and as limber as a common string, and yet very strong, as you will presently see. When it was brought to the Gods, they were full of thanks and acknowledgments to the bringers; and taking the Wolf with them into the isle of a certain lake, they shewed him the string, entreating that he would try to break it, and assuring him that it was somewhat stronger than one would think, on seeing it so slender. They took it themselves, one after another into their hands, attempting in vain to break it; and then told him, that there was none besides himself, who could accomplish such an enterprize. The Wolf replied, That string which you present to me is so slight, that there will be no glory in breaking it; or if there be any artifice in the manner of its formation, although it appear never so brittle, assure yourselves it shall never touch a foot of mine. The Gods assured him that he would easily break so slight a bandage, since he had already burst asunder shackles of iron of the most solid make; adding, that if he should not succeed, he would then have shown the Gods that he was too feeble to excite their terror, and

" mountains; of the nerves of bears; of the breath
" of fishes; and the spittle of birds, &c." *(with much*
more.) T.

there-

therefore they should make no difficulty of setting him at liberty without delay. I am very much afraid, replied the monster, that if you once tye me so fast that I cannot work my deliverance myself, you will be in no haste to unloose me. I would not therefore voluntarily permit myself to be tied, but only to show you, that I am no coward: yet I insist upon it, that one of you put his hand in my mouth, as a pledge that you intend me no deceit. Then the Gods, wistfully looking on one another, found themselves in a very embarrassing dilemma; till Tyr presented himself, intrepidly offering his right hand to the monster. Hereupon the Gods having tied up the Wolf; he forcibly stretched himself, as he had formerly done, and exerted all his powers to disengage himself: but the more efforts he made, the closer and straiter he drew the knot; and all the Gods (except Tyr, ' who ' lost his hand') burst out into loud peals of laughter at the sight. Observing him then so fast tied, as to be unable ever to get loose again, they took one end of the string, and having drilled a hole for it, drew it through the middle of a large broad rock, which they sunk very deep into the earth; afterwards, to make it still more secure, they tied the end of the cord which came through the rock, to a great stone which they sunk

still

still deeper. The Wolf, opening wide his tremendous jaws, endeavoured to devour them, and rushed upon them with violence. Which the Gods seeing, thrust a sword into his mouth, which pierced his under jaw up to the hilt, so that the point touched his palate. The howlings which he then made were horrible; and since that time, the foam flows continually from his mouth, in such abundance that it forms a river, called *Vam*, or The Vices. But that monster shall break his chain at the Twilight of the Gods, that is, at the end of the world (A).

Such is the wicked race engendered by Loke. Hereupon Gangler says to Har, But since the Gods have so much to fear from the Wolf, and from all the other monsters whom ' Loke' hath produced; why have they not put them to death? Har replied, The Gods have so much respect for the sanctity of their tribunals, and cities of peace (B), that they will not have them stained with the blood of the Wolf; although the oracles have intimated to them, that he will one day be destructive to ODIN.

REMARKS on the SEVENTEENTH FABLE.

(A) " At the end of " the world."] It cannot be doubted that the Wolf is the emblem of the Evil Principle, or of some power at enmity with nature. The river of Vices, said to flow from the foam of his mouth, is one of those strokes which manifestly indicate an allegory. I shall show in another place, that the passage we have now read, as well as all of the same kind occurring in the EDDA, are no other than figurative, and poetic ways of propounding that philosophic doctrine of the Celtes, Stoicks, and some eastern sages, which affirms that the world and the inferior Gods must one day yield to their enemies, and be again reproduced, in order to fulfil a new series of destinies.

(B) " The sanctity of " . . . . their cities of " peace."] There were cities, where the holiness of the place forbad all quarrels and bloodshed.

THE EIGHTEENTH FABLE.

Of the Goddesses.

GANGLER asks, Who are the Goddesses? The principal, replies Har, is FRIGGA (A), who hath a magnificent palace, named *Fensaler*, or the Divine Abode. The second is called SAGA. EIRA performs the function of physician to the Gods (B). GEFIONE is a virgin, and takes into her service all chaste maids after their death. FYLLA, who is also a virgin, wears her beautiful locks flowing over her shoulders. Her head is adorned with a golden ribband. She is entrusted with the toilette, and slippers of Frigga *; and admitted into the most important secrets of that Goddess. FREYA is the most illustrious of the Goddesses, next to Frigga.

---

* The Icelandic is, *Ok ber eski Friggiar: Ok gietr skoklætha hennar*, &c. i. e. according to Goranson's Latin version, " *Eique Pyxis Friggæ concredita est, ut " et ejusdem Calcei.*" T.

She

She married a person named *Oder*, and brought him a daughter named *Nossa*, so very handsome, that whatever is beautiful and precious is called by her name. But Oder left her, in order to travel into very remote countries. Since that time Freya continually weeps, and her tears are drops of pure gold. She has a great variety of names; for having gone over many countries in search of her husband, each people gave her a different name; some calling her *Vanadis*, or the Goddess of Hope, &c. &c. She wears a very rich chain of gold. The seventh Goddess is SIONA. She employs herself in turning mens hearts and thoughts to love, and in making young men and maidens well with each other. Hence lovers bear her name. LOVNA is so good and gracious, and accords so heartily to the tender vows of men, that by a peculiar power which Odin and Frigga have given her, she can reconcile lovers the most at variance. VARA, the ninth Goddess, presides over the oaths that men make, and particularly over the promises of lovers. She is attentive to all concealed engagements of that kind, and punishes those who keep not their plighted troth. VORA is prudent, and wise, and so penetrating and curious, that nothing can remain hid from her. SYNIA is the portress of the palace, and shuts the gates against all those who ought not to enter: she also presides in trials, where any thing is about to be denied upon oath; whence the proverb, " Signia is not far from him " who goes about to deny." The twelfth is called LYNA. She has the care of those whom Frigga intends to deliver from peril. SNOTRA is a wise and intelligent Goddess; men and women who are prudent and virtuous bear her name. GNA is the messenger whom Frigga dispatches into the various worlds, to perform her commands. She has a horse which runs over the air (c), and across the waters *. They reckon also SOL and BIL in the number of the ' *Ases*, or' Divinities; but their nature hath been already explained to you †. There are, besides, a great many virgins who officiate in Valhall, pouring out BEER and ALE for the Heroes, and taking care of the cups, and whatever belongs to the table. To this refers what is said in the poem of Grimnis, " I wish *Rista* and " *Mista* would supply me with the drink-" ing horns; for they are the nymphs who " should give cups to the Heroes." These

---

* The curious reader will find an additional passage here in Goranson's Latin translation.   T.

† This, I suppose, refers to FABLE VI, &c.   T.

God-

Goddesses are called *Valkyries*; Odin sends them into the fields of battle, to make choice of those who are to be slain, and to bestow the victory. GUDUR, ROSTA, and the youngest of the 'Destinies or' Fairies * who preside over Time, viz. SKULDA (or the FUTURE) go forth every day on horseback to chuse the dead, and regulate what carnage shall ensue. IORD, or the Earth, the mother of Thor; and RINDA, the mother of *Vale*, ought also to be ranked among the Goddesses.

* Islandic, *Norn en yngsta*, i. e. *Nornarum natu Minima*. Goranson. T.

REMARKS on the EIGHTEENTH FABLE.

(A) "The principal is Frigga."] I have already remarked that FRIGGA was the Earth, the spouse of ODIN, and mother of the inferiour Divinities; and that THOR was her first-born. She, with these two other Gods, made that sacred Triad, who were served and attended with so much respect in the famous Temple of Upsal. *Frigga*, or *Frea*, was there represented as reposing upon cushions between *Odin* and *Thor*; and by various emblems, was denoted to be the Goddess of Plenty, Fruitfulness and Pleasure. The sixth day of the week is Frea's day in all the northern languages, (*sc.* FRIDAY †) She being the mother of the whole human race, the people regarded one another as brethren, and lived in strict unity and concord, during the short time that

† See Vol. I. pag. 95.

her festivals lasted. *Non bella ineunt,* said Tacitus, respecting those seasons, *non arma sumunt, clausum omne ferrum; pax & quies tum tantum amata.* But as soon as these were over, they made themselves amends for this forced state of quiet, and the God of war was only served with the more activity during the rest of the year. I have nothing to remark concerning the other Goddesses, who are only known to us by the EDDA, and who, for the most part, seem to have sprung from the brains of the northern SCALDS.

(B) " EYRA performs " the function of Physi- " cian to the Gods."] Tacitus informs us that the Germans had no other physicians but their women. They followed the armies to stanch and suck the wounds of their husbands. In like manner, all the histories and romances of the north always represent the females, and often princesses, charged with this care. The same thing may be observed of almost all nations in their infancy. But no people had ever a stronger confidence in the women's skill in medicine, than our Celtic ' and Gothic' ancestors. " Persuaded, says Tacitus, that there was " something divine in " that sex," they submitted, when sick, to their opinion and decision with that implicit confidence, which is due to supernatural knowledge. Indeed all the science of medicine that was employed in those times, was little else but magic applied to the cure of diseases. The evils and the remedies were most commonly nothing else but lots, possessions, conjurations and enchantments. And the mountaineers in many parts of Europe, know of no other at this day. The superstition of shepherds and such like people, in this respect, is well known. The prejudices of these poor people, are only reliques of what all heads were once full of. After this, regret who will, the loss of ancient times!

(c) " She hath a horse, " which runs over the " air."]

" air."] The travels of Goddesses and Fairies through the air, are very common in all the poems and fables of the ancient inhabitants of the north, and most of the nations in Europe have thought in this respect along with them. When in procefs of time Christianity became prevalent, what had been formerly looked upon as a precious gift and signal mark of divine favour, was now regarded as the effect only of diabolic arts. The assemblies of ecclesiastics made very severe prohibitions, and denounced their anathemas against all those who should travel through the air in the night-time. In the ancient law of Norway, called " *Gu-* " *lathings Lagen,*" c. I. we find this regulation. " Let the king and the " bishop, with all possi- " ble care, make inquiry " after those who exercise " Pagan superstitions ; " who make use of ma- " gic arts; who adore " the Genii of particu- " lar places, or of tombs, " or rivers ; and who by " a diabolic manner of " travelling, are transported from place to " place through the air, " &c." A council held at Rouen, and cited in Burchard, contains a prohibition of the same nature. (Conc. Rotom. L. I. c. 94. sect. 44.) In some places the people are still of opinion, even in our own days, that witches are carried to their infernal Sabbaths through the midst of the air, on horseback, ' or at least riding ' astride certain animals.' (Vid. Keysler. Antiq. Sept. p. 88, 89.) There are few of our popular superstitions, but what may be traced up to some opinion, which was consecrated by the ancient religion of the ' Goths and' Celts. Nor need we always except those, which seem in some respects to hold a conformity to doctrines or practices, which the Christian religion alone could have taught us. One name substituted for another, and an outside varnish of devotion cannot so disguise their original, but that it is easily discovered by a skilful eye.

THE NINETEENTH FABLE.

Of Frey and Gerde.

THERE was a man named *Gimer*, one of the race of the Giants of the mountains; who had had by his wife *Orboda*, a daughter named *Gerde*, the most beautiful of her sex. One day FREY having ascended the throne of the Universal Father, in order to take a view of the whole world from thence; perceived towards the north a magnificent palace in the middle of a city, and a woman come out of it, whose hair was so bright, that it gave lustre to the air and the waters. At that sight Frey, in just punishment of his audacity in mounting that sacred throne, was struck with sudden sadness, insomuch that upon his return home, he could neither speak, nor sleep, nor drink; nor did any body dare so much as to inquire into the cause. However, NIORD ordered *Skirner*, the confident of Frey, to come to him, and charged him to demand of his

master

master what sworn enemy he had, that thus he renounced all converse with mankind. Skirner promised to do this, and going to Frey, asked him boldly why he was so sad and silent. Frey answered, That he had seen a young woman so beautiful and finely shaped, that if he could not possess her, he should not long survive it; and that this was what rendered him so thoughtful. "Go therefore, adds he, obtain her "for me in marriage, if you bring her to "me, you shall have in recompence what- "ever you desire." Skirner undertook to do this if Frey would make him a present of his Sword, which was so good, that it would of itself strow a field with carnage, whenever the owner ordered it. Frey, impatient of delay, immediately made him a present of the sword; and Skirner setting out, obtained the young woman of her relations, who promised that she should follow him within nine nights after his departure, and that the nuptials should be solemnized in a place called *Barey*. Skirner having reported to Frey the success of his embassy; that God, full of impatience, pronounced these verses. "One night is very long; two nights are "still longer; How then shall I pass the "third? Many a time hath a whole "month appeared to me shorter than the "half

"half of such a night." Frey having thus given away his sword, found himself without arms when he fought against *Bela*; and hence it was, that he slew him with the horn of a stag. Then, said Gangler, It seems to me very astonishing, that so brave a hero as Frey should give his sword away to another, without keeping one equally good for himself. He must have been in very bad plight, when he encountered with Bela; and I'll be sworn, he repented him heartily. That conflict was trifling, replied Har: Frey could have slain Bela with a blow of his fist, had he had a mind to it. But when the sons of Muspell, those wicked Genii, shall come to fight with the Gods, then he will have reason to be sorry indeed that he parted with his sword.

THE TWENTIETH FABLE.

Of the Food of the Gods.

BUT, says Gangler, if every man who has been slain in battle since the beginning of the world, repairs to the palace of ODIN, what food does that God assign to so vast a multitude? Har answered him, You have reason to say it is a vast multitude; yet will it still increase *ad infinitum*; nay, the Gods themselves shall desire, that it were still much more considerable, when the wolf FENRIS arrives at the last day (A). The number, however, never can be so great, but the flesh of the wild boar *Serimner* will suffice to sustain them; which, though dressed every morning, becomes intire again every night. I believe there are but few who are able to explain this matter to you, as it is described in those verses; the sense of which is to this effect;
" The cook, *Andrimner*, dresses the wild
" boar incessantly in his pot: the heroes
" are

" are fed with the lard or fat of this ani-
" mal, which exceeds every thing in the
" world (B)." But, says Gangler, Does
Odin eat at the same table with the heroes?
Har answered, The meat that is set before
him, ODIN distributes to two wolves,
known by the names of *Geri* and *Freki:*
for as to himself, he stands in no need of
food: wine is to him instead of every other
aliment; according to what is said in these
verses; " The illustrious father of armies,
" with his own hands fattens his two
" wolves; the victorious ODIN takes no
" other nourishment to himself, than what
" arises from the unintermitted quaffing of
" wine." Two ravens constantly sit upon
his shoulders, and whisper in his ear
whatever news they have seen or heard.
The one of them is named *Hugin*, or Spirit; the other *Munnin*, or Memory. Odin
lets them loose every day; and they, after
having made their excursions over the
whole world, return again at night about
the hour of repast. Hence it is, that this
God knows so many things, and is called
the God of the Ravens [*]. Gangler proceeds, and demands, And what is the beverage of the heroes, which they have in

---

[*] The reader will find an additional passage here
in the Latin Version of Goranson.   T.

as great abundance as their food? Do they only drink water? Har fays to him, You put a very foolish question. Can you imagine that the Univerfal Father would invite kings, and chiefs *, and great lords; and give them nothing to drink but water? In that cafe, certainly very many of thofe, who arrive at the palace of Odin, and who had endured cruel torments, and received mortal wounds in order to obtain accefs thither, would have reafon to complain: this honour would indeed coft them dear were they there to meet with no better entertainment. But you fhall fee, that the cafe is quite otherwife. For in VALHALL, there is a fhe goat, which feeds on the leaves of the tree *Lerada*. From her paps flows hydromel, or mead, in fuch great abundance, that it every day compleatly fills a pitcher, large enough to inebriate all the heroes (c). Truly, fays Gangler, this is a very ufeful, and very furprizing fhe goat: I fancy the tree fhe feeds upon, muft have many fingular virtues. Har anfwered him, What is related of a particular ftag is much more marvellous. This ftag alfo is in Valhall, and feeds upon the leaves of that fame tree: there iffues from his horns fuch

* The original Icelandic word is *Iarls*, (Lat. *Duces*) whence is derived our title, EARLS; the word *Iarls* however had not acquired fo precife a meaning.
T.

an abundance of vapour, that it forms the fountain of *Vergelmer*, out of which arise the rivers that water the residence of the Gods. Gangler goes on, and says, Valhall must needs be an immense palace; yet I imagine there must often arise struggles and contests at the gate, among such a croud of people as are continually thronging in and out. Har replied, Why do not you inquire, how many gates there are; and what are their dimensions? Then you would be able to judge, whether there be any difficulty in going in and out, or not. Know then, that there is plenty of seats and doors, as it is said in the poem of *Grimnis*; " I know that there are five " hundred and forty gates in Valhall. " Out of each, eight heroes may march " abreast when going to battle, followed " by crouds of spectators." A world of people! says Gangler; and Odin must needs be a great chieftain, to command so numerous an army. But tell me, How do the heroes divert themselves when they are not drinking? Every day, replies Har, as soon as they have dressed themselves, they take their arms; and entering the Lists, fight, till they cut one another in pieces (D): this is their Diversion: but no sooner does the hour of repast approach, than they remount their steeds all safe and sound, and return to drink in the palace

of

of ODIN *. Thus have you good reason to say, that Odin is the greatest and most mighty of Lords; which is also confirmed to us by these verses, composed in honour of the Gods. "The Ash *Udrasil* is the "greatest of Trees; *Skidbladner*, of Vessels; "*Odin*, of Gods; *Sleipner*, of Horses; *Bi-* "*frost*, of Bridges; *Bragè*, of Scalds, or Po- "ets; *Habroc*, of Hawks; and *Garmer*, "of Hounds."

* The reader will find a considerable addition here in Goranson's Latin Version.   T.

REMARKS on the TWENTIETH FABLE.

(A) "When the wolf "FENRIS arrives at the "last day."] I have already remarked, that the EDDA never loses sight of that grand event, the Destruction of the World. The inferior Gods were, at that time, to undergo rude assaults. This was pointed at in the preceding fable; where a reason is assigned why Frey will not be able to resist the attacks of the evil Genii. It was owing to this expectation that the inferior Gods received with pleasure warriors of approved valour, and such as they could depend on at the last times.

(B) "The heroes are "fed with the fat of this "animal."] This description of the palace of Odin is a natural picture of the manners of the ancient Scandinavians and Germans. Prompted by the wants of their climate, and the impulse of their own temperament, they form to themselves a delicious paradise in their own way; where they were to eat and drink, and fight. The women to whom they assign a

place

place there, are introduced for no other purpose, but to fill their cups. One wild boar furnishes out the whole of this celestial banquet: for, not very nice, they were only solicitous about the quantity of their food. The flesh of this animal, as well as that of the Hog, was formerly the favourite meat of all these nations. The ancient Franks were no less fond of it; a herd of swine was, in their eyes, an affair of such importance, that the second chapter of the Salic Law, consisting of twenty articles, is wholly taken up in inflicting penalties on those who stole them. In Gregory of Tours, queen Fredegond, in order to alienate the mind of the king from one Nectarius, blackens him with the crime of having stolen a great many Gammons or Hams, from the place where K. Chilperic laid up his provisions. The king did not consider this at all as a laughing matter, but took it in a very grave and serious light.

(c) " To inebriate all " the Heroes."] Wine was very scarce in those times, and almost unknown. BEER was, ' perhaps,' a liquor too vulgar for the Heroes †; the EDDA therefore makes them drink Hydromel, or MEAD, a beverage in great esteem among all the German nations. The ancient Franks made great use of it. Gregory of Tours, speaking of a certain lord who generally drank it, adds, *Ut mos barbarorum habet*. Greg. Turon. L. 8. c. 3.

(D) " They cut one " another in pieces."] From this passage of the EDDA, we may form to ourselves an idea of the amusements of the ancient ' Goths and' Celtes. When they were not engaged in any real war, they endeavoured by the representation of battles, to gratify that fierce disposition which made them

† Yet we find in some of the Icelandic odes, the Heroes rejoicing in the expectation that they should quaff BEER out of the sculls of their enemies, when once they were received into Valhall, or the palace of ODIN. See below, Regner Lodbrog's Ode in this Volume.   T.

fond

fond of the profession of arms. "The Goths are extremely fond of throwing their darts, and handling their arms; and it is their daily practice, to divert themselves with mock-fights:" says Isidore in his Chronic. The same prevailed among the Gauls and Germans, as is plain from a passage in the fragments of Varro. To this custom we may ascribe the rise and establishment of Justings and Turnaments. There are many institutions of this kind, whose origin is no less ancient, lost in the clouds of a very remote antiquity, whatever some learned men may assert, who assign them much later eras; not considering that customs are commonly more ancient than the first historian who speaks of them; and that a new name, or more regular form, which may have been given them, imply not necessarily their first beginning. In fact, we have never seen, nor ever shall see, any important custom spring up all at once, and establish itself with success, without there having existed something analogous to it beforehand, to prepare and lead men's minds to adopt it.

To return to the PALACE of ODIN; in order that the Heroes might repair betimes in the morning to the celestial Tilt-Yard, there was a Cock in the neighbourhood, which awaked them. At the great day of the overthrow of the world, the shrill screams of this bird will be the first signal of the approach of the evil Genii. This particular is related in the VOLUSPA, a poem wherein we have some flashes of true poetic fire, amidst a great deal of smoke. The passage is this:

"That animal which gives such a brilliancy to his golden crest, hath already pierced with his cries the abode of the Gods: he hath awakened the Heroes; they run to their arms; they run to the Father of Armies. To his screams answer, under ground, the dismal cries of the Black Cock, which dwells in the palace of Death." See Barthol. Antiq. Dan. p. 563

THE TWENTY-FIRST FABLE.

Of the Horse Sleipner, and his Origin.

GANGLER asked; Whence comes the horse *Sleipner*, which you mentioned; and to whom does he belong? Har replied, His origin is very wonderful. One day a certain architect came, and offered his service to the Gods, to build them, in the space of two years, a city so well fortified that they should be perfectly safe from the incursions of the Giants, even although they should have already penetrated within the inclosure of Midgard; but he demanded for his reward the Goddess Freya, together with the Sun and Moon. After long deliberation, the Gods agreed to his terms, provided he would finish the whole himself without any one's assistance; and all within the space of one single winter. But if any thing should remain to be finished on the first day of summer, he should intirely forfeit the recompense agreed on. On being acquainted with this, the architect stipulated that he should be allowed the use of his horse. And to this the Gods, by the advice of Loke, assented. This agreement was confirmed by many oaths, and concluded in the presence of many witnesses; for without this precaution, a Giant would not have thought himself safe among the Gods, especially if Thor had been returned from the expedition he had then taken into the east, to conquer the Giants. From the very first night then this workman caused his horse to draw stones of an immense bulk; and the Gods saw with surprize, that this creature did much more work, than his master himself. The winter however was far advanced, and towards the latter end of it, this impregnable city had almost attained the summit of perfection. In short, when the full time was now expired all but three days, nothing was wanting to compleat the work, except the gates, which were not yet put up. Then the Gods entered into consultation, and inquired of one another who among them it was that could have advised to marry Freya into the country of the Giants; and to plunge the sky and heavens into darkness, by permitting the Sun and Moon to be carried away. They all agreed that Loke was the author of that bad counsel, and that he should be put to a most cruel death, if he did not contrive some way or other to prevent the workman from accomplishing his undertaking, and obtaining the promised reward. Immediately they laid hands on Loke; who in his fright, promised upon oath to do whatever they desired, let it cost him what it would. That very night, while the architect was employing his horse, as usual, to convey stones to the place, there suddenly leaped forth a mare from the neighbouring forest, which allured the horse with her neighings. That animal no sooner saw her, but giving way to his ardour, he broke his bridle, and began to run after the mare. This obliged the workman also to run after his horse, and thus, between one and the other, the whole night was lost, so that the progress of the work must have been delayed till next morning. Then the architect perceiving that he had no other means to finish his undertaking, resumed his own proper shape and dimensions; and the Gods now clearly perceiving that it was really a Giant with whom they had made their contract, paid no longer any regard to their oath *, but

---

* The Gothic Deities seem to be guided by no very nice principles of Morality, any more than those of the Greeks and Romans. It is needless to observe what a dreadful effect, such an example as the above, must have on the conduct of their blind votaries. T.

calling the God Thor, he immediately ran to them, and paid the workman his falary by a blow of his mace, which ſhattered his head to pieces, and ſent him headlong into hell. Shortly after Loke came and reported, that the architect's horſe had be-got a foal with eight feet. This is the horſe named SLEIPNER, which excels all the horſes that ever were poſſeſſed by Gods or men *.

* In Goranſon's Latin Verſion, the reader will find ſome lines that are here omitted. T.

THE TWENTY-SECOND FABLE.

Of the Ship of the Gods.

GANGLER says to Har, You have told me of a vessel called *Skidbladner*, that was the best of all ships. Without doubt, replies Har, it is the best, and most artfully constructed of any; but the ship *Nagelfara* is of larger size. They were Dwarfs who built Skidbladner, and made a present of it to Frey. It is so large, that all the Gods compleatly armed may sit in it at their ease. As soon as ever its sails are unfurled, a favourable gale arises, and carries it of itself to whatever place it is destined. And when the Gods have no mind to sail, they can take it into pieces so small, that being folded upon one another, the whole will go into a pocket. This is indeed a very well-contrived vessel, replied Gangler, and there must doubtless have been a great deal of art and magic employed in bringing it to perfection.

THE TWENTY-THIRD FABLE.

Of the God Thor.

GANGLER proceeds, and says, Did it never happen to THOR in his expeditions to be overcome, either by enchantment or downright force? Har replied to him, Few can take upon them to affirm that ever any such accident befel this God; nay, had he in reality been worsted in any rencounter, it would not be allowable to make mention of it, since all the world ought to believe, that nothing can resist his power. I have put a question then, says Gangler, to which none of you can give any answer *. Then Jafnhar took up the discourse, and said; True indeed, there are some such rumours current among us; but they are hardly credible: yet there is one

---

* The reader will remember that Gangler would have considered himself as victor in this contest, if he had proposed any question they could not have answered. Vide page 3, 4, &c.   T.

present who can impart them to you; and you ought the rather to believe him, in that having never yet told you a lie, he will not now begin to deceive you with false stories. Come then, says Gangler interrupting him, I await your explication; but if you do not give satisfactory answers to the questions I have proposed, be assured I shall look upon you as vanquished. Here then, says Har, begins the history you desire me to relate:

One day the God THOR set out with LOKE, in his own chariot, drawn by two He-Goats; but night coming on, they were obliged to put up at a peasant's cottage. The God Thor immediately slew his two He-Goats, and having skinned them, ordered them to be dressed for supper. When this was done, he sat down to table, and invited the peasant and his children to partake with him. The son of his host was named *Thialfe*, the daughter *Raska*. Thor bade them throw all the bones into the skins of the goats, which he held extended near the table; but young Thialfe, to come at the marrow, broke with his knife one of the shank bones of the goats. Having passed the night in this place, Thor arose early in the morning, and dressing himself, reared the handle of his mace; which he had no sooner done, than the

two

two goats reaſſumed their wonted form, only that one of them now halted upon one of his hind legs. The God ſeeing this, immediately judged that the peaſant, or one of his family, had handled the bones of this goat too roughly. Enraged at their folly, he knit his eye-brows, rolled his eyes, and ſeizing his mace, graſped it with ſuch force, that the very joints of his fingers were white again. The peaſant trembling, was afraid of being ſtruck down by one of his looks; he therefore, with his children, made joint ſuit for pardon, offering whatever they poſſeſſed in recompence of any damage that had been done. Thor at laſt ſuffered himſelf to be appeaſed, and was content to carry away with him Thialfe and Raſka. Leaving then his He-Goats in that place, he ſet out on his road for the country of the Giants; and coming to the margin of the ſea, ſwam acroſs it, accompanied by Thialfe, Raſka, and Loke. The firſt of theſe was an excellent runner, and carried Thor's wallet or bag. When they had made ſome advance, they found themſelves in a vaſt plain, through which they marched all day, till they were reduced to great want of proviſions. When night approached, they ſearched on all ſides for a place to ſleep in, and at laſt, in the dark, found the houſe of a certain Giant; the gate of which was so large, that it took up one whole side of the mansion. Here they passed the night; but about the middle of it were alarmed by an earthquake, which violently shook the whole fabrick. Thor, rising up, called upon his companions to seek along with him some place of safety. On the right they met with an adjoining chamber, into which they entered; but Thor remained at the entry, and whilst the others, terrified with fear, crept to the farthest corner of their retreat, he armed himself with his mace, to be in readiness to defend himself at all events. Meanwhile they heard a terrible noise: and when the morning was come, Thor went out, and observed near him a man of enormous bulk, who snored pretty loud. Thor found that this was the noise which had so disturbed him. He immediately girded on his Belt of Prowess, which hath the virtue of increasing strength: but the Giant awaking; Thor affrighted, durst not lanch his mace, but contented himself with asking his name. My name is *Skrymner*, replied the other; as for you, I need not inquire whether you are the God Thor: pray, tell me, have not you picked up my Glove? Then presently stretching forth his hand to take it up, Thor perceived that the house wherein they had passed the night, was that very Glove; and the chamber, was only one of its fingers. Hereupon Skrymner afked, whether they might not join companies; and Thor confenting, the Giant opened his cloak-bag, and took out fomething to eat. Thor and his companions having done the fame, Skrymner would put both their wallets together, and laying them on his fhoulder, began to march at a great rate. At night, when the others were come up, the Giant went to repofe himfelf under an oak, fhewing Thor where he intended to lie, and bidding him help himfelf to victuals out of the wallet. Meanwhile he fell to fnore ftrongly. But what is very incredible, when Thor came to open the wallet, he could not untie one fingle knot. Vexed at this, he feized his mace, and lanched it at the Giant's head. He awaking, afks, what leaf had fallen upon his head, or what other trifle it could be. Thor pretended to go to fleep under another oak; but obferving about midnight that Skrymner fnored again, he took his mace and drove it into the hinder part of his head. The Giant awaking, demands of Thor, whether fome fmall grain of duft had not fallen upon his head, and why he did not go to fleep. Thor anfwered, he was going; but prefently after, refolving to have a third blow

at

at his enemy, he collects all his force, and lanches his mace with so much violence against the Giant's cheek, that it forced its way into it up to the handle. Skrymner awaking, slightly raises his hand to his cheek, saying, Are there any birds perched upon this tree? I thought one of their feathers had fallen upon me. Then he added, What keeps you awake, Thor? I fancy it is now time for us to get up, and dress ourselves. You are now not very far from the city of *Utgard*. I have heard you whisper to one another, that I was of a very tall stature; but you will see many there much larger than myself. Wherefore I advise you, when you come thither, not to take upon you too much; for in that place they will not bear with it from such little men as you*. Nay, I even believe, that your best way is to turn back again; but if you still persist in your resolution, take the road that leads eastward; for as for me, mine lies to the north. Hereupon he threw his wallet over his shoulder, and entered a forest. I never could hear that the God Thor wished him a good journey; but proceeding on his way along with his companions, he perceived,

* To conceive the force of this raillery, the Reader must remember that THOR is represented of gigantic size, and as the stoutest and strongest of the Gods. The HERCULES of the northern nations. T.

about

about noon, a city situated in the middle of a vast plain. This city was so lofty, that one could not look up to the top of it, without throwing one's head quite back upon the shoulders. The gate-way was closed with a grate, which Thor never could have opened; but he and his companions crept through the bars. Entering in, they saw a large palace, and men of a prodigious stature. Then addressing themselves to the king, who was named *Utgarda-Loke*, they saluted him with great respect. The king having at last discerned them, broke out into such a burst of laughter, as discomposed every feature of his face. It would take up too much time, says he, to ask you concerning the long journey you have performed; yet if I do not mistake, that little man whom I see there, should be Thor: perhaps indeed he is larger than he appears to me to be; but in order to judge of this, added he, addressing his discourse to Thor, let me see a specimen of those arts by which you are distinguished, you and your companions; for no body is permitted to remain here, unless he understand some art, and excel in it all other men. LOKE then said, that his art consisted in eating more than any other man in the world, and that he would challenge any one at that kind of combat. It must
indeed

indeed be owned, replied the king, that you are not wanting in dexterity, if you are able to perform what you promife. Come then, let us put it to the proof. At the fame time he ordered one of his courtiers who was fitting on a fide-bench, and whofe name was *Loge* (i. e. Flame) to come forward, and try his fkill with Loke in the art they were fpeaking of. Then he caufed a great tub or trough full of provifions to be placed upon the bar, and the two champions at each end of it: who immediately fell to devour the victuals with fo much eagernefs, that they prefently met in the middle of the trough, and were obliged to defift. But Loke had only eat the flefh of his portion; whereas the other had devoured both flefh and bones. All the company therefore adjudged that Loke was vanquifhed.

THE

THE TWENTY-FOURTH FABLE.

Of Thialfe's Art.

THEN the king afked, what that young man could do, who accompanied Thor. THIALFE anfwered, That in running upon fcates, he would difpute the prize with any of the courtiers. The king owned, that the talent he fpoke of was a very fine one; but that he muft exert himfelf, if he would come off conqueror. He then arofe and conducted Thialfe to a ' fnowy' plain, giving him a young man named *Hugo* (Spirit or Thought) to difpute the prize of fwiftnefs with him. But this Hugo fo much outftript Thialfe, that in returning to the barrier whence they fet out, they met face to face. Then fays the king; Another trial, and you may perhaps exert yourfelf better. They therefore ran a fecond courfe, and Thialfe was a full bow-fhot from the boundary, when Hugo arrived at it. They ran a third time; but Hugo had already reached the goal, before Thialfe had got half way. Hereupon all who were prefent cried out, that there had been a fufficient trial of fkill in this kind of exercife.

THE TWENTY-FIFTH FABLE.

Of the Trials that Thor underwent.

THEN the king afked THOR, in what art HE would chufe to give proof of that dexterity for which he was fo famous. Thor replied, That he would conteft the prize of Drinking with any perfon belonging to his court. The king confented, and immediately went into his palace to look for a large Horn, out of which his courtiers were obliged to drink when they had committed any trefpafs againft the cuftoms of the court*. This the cupbearer filled to the brim, and prefented to Thor, whilft the king fpake thus: Whoever is a good drinker, will empty that horn at a fingle draught; fome perfons make two of it; but the moft puny drinker of all can do it at three. Thor looked at the horn, and was aftonifhed at its length †; however, as he was very thirfty, he fet it to his mouth, and without drawing breath,
pulled

---

* Our modern Bachanals will here obferve, that punifhing by a Bumper is not an invention of thefe degenerate days. The ancient Danes were great Topers.   T.

† The Drinking Veffels of the northern Nations were the Horns of animals, of their natural length,
only

pulled as long and as deeply as he could, that he might not be obliged to make a fecond draught of it: but when he withdrew the cup from his mouth, in order to look in, he could fcarcely perceive any of the liquor gone. To it he went again with all his might, but fucceeded no better than before. At laft, full of indignation, he again fet the horn to his lips, and exerted himfelf to the utmoft to empty it entirely: then looking in, he found that the liquor was a little lowered: upon this, he refolved to attempt it no more, but gave back the horn. I now fee plainly, fays the king, that thou art not quite fo ftout as we thought thee; but art thou willing to make any more trials? I am fure, fays Thor, fuch draughts as I have been drinking, would not have been reckoned fmall among the Gods: but what new trial have you to propofe? We have a very trifling game, here, replied the king, in which we exercife none but children: it confifts in only lifting my Cat from the ground; nor fhould I have mentioned it, if I had not already obferved, that you are by no means what we took you for. Immediately a large iron-coloured Cat leapt into the middle of the hall.

only tipt with filver, &c. In York-Minfter is preferved one of thefe ancient Drinking Veffels, compofed of a large Elephant's Tooth, of its natural dimenfions, ornamented with fculpture, &c. See Drake's Hift.

Thor

Thor advancing, put his hand under the Cat's belly, and did his utmost to raise him from the ground; but the Cat bending his back, had only one of his feet lifted up. The event, says the king, is just what I foresaw; the Cat is large, but Thor is little in comparison of the men here. Little as I am, says Thor, let me see who will wrestle with me. The king looking round him, says, I see no body here who would not think it beneath him to enter the lists with you; let somebody, however, call hither my nurse *Hela* (i. e. Death) to wrestle with this God Thor: she hath thrown to the ground many a better man than he. Immediately a toothless old woman entered the hall. This is she, says the king, with whom you must wrestle*. I cannot, 'says 'Jafnhar,' give you all the particulars of this contest, only in general, that the more vigorously Thor assailed her, the more immoveable she stood. At length the old woman had recourse to stratagems, and Thor could not keep his feet so steadily, but that she, by a violent struggle, brought him upon one knee. Then the king came to them and ordered them to desist: adding, there now remained no body in his court, whom he could ask with honour to condescend to fight with Thor.

* I here follow the Latin Version of Goranson, rather than the French of M. Mallet.   T.

THE

THE TWENTY-SIXTH FABLE.

The Illusions accounted for.

THOR passed the night in that place with his companions, and was preparing to depart thence early the next morning; when the king ordered him to be sent for, and gave him a magnificent entertainment. After this he accompanied him out of the city. When they were just going to bid adieu to each other, the king asked Thor what he thought of the success of his expedition. Thor told him, he could not but own that he went away very much ashamed and disappointed. It behoves me then, says the king, to discover now the truth to you, since you are out of my city; which you shall never re-enter whilst I live and reign. And I assure you, that had I known before-hand, you had been so strong and mighty, I would not have suffered you to enter now. But I enchanted you by my illusions; first of all in the forest, where I arrived before you.

And there you were not able to untie your wallet, becaufe I had faftened it with a magic chain. You afterwards aimed three blows at me with your mace: the firft ftroke, though flight, would have brought me to the ground, had I received it: but when you are gone hence, you will meet with an immenfe rock, in which are three narrow valleys of a fquare form, one of them in particular remarkably deep: thefe are the breaches made by your mace; for I at that time lay concealed behind the rock, which you did not perceive. I have ufed the fame illufions in the contefts you have had with the people of my court. In the firft, LOKE, like Hunger itfelf, devoured all that was fet before him: but his opponent, LOGE, was nothing elfe but a wandering Fire, which inftantly confumed not only the meat, but the bones, and very trough itfelf. HUGO, with whom THIALFE difputed the prize of fwiftnefs, was no other than Thought or Spirit; and it was impoffible for Thialfe to keep pace with that. When you attempted to empty the Horn, you performed, upon my word, a deed fo marvellous, that I fhould never have believed it, if I had not feen it myfelf; for one end of the Horn reached to the fea, a circumftance you did not obferve: but the firft time you go to the feafide, you will fee how much it is diminifhed.

nished. You performed no less a miracle in lifting the Cat, and to tell you the truth, when we saw that one of her paws had quitted the earth, we were all extremely surprized and terrified; for what you took for a Cat, was in reality the great Serpent of Midgard, which encompasses the earth; and he was then scarce long enough to touch the earth with his head and tail; so high had your hand raised him up towards heaven. As to your wrestling with an old woman, it is very astonishing that she could only bring you down upon one of your knees; for it was DEATH you wrestled with, who first or last will bring every one low. But now, as we are going to part, let me tell you, that it will be equally for your advantage and mine, that you never come near me again; for should you do so, I shall again defend myself by other illusions and enchantments, so that you will never prevail against me.—As he uttered these words, Thor in a rage laid hold of his mace, and would have lanched it at the king, but he suddenly disappeared; and when the God would have returned to the city to destroy it, he found nothing all around him but vast plains covered with verdure. Continuing therefore his course, he returned without ever stopping, to his palace.

REMARKS on the TWENTY-THIRD, and following FABLES.

I was unwilling to suppress the fables we have been reading, however trifling they may appear at first sight; partly that I might give the original compleat, and partly because I thought them not altogether useless, as they would contribute still farther to lay open the turn of mind and genius of the ancient inhabitants of Europe. We have seen above, that THOR was regarded as a Divinity favourable to mankind, being their protector against the attacks of Giants and evil Genii. It is pretty remarkable, that this same God should here be liable to illusions, snares and trials; and that it should be the Evil Principle, that persecutes him. *Ut-garda Loke*, signifies "the LOKE, or Demon "from without." "But may not all this fable have been invented in imitation of the labours of Hercules?" The analogy is so small in general between the mythology of the Greeks, and that of the northern nations, that I cannot think the imperfect resemblance which is found between these two stories deserves much attention. I am of opinion that we shall be more likely to succeed, if we look for the origin of this fable in the religion formerly spread throughout Persia and the neighbouring countries; whence, as the ancient Chronicles inform us, ODIN and his companions originally came. There first arose the doctrine of a Good and Evil Principle, whose conflicts we here see described after an allegorical manner.

It appears probable to me that this doctrine, which was carried into the north by the Asiatics who established themselves there, hath had many puerile circumstances added to it, in successively passing through the mouths

of

of the Poets, the sole depositaries of the opinions of those times. In reality, we find in every one of those additions, somewhat that strongly marks the soil from whence they sprung. Such, for example, are the contests about eating and drinking most; who should scate best on the 'snow;' and the horns out of which the courtiers were obliged to drink, when they committed a fault. These, and some other strokes of this kind, strongly favour of the north. But what most of all shows somewhat of mystery after the Oriental manner, is THOR's wrestling with Death, or Old Age; to whom he seems to pay a slight tribute, in falling down upon one of his knees, and immediately again raising up himself. In the next fable he preserves and continues, as indeed throughout all this Mythology, the character and functions which were at first ascribed to him. He enters into conflict with the great Serpent, a monster descended from that Evil Principle, who is at enmity with Gods and men: but he will not be able perfectly to triumph over him, till the last day; when recoiling back nine paces, he strikes him dead with his thunder, and destroys him for ever.

There are few methods of interpretation more equivocal, more subject to abuse, and more discredited, than that which hath recourse to allegory. But the turn of genius which seems to have dictated all this Mythology, and the significant words it affects to employ, seem to prescribe this method to us on this occasion. Besides, we are to remember that the whole of it hath been transmitted to us by Poets, and that those Poets, in their manner, have been partly Oriental and partly Celtic. We have therefore abundant reason to be convinced, that we ought not to interpret any thing here in a simple or literal sense.

THE TWENTY-SEVENTH FABLE.

Of the Journey undertaken by Thor, to go to fish for the great Serpent.

I Find by your account, says Gangler, that the power of this King, you have been mentioning, muſt be very great, and there cannot be a ſtronger proof it, than his having courtiers ſo ſkilful and dexterous in all reſpects. But, tell me, did THOR never revenge this affront? 'Tis well known, ſays Har, (though no body has talked of it) that Thor had reſolved to attack the great Serpent, if an opportunity offered: with this view he ſet out from ASGARD a ſecond time, under the form of a young boy, in order to go to the Giant EYMER *. When he was got there, he beſought the Giant, to permit him to go

---

* I here give this name as it is in the Icelandic: M. Mallet writes it HYMER. The Reader muſt not confound this name with that of the Giant YMI, or YMIR, mentioned in the ſecond fable, &c. T.

aboard

aboard his bark along with him, when he went a fishing. The Giant answered, that a little puny stripling like him, could be of no use to him; but would be ready to die of cold, when they should reach the high seas, whither he usually went. Thor assured him that he feared nothing: and asked him what bait he intended to fish with. Eymer bade him to look out for something. Thor went up to a herd of cattle which belonged to the Giant, and seizing one of the oxen, tore off his head with his own hands; then returning to the bark where Eymer was, they sate down together. Thor placed himself in the middle of the bark, and plied both his oars at once: Eymer, who rowed also at the prow, saw with surprize how swiftly Thor drove the boat forward, and told him, that by the land-marks on the coasts, he discovered that they were come to the most proper place to angle for flat fish. But Thor assured him that they had better go a good way further: accordingly they continued to row on, till at length Eymer told him if they did not stop, they would be in danger from the great Serpent of Midgard. Notwithstanding this, Thor persisted in rowing further, and spite of the Giant, was a great while before he would lay down his oars. Then taking out a fishing line extremely strong, he fixed to it the ox's head, unwound it, and cast it into the sea. The bait reached the bottom, the Serpent greedily devoured the head, and the hook stuck fast in his palate. Immediately the pain made him move with such violence, that Thor was obliged to hold fast with both his hands by the pegs which bear against the oars: but the strong effort he was obliged to make with his whole body, caused his feet to force their way through the boat, and they went down to the bottom of the sea; whilst with his hands, he violently drew up the Serpent to the side of the vessel. It is impossible to express the dreadful looks that the God darted at the Serpent, whilst the monster, raising his head, spouted out venom upon him: in the meantime the Giant Eymer seeing, with affright, the water enter his bark on all sides, cut with his knife the string of the fishing-line, just as Thor was going to strike the Serpent with his mace. Upon this the monster fell down again to the bottom of the sea: nevertheless, some add that Thor darted his mace after him, and bruised his head in the midst of the waves. But one may assert with more certainty, that he lives still in the waters *.

Then

---

* We see plainly in the above fable the origin of those vulgar opinions entertained in the north, and which

Pon-

Then Thor ſtruck the Giant a blow with his fiſt, nigh the ear, and throwing his head into the ſea, waded afterwards on foot to land.

Pontoppidan has recorded, concerning the CRAKEN, and that monſtrous Serpent, deſcribed in his Hiſtory of NORWAY.   T.

THE TWENTY-EIGHTH FABLE.

Of Balder the Good.

CERTAINLY, fays Gangler, this was a very great victory of THOR's. The dream which BALDER had one night, replies Har, was fomething ftill more remarkable. This God thought that his life was in extreme danger: wherefore, telling his dream to the other Gods, they agreed to conjùre away all the dangers with which Balder was threatened. Then FRIGGA exacted an oath of Fire, Water, Iron and other Metals, as alfo of Stones, Earth, Trees, Animals, Birds, Difeafes, Poifon and Worms, that none of them would do any hurt to Balder (A). This done, the Gods, together with Balder himfelf, fell to diverting themfelves in their grand affembly, and Balder ftood as a mark at which they threw, fome of them darts, and fome ftones, while others ftruck at him with a fword. But whatever they could do, none of them could

could hurt him; which was considered as a great honour to Balder. In the meantime, LOKE, moved with envy, changed his shape into that of a strange old woman, and went to the palace of Frigga. That Goddess seeing her, asked if she knew what the Gods were at present employed about in their assembly. The pretended old woman answered, That the Gods were throwing darts and stones at Balder, without being able to hurt him. Yes, said Frigga, and no sort of arms, whether made of metal or wood, can prove mortal to him: for I have exacted an oath from them all. What, said the woman, have all substances then sworn to do the same honours to Balder? There is only one little shrub, replied Frigga, which grows on the western side of Valhall, and its name is *Miſtiltein*, (the Misseltoe;) of this I took no oath, because it appeared to me too young and feeble. As soon as Loke heard this, he vanished, and resuming his natural shape, went to pluck up the shrub by the roots, and then repaired to the assembly of the Gods. There he found HODER standing apart by himself, without partaking of the sport, because he was blind. Loke came to him, and asked him, Why he did not also throw something at Balder, as well as the rest? Because I am blind,

blind, replied the other, and have nothing to throw with. Come then, fays Loke, do like the reft, fhew honour to Balder by toffing this little trifle at him; and I will direct your arm towards the place where he ftands. Then Hoder took the Miffeltoe (B), and Loke guiding his hand, he darted it at Balder; who, pierced through and through, fell down devoid of life: and furely never was feen, either among Gods or men, a crime more fhocking and attrocious than this. Balder being dead, the Gods were all filent and fpiritlefs: not daring to avenge his death, out of refpect to the facred place in which it happened. They were all therefore plunged in the deepeft mourning, and efpecially ODIN, who was more fenfible than all the reft of the lofs they had fuffered. * After their forrow was a little appeafed, they carried the body of Balder down towards the fea, where ftood the veffel of that God, which paffed for the largeft in the world. But when the Gods wanted to lanch it into the water, in order to make a funeral pile for Balder †, they could never make it ftir: wherefore they caufed to

---

* What follows is different in the Latin Verfion of Goranfon.   T.

† The fenfe of Goranfon's Verfion is, " In order " to carry the body of Balder, together with his fu- " neral pile."   T.

come from the country of the Giants, a certain Sorceress, who was mounted on a wolf, having twisted serpents by way of a bridle. As soon as she alighted, Odin caused four Giants to come, purely to hold her steed fast, and secure it: which appeared to him so dreadful, that he would first see whether they were able to overthrow it to the ground: for, says he, if you are not able to overthrow it to the earth, I shall never be secure that you have strength to hold it fast. Then the Sorceress bending herself over the prow of the vessel, set it afloat with one single effort; which was so violent, that the fire sparkled from the keel as it was dragging to the water, and the earth trembled. Thor, enraged at the sight of this woman, took his mace and was going to dash her head to pieces, had not the Gods appeased him by their intercessions. The body of BALDER being then put on board the vessel, they set fire to his funeral pile; and NANNA, his wife, who had died of grief, was burnt along with him. There were also at this ceremony, besides all the Gods and Goddesses, a great number of Giants. Odin laid upon the pile, a ring of gold, to which he afterwards gave the property of producing every ninth night, eight rings of equal weight.

Balder's

Balder's horſe was alſo conſumed in the ſame flames with the body of his maſter *.

* For an Account of the Funerals of the ancient Scandinavians, and of the Piles in which the wife, ſlave and horſe were buried along with the Owner, ſee Vol. I. p. 341, &c. ——In the firſt part of this work, our Author promiſed to give proofs of whatever he had advanced concerning the manners and cuſtoms of the ancient Danes; and whoever examines with attention, the original pieces contained in this ſecond Volume, cannot but acknowlege he has kept his word.

REMARKS ON THE TWENTY-EIGHTH FABLE.

(A) " That none of " them would do any hurt " to Balder."] It is well known to ſuch as have dipt into the ancient romances, that there were formerly Necromancers and Sorcereſſes, who could ſo throughly enchant lances and ſwords, that they could do no hurt. This ridiculous opinion is not entirely eradicated out of the minds of the common people every where, to this day. Our ancient northern hiſtorians are full of alluſions to feats of this kind. Saxo, lib. 6. aſſures us, that a certain champion, named *Wiſin*, was able to charm his enemies ſwords with a ſingle look. There were certain Runic characters, which produced this effect; but in general they were the Fairies and Goddeſſes who excelled in this fine art. Frigga herſelf was particularly diſtinguiſhed for it. We ſee in the text, that ſhe could charm and inchant whatever ſhe pleaſed. Tacitus, who deſcribes her under the title of the " Mother of the Gods," (a name which is alſo given her in the EDDA in more places than one) ſpeaks in like manner of the power ſhe had to protect her votaries in the midſt of darts thrown by their enemies. *Matrem deûm*

deûm venerantur (Æstyi): Insigne superstitionis, formas aprorum gestant. Id pro armis omniumque tutelâ, securum Deæ cultorem etiam inter hostes præstat, c. 45.

(B) " Then Hoder " took the Misseltoe."] If the Scandinavians had been a different nation from the Germans, the Germans from the Gauls, and the Gauls from the Britons; whence could arise this striking conformity which is found between them, even in those arbitrary opinions, to which caprice alone could have given rise? I lay particular stress upon this remark, as what justifies me in calling the EDDA a System of CELTIC MYTHOLOGY; and I recall it on occasion of this passage. We see here, that the Scandinavians, as well as the Gauls and Britons, attributed to the MISSEL- TOE a certain divine power. This plant, particularly such of it as grew upon the oak, hath been the object of veneration, not among the Gauls only, (as hath been often advanced without just grounds) but also among all the Celtic nations of Europe. The people of Holstein, and the neighbouring countries, call it at this day *Marentaken,* or the " Branch of Spec- " tres;" doubtless on account of its magical virtues. In some places of Upper Germany, the people observe the same custom, which is practised in many provinces of France. Young persons go at the beginning of the year, and strike the doors and windows of houses, crying *Guthyl,* which signifies Misseltoe. (See Keysler. Antiq. Sept. and Celt. p. 304, & seq.) Ideas of the same kind prevailed among the ancient inhabitants of Italy. Apuleius hath preserved some verses of the ancient poet Lælius, in which Misseltoe is mentioned as one of the ingredients which will convert a man into a Magician. (Apul. Apolog. Prior.)

※ As so much stress is laid here on the circumstance of Balder's being slain by the MISSELTOE, it deserves a particular discussion: and as almost every thing advanced in this note is borrowed confessedly from

Keysler's *Antiquitates Selectæ Septentrionales* (p. 364, &c.) it will be proper to examine the arguments produced in that book; to which our ingenious Author, M. Mallet, has, I fear, rather given his assent too hastily.

Pliny is the writer of Antiquity, from whom we learn the particular account of the veneration paid to this Plant by the Druids of Gaul. Nat. Hist. lib. 16. c. 44. *Non est omittenda in ea re & Galliarum admiratio. Nihil habent Druidæ (ita suos appellant Magos) Visco & Arbore in qua gignatur (si modo sit Robur) sacratius. Jam per se Roborum eligunt Lucos, nec ulla sacra sine ea fronde conficiunt, et inde appellati quoque interpretatione Græca possint Druidæ videri. Enimvero quidquid adnascatur illis, e cælo missum putant, signumque esse electæ ab ipso Deo Arboris. Est autem id rarum admodum inventu, & repertum magna religione petitur: et ante omnia sexta Lunâ, quæ principia mensium annorumque his facit, et seculi post tricessimum annum, quia jam virium abunde habeat, nec sit sui dimidia. Omnia-Sanantem appellantes suo vocabulo, sacrificiis epulisque rite sub arbore præparatis duos admovent candidi coloris tauros, quorum cornua tunc primum vinciantur. Sacerdos candida veste cultus arborem scandit. Falce aurea demittit. Candido id excipitur sago. Tum deinde victimas immolant, precantes, ut suum donum Deus prosperum faciat his quibus dederit. Fæcunditatem eo poto dari cuicunque animali sterili arbitrantur, contraque venena omnia esse* remedio. *Tanta gentium in rebus frivolis plerunque religio est.*" So again in lib. 24. c. 4. " Viscum *e robore præcipuum diximus haberi, & quo conficeretur modo, &c. Quidam id religione efficacius fieri putant, prima luna collectum e Robore sine ferro. Si terram non attigit, comitialibus* mederi. *Conceptum fœminarum* adjuvare, *si omnino secum habeant. Ulcera commanducato impositoque efficacissimè* sanari."

Here we see the Misseltoe is revered among the Gauls as a Divine Plant, producing most salutary effects; "curing barrenness, repelling poison, assisting "women in labour, and curing ulcers;" and for its great beneficial qualities in general, called All-..eal, and honoured with peculiar marks of reverence.——

Was

Was this plant confidered in the fame favourable light among the Scandinavians; or honoured by them with the fame obfervances? Nothing like this appears. It is mentioned in this one place of the EDDA, as a little inconfiderable fhrub, that was made ufe of by a malicious Being to perpetrate great mifchief. I am afraid therefore, that the reafoning of our elegant and learned Author will be found here to amount to this, viz. " In GAUL the Miffeltoe was the Inftrument of GOOD; in the north the inftrument of EVIL; therefore the Gauls and the northern nations muft have been the fame people; and there appears a ftriking conformity between them both in their opinions on this fubject."——One might rather infer that there was an effential difference and oppofition between the religious tenets of thefe two nations: and that therefore they were, *ab origine*, two diftinct races of men.—But it will perhaps be urged, How fhould the followers of ODIN think of affixing any peculiar arbitrary qualities to the MISSELTOE at all, if they had not this notion from the Celtic Druids?—I anfwer, From the Celtes they probably learnt all they knew about the Miffeltoe: but as they entertained fo different an opinion concerning this plant, it is plain they could never have the Druids for their inftructors. The truth probably is; The Gothic nations, in their firft incurfions upon the neighbouring Celtes, had obferved the fuperftitious veneration that was paid to this plant by their enemies; and their own religious modes being different, they therefore held it in contempt and abhorrence:—So in fucceeding ages, when Chriftianity was eftablifhed in Gaul and Britain, the Scandinavians (ftill Pagans) turned ther facred rites into ridicule. Thus Regner Lodbrog, in his DYING ODE, fpeaking of a battle, (fought perhaps againft Chriftians) fays, in ridicule of the Eucharift,

" There we celebrated a MASS [*Mi-Ja. Isl.*] of
" weapons * !"

* Five Pieces of Runic Poetry, p. 32.

Some of the Celtic nations (the Britons for inftance) have a traditionary opinion that the dominions of their anceftors were once extended much farther north, than they were in the time of the Romans; and that they were gradually difpoffeffed by the Gothic or Teutonic nations, of many of thofe countries, which the latter afterwards inhabited.——Whether this tradition be admitted or not, it is certain that the Gothic and Celtic tribes bordered on each other; and this, no lefs than through the whole boundary of Gaul and Germany. Now the frequent wars, renewals of peace, and other occafions of intercourfe in confequence of this vicinage, will account to us for all that the Gothic nations knew or practifed of the Celtic cuftoms and opinions. Perhaps it would be refining too much upon the paffage in the EDDA, to explain it as an allegory; or to fuppofe that the difturbance wrought among the Gods by the Miffeltoe, was meant to exprefs the oppofition which Odin's religion found from the Druids of the Celtic nations. Such an Interpretation of this ancient piece of Mythology would be neither forced nor unnatural: but it is not worth infifting upon.

To return to KEYSLER, he fays (p. 305.) that there are " plain veftiges of this ancient Druidical " reverence for the MISSELTOE ftill remaining in fome " places in Germany; but principally in Gaul and " Aquitain: in which latter countries, it is cuftomary " for the boys and young men on the laft day of De- " cember, to go about through the towns and villa- " ges, finging and begging money, as a kind of New- " year's gift, and crying out, AU GUY! L' AN NEUF! " To the Miffeltoe! The New Year is at hand!"— This is a curious and ftriking inftance; and to it may be added that rural cuftom ftill obferved in many parts of England, of hanging up a Miffeltoe-bufh on Chriftmas Eve, and trying lots by the crackling of the leaves and berries in the fire on Twelfth Night.— All thefe will eafily be admitted to be reliques of Druidical

idical superstition, because all practised in those very countries, in which the Druids were formerly established.—KEYSLER then proceeds to attribute to the same Druidic origin, a custom practised in Upper Germany by the vulgar at Christmas, of running through the streets, &c. and striking the doors and windows (not with MISSELTOE, for that plant does not appear to be at all used or attended to upon the occasion, but) with HAMMERS *(Malleis,* Lat.) crying GUTHYL, GUTHYL.——Now *Guthyl* or *Gut Heyl* ‡, he owns is literally *Bona Salus* ; and therefore might most naturally be applied to the birth of Christ then celebrated : but, because the words have a distant resemblance in meaning to the *Omnia-Sanans,* by which the Gauls expressed the MISSELTOE, according to Pliny; therefore he (without the least shadow of authority) will have this German term *Guthyl,* to be the very Gallic name meant by that author : And his reasons are as good as his authority : viz. " Because, (1st) he says, The language of the Gauls, Germans, Britons, and northern nations, were only different dialects of ONE COMMON tongue; (2dly) Because the German name for this plant *Mistel,* as well as our English *Misseltoe,* are foreign words, and BOTH DERIVED from the Latin *Viscum.*"— That the ancient language of the Gauls, still preserved in the Welsh, Armoric, &c. is or ever was the same with those dialects of the Gothic, the Saxon, German and Danish, &c. believe who will. But that our English name *Misseltoe,* as well as the German *Mistel,* are words of genuine Gothic original, underived from any foreign language, is evident from their being found in every the most ancient dialect of the Gothic tongue: viz. *Ang.-Sax.* Miꞅtiltan. *Island.* [*in* EDDA] Mistilteinn. *Dan. & Belg.* Mistel, *&c. &c.*

We see then what little ground this passage of the EDDA now affords us for supposing the Gothic nations of Scandinavia and Germany, to be the same people

‡ *Angliæ* Good Heal; or Good Health.

with the Celtic tribes of Britain and Gaul; or for calling the Icelandic and Gothic EDDA, a Syſtem of Druidical or CELTIC MYTHOLOGY: For as for the preſent German inhabitants of Holſace calling the MISSELTOE " the branch of ſpectres," that proves no more that their anceſtors revered it as ſalutary and divine; than its being anciently repreſented in the north as the death of Balder proves it to have been intitled there to the Druidical character of *Omnia Sanans*.

T.

THE TWENTY-NINTH FABLE.

Hermode's Journey to Hell.

* BALDER having thus perished, FRIG-
GA, his mother, caused it to be published every where, that whosoever of the Gods would go to Hell in search of Balder, and offer DEATH such a ransom as she would require for restoring him to life, would merit all her love. HERMODE, surnamed the Nimble or Active, the son of Odin, offered to take this commission upon him. With this view he took Odin's horse, and mounting him, departed. For the space of nine days and as many nights, he travelled through deep vallies, so dark, that he did not begin to see whither he was going, till he arrived at the river of *Giall*,

---

* In this, as well as the preceding chapter, the Latin Version of Goranson differs exceedingly from the French of M. Mallet (which is here followed) owing, I suppose, to the great variations in the different copies, which they respectively adopted. T.

that he paſſed over a bridge, which was all covered with ſhining gold. The keeping of this bridge was committed to a damſel named *Modguder*, or Audacious War. When ſhe ſaw Hermode, ſhe demanded his name and family, telling him that the preceding day ſhe had ſeen paſs over the bridge five ſquadrons of dead perſons, who all together did not make the bridge ſhake ſo much as he alone; and beſides, added ſhe, you have not the colour of a dead corpſe: what brings you then to the infernal regions? Hermode anſwered, I go to ſeek Balder: Have not you ſeen him paſs this way? Balder, ſaid ſhe, hath paſſed over this bridge; but the road of the dead is there below, towards the north. Hermode then perſued his journey, till he came near to the entrance of Hell, which was defended by a large grate. Hermode now alighted, and girthed his ſaddle tighter; then mounting again, clapped both ſpurs to his horſe; who immediately leaped over the grate, without touching it the leaſt in the world with his feet. Entering in, he ſaw his brother Balder ſeated in the moſt diſtinguiſhed place in the palace; and there he paſſed the night. The next morning he beſought HELA (or DEATH) to ſuffer Balder to return back with him, aſſuring her that the Gods had been all moſt ſeverely

afflicted

afflicted for his death. But Hela told him, she would know whether it was true that Balder was so much beloved by all things in the world, as he had represented: she required therefore that all beings, both animate and inanimate, should weep for his death; and in that case she would send him back to the Gods: but on the other hand, she would keep him back, if one single thing should be found which refused to shed tears. Upon this Hermode got up, and BALDER re-conducting him out of the palace, took off his ring of gold, and gave it to convey to Odin as a token of remembrance. NANNA also sent Frigga a golden Die, and many other presents. Hermode then set out back again for Asgard; and as soon as he got thither, faithfully reported to the Gods all he had seen and heard.

The Gods, upon this, dispatched messengers throughout the world, begging of every thing to weep, in order to deliver Balder from Hell. All things willingly complied with this request, both men, and beasts, and stones, and trees, and metals, and earth: and when all these wept together, the effect was like as when there is a universal thaw. Then the messengers returned, concluding they had effectually performed their commission: but as they were

were travelling along, they found, in a cavern, an old witch, who called herself *Thok*; the meſſengers having beſought her that ſhe would be ſo good as to ſhed tears for the deliverance of Balder; ſhe anſwered in verſes to this effect, " Thok will weep " with dry eyes the funeral of Balder; Let " all things living or dead weep if they " will: But let Hela keep her prey." It was conjectured that this curſed witch muſt have been LOKE himſelf, who never ceaſed to do evil to the other Gods. He was the cauſe that Balder was ſlain; he was alſo the cauſe that he could not be reſtored to life.

REMARK ON THE TWENTY-NINTH FABLE.

Balder, not having the good fortune to be ſlain in battle, was obliged to go, like all thoſe that died of diſeaſes, to the abode of DEATH. Saxo Grammaticus relates the ſame adventure, with ſome different circumſtances, (L. III. p. 43.) Which ſeems to prove that there had paſſed among the deified Aſiatics, ſome event, out of which the Poets had compoſed the Fable we have been reading.

LOKE and HELA play their part here very well. It is a cuſtom, not yet laid aſide among the people of the Dutchy of Sleſwick, if we will believe Arnkiel, to perſonify DEATH, and to give her the name of *Hell* or *Hela*. Thus, when they would ſay that a contagion rages in any place, they ſay that *Hela* walks there, or *Hela* is come there; and that a man hath made up the matter with *Hela*; when

when he is relieved from a diftemper which was judged to be mortal. From the fame word is derived the prefent name for the Infernal Region in all the languages of Germany and the north *. Vide Arnkiel in Cimbria, c. 9. § 2. p. 55. Keyfl. Antiq. p. 180.

* In all the other Teutonic dialects, as well as in our Englifh, the name for it is HELL, or fome word derived from the fame root. And indeed Goranfon has generally rendered the name *Hela*, throughout this EDDA, not as our French author does by the word *Mort*, or DEATH, but by *Infernum*, HELL. T.

THE THIRTIETH FABLE.

The Flight of Loke.

AT length the Gods being exasperated against LOKE, he was obliged to fly and hide himself in the mountains: there he built him a house open on four sides, whence he could see every thing that passed throughout the world. Often in the day time, he concealed himself in the shape of a Salmon within the waters of a river, where he employed himself in foreseeing and preventing whatever stratagems the Gods might employ to catch him there. One day, as he was in his house, he took thread or twine, and made nets of it, like those which fishermen have since invented. In the mean time, ODIN having discovered, from the height of his all-commanding throne, the place whither Loke had retired, repaired thither with the other Gods. But Loke being aware of their approach, threw his net with all speed into the fire, and ran to conceal himself in the river. As soon as the Gods got there, *Kuafer*, who was the most distinguished among them all for his quickness and penetration, traced out in the hot embers, the vestiges and remains of the net which had been burnt, and by that means found out Loke's invention. Having made all the other Gods remark the same thing, they set themselves to weave a net after the model which they saw imprinted in the ashes. This net, when finished, they threw into the water of the river in which Loke had hid himself. Thor held one end of the net, and all the Gods together laid hold of the other, thus jointly drawing it along the stream. Nevertheless, Loke concealing himself between two stones, the net passed over him without taking him; and the Gods only perceived that some living thing had touched the meshes. They cast it in a second time, after having tied so great a weight to it, that it every where raked the bottom of the stream. But Loke saved himself by suddenly mounting up to the top of the water, and then plunging in again, in a place where the river formed a cataract. The Gods betook themselves afresh towards that place, and divided into two bands: Thor walking in the water followed the net, which they dragged thus to the very margin of the sea.

Then

Then Loke perceived the danger that threatned him, whether he saved himself in the sea; or whether he got back over the net. However, he chose the latter, and leaped with all his might over the net: but Thor running after him, caught him in his hand: but for all this, being extremely flippery, he had doubtless escaped, had not Thor held him fast by the tail; and this is the reason why Salmons have had their tails ever since so fine and thin.

THE THIRTY-FIRST FABLE.

The Punishment of Loke.

LOKE being thus taken, they dragged him without mercy into a cavern. The Gods also seized his children, *Vali* and *Nari:* the first being changed by the Gods into a savage beast, tore his brother in pieces and devoured him. The Gods made of his intestines cords for Loke, tying him down to three sharp stones; one of which pressed his shoulder, the other his loyns; and the third his hams. These cords were afterwards changed into chains of iron. Besides this, *Skada* suspended over his head a serpent, whose venom falls upon his face, drop by drop. At the same time his wife, *Siguna*, sits by his side, and receives the drops as they fall, into a bason, which she empties as often as it is filled. But while this is doing, the venom falls upon Loke, which makes him howl with horror, and twist his body about with such violence, that all the earth is shaken with it; and this produces what men call Earth-quakes. There
will

will Loke remain in irons till the laſt day of the darkneſs of the Gods.

REMARKS ON THE THIRTY-FIRST FABLE.

Loke having at length tired out the patience of the Gods, they ſeize and puniſh him. This idea, at the bottom, hath prevailed among almoſt all the ancient nations; but they have each of them imbelliſhed it after their own manner. One cannot doubt but our Scandinavians brought with them from Aſia this belief, which appears to have been very widely eſtabliſhed there from the earlieſt antiquity. In the Book of the pretended prophecy of Enoch, we find many particulars very much reſembling theſe of the Edda. The rebel angels cauſing inceſſantly a thouſand diſorders, God commanded the Arch-Angel, Raphael, to bind hand and foot one of the principal among them, named *Azael*, and caſt him into an obſcure place in a deſert, there to keep him bound upon ſharp pointed ſtones to the laſt day. One may alſo ſafely conjecture that the fables of *Promitheus, Typhon* and *Enceladus*, are derived from the ſame original: whether one is to look for this in the Hiſtory of Holy Writ, miſunderſtood and disfigured, or in other forgotten events, or only in the ancient cuſtom of concealing all inſtructions under the veil of allegory; a cuſtom common in all nations, while their reaſon is in its infancy, but peculiarly proper to thoſe of the eaſt. As all the diligence of the learned cannot ſupply the want of neceſſary monuments, I ſhall not venture to do more than juſt barely to point out the principal grounds of their conjectures: to enumerate them all, to weigh their reſpective merits, and to apply each of them to this fable of the Edda, would be a taſk as laborious, as diſagreeable and uſeleſs: and for which very few of my readers would think themſelves obliged to me.

THE

THE THIRTY-SECOND FABLE;

Of the Twilight of the Gods.

GANGLER then inquired; What can you tell me concerning that day? Har replied; There are very many and very notable circumstances which I can impart to you. In the first place, will come the grand, 'the desolating' Winter; during which the snow will fall from the four corners of the world: the frost will be very severe; the tempest violent and dangerous; and the Sun will withdraw his beams. Three such winters shall pass away, without being softened by one summer. Three others shall follow, during which War and Discord will spread through the whole globe. Brothers, out of hatred, shall kill each other; no one shall spare either his parent, or his child, or his relations. See how it is described in the VOLUSPA; " Bro-
" thers becoming murderers, shall stain
" themselves with brothers blood; kindred
" shall

" shall forget the ties of consanguinity;
" life shall become a burthen; adultery
" shall reign throughout the world. A
" barbarous age! an age of swords! an
" age of tempests! an age of wolves!
" The bucklers shall be broken in pieces;
" and these calamities shall succeed each
" other till the world shall fall to ruin."
Then will happen such things as may well
be called Prodigies. The Wolf FENRIS
will devour the Sun; a severe loss will it be
found by mankind. Another monster will
carry off the Moon, and render her totally
useless: the Stars shall fly away and vanish
from the heavens *: the earth and the
mountains shall be seen violently agitated;
the trees torn up from the earth by the
roots; the tottering hills to tumble headlong from their foundations; all the chains
and irons of the prisoners to be broken
and dashed in pieces. Then is the Wolf
Fenris let loose; the sea rushes impetuously
over the earth, because the great Serpent,
changed into a Spectre, gains the shore.
The ship *Naglefara* is set afloat: this vessel
is constructed of the nails of dead men;
for which reason great care should be taken

---

* Goranson has it, *Stellæ de cælo cadunt.* See other variations in his Latin Version; which seems, in some respects, more spirited than that of M. Mallet, here followed.   T.

not to die with unpared nails; for he who dies so, supplies materials towards the building of that vessel, which Gods and men will wish were finished as late as possible. The Giant *Rymer* is the pilot of this vessel, which the sea breaking over its banks, wafts along with it. The Wolf Fenris advancing, opens his enormous mouth; his lower jaw reaches to the earth, and his upper jaw to the heavens, and would reach still farther, were space itself found to admit of it. The burning fire flashes out from his eyes and nostrils. The Great Serpent vomits forth floods of poison; which overwhelm the air and the waters. This terrible monster places himself by the side of the Wolf. In this confusion the heaven shall cleave asunder; and by this breach the Genii of Fire enter on horseback. *Surtur* is at their head: before and behind him sparkles a bright glowing fire. His sword outshines the Sun itself. The army of these Genii passing on horseback over the bridge of heaven, break it in pieces: Thence they direct their course to a plain; where they are joined by the Wolf Fenris, and the Great Serpent. Thither also repair LOKE, and the Giant RYMER, and with them all the Giants of the Frost, who follow Loke even to Death. The Genii of Fire march first in battle array, forming a most brilliant squadron on this plain;

plain; which is an hundred degrees square on every side. During these prodigies, HEIMDAL, the door-keeper of the Gods, rises up; he violently sounds his clanging trumpet to awaken the Gods: who instantly assemble. Then ODIN repairs to the fountain of *Mimis*, to consult what he ought to do, he and his army. The great Ash Tree of *Ydrasil* is shaken; nor is any thing in heaven or earth exempt from fear and danger. The Gods are clad in armour; ODIN puts on his golden helmet, and his resplendent cuirass; he grasps his sword, and marches directly against the Wolf Fenris. He hath THOR at his side: but this God cannot assist him; for he himself fights with the Great Serpent. FREY encounters SURTUR, and terrible blows are exchanged on both sides; 'till Frey is beat down; and he owes his defeat to his having formerly given his sword to his attendant *Skyrner*. That day also is let loose the dog named *Garmer*, who had hitherto been chained at the entrance of a cavern. He is a monster dreadful even to the Gods; he attacks TYR, and they kill each other. THOR beats down the Great Serpent to the earth, but at the same time recoiling back nine steps, he falls dead upon the spot *,

* The Reader will observe that our ingenious Author has represented this somewhat differently above, in p. 133.   T.

suffocated with floods of venom, which the Serpent vomits forth upon him. ODIN is devoured by the Wolf Fenris. At the same instant VIDAR advances, and pressing down the monster's lower jaw with his foot, seizes the other with his hand, and thus tears and rends him till he dies. LOKE and HEIMDAL fight, and mutually kill each other. After that, SURTUR darts fire and flame over all the earth; the whole world is presently consumed. See how this is related in the VOLUSPA. "Heimdal
" lifts up his crooked trumpet, and sounds
" it aloud. Odin consults the head of
" Mimis; the great Ash, that Ash sublime
" and fruitful, is violently shaken, and sends
" forth a groan. The Giant bursts his
" irons. What is doing among the Gods?
" What is doing among the Genii? The
" land of the Giants is filled with uproar:
" the Deities collect and assemble together.
" The Dwarfs sigh and groan before the
" doors of their caverns. Oh! ye inha-
" bitants of the mountains; can you say
" whether any thing will yet remain in
" existence? [The Sun is darkened; the
" earth is overwhelmed in the sea; the
" shining stars fall from heaven; a vapour,
" mixed with fire, arises: a vehement heat
" prevails, even in heaven itself *."]

* The passage in Brackets is given from the Latin of Goranson, being omitted by M. Mallet.   T.

THE THIRTY-THIRD FABLE.

The Sequel of the Conflagration of the World.

ON hearing the preceding relation, Gangler asks, What will remain after the world shall be consumed; and after Gods, and Heroes, and Men shall perish? For I understood by you, adds he, that mankind were to exist for ever in another world. Thridi replies, After all these prodigies, there will succeed many new abodes, some of which will be agreeable and others wretched: but the best mansion of all, will be *Gimle* (or HEAVEN) where all kinds of liquors shall be quaffed in the Hall called *Brymer* (A), situated in the country of *Okolm*. That is also a most delightful palace which is upon the mountains of *Inda* *, and which is built of shining gold. In this palace good and just men shall abide. In *Nastrande* (i. e. the shore of the dead) there is a vast and direful structure, the portal of which faces the

---

* This and the preceding names are very different in the Edition of Goranson. T.

north. It is compiled of nothing but the carcafes of Serpents, all whofe heads are turned towards the infide of the building: there they vomit forth fo much venom, that it forms a long river of poifon: and in this float the perjured and the murderers; as is faid in thofe verfes of the VOLUSPA:
" I know that there is in *Naftrande*, an
" abode remote from the Sun, the gates
" of which look towards the north; there
" drops of poifon rain through the win-
" dows. It is all built of the carcafes of
" ferpents. There, in rapid rivers, fwim
" the perjured, the affaffins, and thofe who
" feek to feduce the wives of others. In an-
" other place, their condition is ftill worfe;
" for a wolf, an all-devouring monfter,
" perpetually torments the bodies who are
" fent in thither (B)." Gangler refumes the difcourfe, and fays, Which then are the Gods that fhall furvive? Shall they all perifh, and will there no longer be a heaven nor an earth? Har replies, There will arife out of the fea, another earth moft lovely and delightful: covered it will be with verdure and pleafant fields: there the grain fhall fpring forth and grow of itfelf, without cultivation. VIDAR and VALE fhall alfo furvive, becaufe neither the flood, nor the black conflagration fhall do them any harm. They fhall dwell in the plains

of *Ida*; where was formerly the residence of the Gods. The sons of Thor, Mode and Magne repair thither: thither come Balder and Hoder, from the mansions of the dead. They sit down and converse together; they recal to mind the adversities they have formerly undergone. They afterwards find among the grass, the golden Dice *, which the Gods heretofore made use of. And here be it observed, that while the fire devoured all things, two persons of the human race, one male and the other female, named *Lif* and *Lifthraser*, lay concealed under an hill. They feed on the dew, and propagate so abundantly, that the earth is soon peopled with a new race of mortals. What you will think still more wonderful is, that *Sunna* (the Sun) before it is devour'd by the Wolf Fenris, shall have brought forth a daughter as lovely and as resplendant as herself; and who shall go in the same track formerly trode by her mother: according as it is described in these verses: " The brilliant monarch of " Fire †, shall beget an only daughter, be-
" fore

---

* Goranson renders it *Crepidas*, " Sandals." But M. Mallet's Version is countenanced by Bartholin. *Deaurati orbes aleatorij*, p. 597.   T.

† There seems to be a defect or ambiguity in the Original here, which has occasioned a strange confusion of genders, both in the French of M. Mallet, and the Latin
Ver-

" fore the Wolf commits his devaſtation.
" This young Virgin, after the death of the
" Gods, will purſue the ſame track as her
" parent (c)."

Now, continues Har, If you have any new queſtions to aſk me, I know not who can reſolve you; becauſe I have never heard of any one who can relate what will happen in the other ages of the world: I adviſe you therefore to remain ſatisfied with my relation, and to preſerve it in your memory.——

Upon this, Gangler heard a terrible noiſe all around him; he looked every way, but could diſcern nothing, except a vaſt extended plain. He ſet out therefore on his return back to his own kingdom; where he related all that he had ſeen and heard: and ever ſince that time, this relation hath been handed down among the people by Oral Tradition (D).

Verſion of Goranſon. The former has " LE ROI
" brillant du feu engendrera une fille unique avant que
" d'etre englouti par le loup; cette fille ſuivra le traces de
" SA MERE, apres la mort des dieux." The latter,
Unicam filiam genuit rubicundiſſimus ILLE REX antiquam
EUM Fenris devoraverit; quæ curſura eſt, mortuis Diis,
viam MATERNAM. I have endeavoured to avoid this,
by expreſſing the paſſage in more general terms. T.

REMARKS ON THE TWO LAST FABLES.

Had the EDDA had no other claim to our regard, than as having preserved to us the opinions and doctrines of the 'ancient 'northern nations *' on that important subject, an existence after this life, it would have merited, even on that account, to have been preserved from oblivion. And really on this head it throws great light on History: whether we consider that branch of it which principally regards the ascertainment of facts; or that which devotes itself rather to trace the different revolutions of manners and opinions. Such as are only fond of the former species of History, will find in these concluding Fables, the principles of that wild enthusiastic courage which animated the ravagers of the Roman Empire, and conquerors of the greatest part of Europe. Such as interest themselves more in the latter, will see (not without pleasure and astonishment) a people whom they were wont to consider as barbarous and uncultivated, employed in deep and sublime speculations; proceeding in them more conclusively, and coming, possibly, much nearer to the end, than those celebrated nations who have arrogated to themselves an exclusive privilege to reason and knowlege.

I have before observed, that ' the philosophers of ' the north †' considered nature as in a state of perpetual labour and warfare. Her strength was thus continually wasting away by little and little; and her approaching dissolution could not but become every day more and more perceptible. At last, a confusion of the seasons, with a long and preternatural winter, were to be the final marks of her decay. The moral world is to be no less disturbed and troubled than the natural. The voice of dying Nature will be no

* *Les Celtes.* Fr. Orig.

† *Les Celtes.* Fr.

longer heard by man. Her senfations being weakened, and as it were, totally extinct, shall leave the heart a prey to cruel and inhuman paffions. Then will all the malevolent and hoftile powers, whom the Gods have heretofore with much difficulty confined, burft their chains, and fill the univerfe with diforder and confufion. The hoft of Heroes from VALHALL shall in vain attempt to affift and fupport the Gods; for though the latter will deftroy their enemies, they will neverthelefs fall along with them: that is, in other words, In that great day all the inferior Divinities, whether good or bad, shall fall in one great conflict back again into the bofom of the Grand Divinity; from whom all things have proceeded, as it were emanations of his effence, and who will furvive all things. After this, the world becomes a prey to flames: which are, however, deftined rather to purify than deftroy it; fince it afterwards makes its appearance again more lovely, more pleafant, and more fruitful than before. Such, in a few words, is the doctrine of the EDDA, when divefted of all thofe poetical and allegorical ornaments, which are only accidental to it. One fees plainly enough, that the poem called VOLUSPA hath been the text, of which this Fable is the comment: fince in reality the fame ideas, but expreffed with a fuperior pomp and ftrength, are found in that old poem. It may perhaps afford fome pleafure to perufe the following extracts, given literally from the tranflation of Bartholin *.

" THE Giant Rymer arrives from the eaft, car-
" ried in a chariot: the ocean fwells: the Great Ser-
" pent rolls himfelf furioufly in the waters, and lifteth
" up the fea. The eagle fcreams, and tears the dead

* Vid. CAUSÆ Contemptæ a Danis Mortis, 4to. 1689. Lib. II. cap. 14. p. 597, & feq. I have rather followed the Latin of Bartholin, than the French Verfion of our author. T.

" bodies

"bodies with his horrid beak. The veſſel of the Gods is ſet afloat.

"The veſſel comes from the eaſt: the hoſt of Evil Genii † arrives by ſea: Loke is their pilot and director. Their furious ſquadron advances, eſcorted by the Wolf Fenris: Loke appears with them ‡.

"The black prince of the Genii of Fire § iſſues forth from the ſouth, ſurrounded with flames: the ſwords of the Gods beam forth rays like the Sun. The rocks are ſhaken, and fall to pieces. The female Giants wander about 'weeping.' Men tread in crowds the paths of death. The heaven is ſplit aſunder.

"New grief for the Goddeſs who defends Odin. For Odin advances to encounter Fenris; the ſnow-white ſlayer of Bela ‖, againſt the 'black' prince of the Genii of Fire *. Soon is the ſpouſe of Frigga beaten down.

"Then runs Vidar, the illuſtrious ſon of Odin, to avenge the death of his father. He attacks the murderous monſter, that monſter born of a Giant; and with his ſword he pierces him to the heart.

"The Sun is darkened: the ſea overwhelms the earth: the ſhining ſtars vaniſh out of heaven: the fire furiouſly rages: the ages draw to an end: the flame aſcending, licks the vault of heaven."

† *Muſpelli Incolæ.* Bartholin.
‡ A ſtanza is here omitted, being part of what is quoted above in the 32d fable, p. 163: as alſo one or two ſtanzas below.   T.
§ *Surtur.* Iſland. orig.—The reader will obſerve ſome variations between the verſion here, and that given of this ſame ſtanza in p. 13. they are owing to the different readings of the original.   T.
‖ Sc. Frey.   * Sc. Surtur.

Many

Many other pieces of poetry might be quoted to shew, that the Scandinavians had their minds full of all these prophecies, and that they laid great stress upon them. But the generality of readers may possibly rather take my word for it, than be troubled with longer extracts. It will be of more importance to remark, that what we have been reading is, for the most part, nothing else, but the doctrine of ZENO and the Stoics. This remarkable resemblance hath never been properly considered, and highly deserves a discussion.

The ancients universally assure us, that the Stoic philosophy established the existence of an eternal divinity, diffused through and pervading all nature; and being, as it were, the soul and primum mobile of matter. From this divinity, proceeded as emanations from his essence, together with the world, certain intelligences ordained to govern under his directions, and who were to undergo the same revolutions as the world itself until the day appointed for the renovation of this universe. The fires concealed in the veins of the earth, never cease to dry up the moisture contained therein, and will, in the end, set it all on flames. " A " time will come, says " SENECA, when the " world, ripe for a re- " novation, shall be " wrapt in flames; when " the opposite powers " shall in conflict mutu- " ally destroy each other; " when the constellations " shall dash together: " and when the whole " universe, plunged in " the same common fire, " shall be consumed to " ashes." (Senec. Consol. ad Marciam. cap. ult.) This general destruction was to be preceded by an inundation: And in this respect, the EDDA perfectly agrees with Zeno. SENECA treats this subject of a future deluge at large, in his Quæst. Natural. Lib. 3. c. 29. which he asserts must contribute to purify and prepare the earth for a new race of inhabitants, more innocent and virtuous than the present.

But

But the confummation of the world by fire, was the point moſt ſtrongly inſiſted on by the Stoics. Theſe verſes of Seneca's kinſman Lucan are well known.

———" *Hos populos ſi nunc non uſſerit Ignis,*
" *Uret cum terris, uret cum gurgite ponti ;*
" *Communis Mundo fupereſt Rogus.*"———

That is, " I F theſe people are not as yet to periſh
" by fire ; the time will neverthelefs come when they
" ſhall be conſumed along with the Earth and the
" Sea : the whole world will become one common
" funeral pile."

But the ſtrongeſt proof of the agreement between theſe two ſyſtems is this, that the deſtruction of the world will involve in it that of the Gods; that is to ſay, all thoſe created or inferior Divinities. This is expreſſed by Seneca the Tragedian, in moſt clear and preciſe terms, in thoſe remarkable verſes, which I have already quoted in the firſt Volume, p. 115. and which I ſhall again repeat here.

Jam jam legibus obrutis
Mundo cum veniet dies
Auſtralis Polus obruet
Quicquid per Libyam jacet . .
Arctous Polus obruet
Quicquid ſubjacet axibus :
Amiſſum trepidus polo
Titan excutiet diem,
Cœli Regia concidens
Ortus atque Obitus trahet,
Atque Omnes pariter Deos
Perdet Mors aliqua, *et*
Chaos, &c.   Hercul. Oet. ver. 1102.

i. e. " When the laws of nature ſhall be buried in
" ruin, and the laſt day of the world ſhall come, the
" ſouthern pole ſhall cruſh, as it falls, all the regions
" of Africa. The north pole ſhall overwhelm all the
" coun-

"countries beneath it's axis. The affrighted Sun shall be deprived of its light; the palace of heaven falling to decay, shall produce at once both life and death, and some KIND OF DISSOLUTION SHALL IN LIKE MANNER SEIZE ALL THE DEITIES, and they shall return into their original chaos, &c."

In another place, SENECA explains what he means by this Death of the Gods. They were not to be absolutely annihilated; but to be once more re-united, by dissolution, to the soul of the world; being resolved and melted into that intelligence of fire, into that eternal and universal principle, from which they had originally been emanations. It was, without doubt, in this sense also that our northern philosophers understood the matter. We may, from analogy, supply this circumstance with the greater confidence, as the poets have been ever more attentive to adorn and embellish the received doctrines, than to deliver them with precision. But lastly, what must render this parallel more compleat and striking, is, that according to the school of ZENO, no less than in the Icelandic prophecies, this tremendous scene is succeeded by a new creation, evidently drawn in the same colours by both.

The world, says SENECA, being melted and re-entered into the bosom of Jupiter, this God continues for some time totally concentered in himself, and remains concealed, as it were, wholly immersed in the contemplation of his own ideas: Afterwards we see a new world spring from him, perfect in all its parts; animals are produced anew; an innocent race of men are formed under more favourable auspices, in order to people this earth, the worthy abode of virtue. In short, the whole face of Nature becomes more pleasing and lovely. (Senec. Epist. 9. & Quæst. Nat. L. 3. c. ult.)

The EDDA gives us the same descriptions in other words. They likewise occur in the poem of the Voluspa, above quoted; and the same doctrine is very conspicuous in the following stanzas from the same piece †.

"THEN" (i. e. after the death of the Gods, and the conflagration of the world) "we see emerge
"from the bosom of the waves, an earth cloathed
"with a most lovely verdure. The floods retire: the
"eagle soars wheresoever he lifts, and seizes his fishy
"prey on the tops of the mountains.

"The fields produce their fruits without culture;
"misfortunes are banished from the world. Balder
"and his brother ‖, those warrior Gods, return to
"inhabit the ruined palaces of Odin. Do ye con-
"ceive what will then come to pass?

"The Gods assemble in the fields of Ida; they
"discourse together concerning the heavenly palaces,
"whose ruins are before them: they recollect their
"former conversations, and the ancient discourses of
"Odin.

"A palace more resplendant than the Sun rises to
"view; it is adorned with a roof of gold: there the
"assemblies of good men shall inhabit; and give
"themselves up to joy and pleasure, throughout all
"ages."

The distance between Scandinavia and those countries where the Stoic philosophy prevailed, is certainly great, and must have been greater still in former ages than the present, when commerce and books lend wings to opinions, and diffuse them in a short time thro' the world. On the other hand, the system now under consideration is not such as

† Vid. Bartholin, *ubi supra*, p. 596. where the original and a literal Latin Version may be seen: our French author has only selected some of the stanzas, which he has taken the liberty to transpose. T.
‖ Hoder.

all

all men would arrive at by meer dint of reflection. It appears then probable, that all thofe who adopted it, muft have had it from the fame hands; namely, from the eaftern philofophers, and more particularly from the Perfians. And hiftory affords a fanction to this conjecture. We know that the Scandinavians came from fome country of Afia. ZENO, who was born in Cyprus, of Phænician parents, borrowed in all probability the principal tenets of his doctrine from the philofophers of the eaft. This doctrine was in many refpects the fame with that of the Magi. ZOROASTRE had taught that the conflict between *Oromafdes* and *Arimanes*; (i. e. Light and Darknefs, the Good and Evil Principle) fhould continue till the laft day; and that then the Good Principle fhould be re-united to the fupreme God, from whom it had firft iffued: the Evil fhould be overcome and fubdued; darknefs fhould be deftroyed, and the world, purified by an univerfal conflagration, fhould become a luminous and fhining abode, into which Evil fhould never more be permitted to enter. (Vid. Brücker Hift. Crit. Philof. Vol. I. Lib. 2. c. 3.)

Arts, Sciences and Philofophy have heretofore taken their flight from eaft to weft. The doctrine of the renovation of the world was current among fome of the Celtic nations long ere ODIN migrated from Afiatic Scythia into the north. ORPHEUS had taught it among the Thracians, according to Plutarch and Clemens Alexandrinus; and we find traces of it in verfes attributed to that ancient bard. The Greeks and Romans had alfo fome idea of it; but the greateft part of them did not adopt the whole compleat fyftem, but were content to detach from it, what regarded the conflagration of the world, in order to augment the confufed and incoherent mafs of their own religious opinions.

I muft not finifh this note, without juftifying the length of it: one
word

word will be sufficient. Some of the points of doctrine which I have been displaying after the EDDA, have been consecrated by Revelation. Here follow some of the principal passages:

"BUT the heavens and the earth which are now, are reserved unto fire against the day of judgment and perdition of ungodly men." (2 Pet. ch. iii. ver. 7.)

"The day of the Lord will come as a thief in the night, in the which the heavens shall pass away with a great noise, and the elements shall melt with fervent heat, and the earth also, and the works that are therein shall be burnt up." (Ver. 10.) "Nevertheless we look for new heavens and a new earth, wherein dwelleth righteousness." (Ver. 13.)

"THEN" (i. e. in the last day) "shall many be offended, and shall betray one another, and shall hate one another." (Mat. ch. xxiv. ver. 10.) "And because iniquity shall abound, the love of many shall wax cold." (Ver. 12.)

"But in those days, after that tribulation, the Sun shall be darkened, and the Moon shall not give her light: and the Stars of heaven shall fall, and the powers that are in heaven shall be shaken." (Mark, ch. xiii. ver. 24, 25.)

"And there shall be signs in the Sun and in the Moon and in the Stars; and upon the earth distress of nations with perplexity; the sea and waves roaring; mens hearts failing them for fear." (Luke, ch. xxi. ver. 25, 26.)

The Apocalypse adds other circumstances to the above description.

"AND lo!" (i. e. in the terrible day of the anger of the Lord) "there was a great earthquake: and the Sun became black as sackcloth of hair, and the Moon became as blood; and the Stars of heaven fell unto the earth. And the heaven departed as a
"scrowl

"scrowl when it is rolled together; and every mountain and ifland were moved out of their places."
(Rev. ch. vi. ver. 12, 13, 14.)

"And there was war in heaven; Michael and his Angels fought againſt the Dragon: and the Dragon fought and his Angels; and prevailed not, neither was their place found any more in heaven. And the great Dragon was caſt out, that old Serpent, called the Devil and Satan, which deceiveth the whole world: he was caſt out into the earth, and his Angels were caſt out with him. And I heard a loud voice faying in heaven, Now is come falvation and ſtrength, and the kingdom of our God, and the power of his Chriſt: for the accufer of our brethren is caſt down, which accufed them before our God day and night!"
(Rev. ch. xii. ver. 7, 8, 9, 10.)

"And I faw an Angel come down from heaven, having the key of the bottomlefs pit, and a great chain in his hand: and he laid hold on the Dragon, that old Serpent, which is the Devil and Satan, and bound him. .... And I faw the fouls of them that were beheaded for the witnefs of Jefus, and for the Word of God. .... And they lived and reigned with Chriſt a thoufand years." (Ibid. ch. xx. ver. 1, 2, 4.)

"And I faw a new heaven and a new earth: for the firſt heaven and the firſt earth were paſſed away, and there was no more fea. ... And God ſhall wipe away all tears from their eyes; and there ſhall be no more death, neither forrow, nor crying; neither ſhall there be any more pain. .... And the building of the wall of it was of jafper; and the city was pure gold, like unto clear glafs. .... And the city had no need of the Sun, neither of the Moon to ſhine in it; for the glory of God did lighten it. ... And there ſhall in no wife enter into it any thing that defileth." (Ibid. ch. xxi. ver. 1, 4, 18, 23, 27.)

After these general observations, nothing more remains but to clear up some particular passages of the last fable of the EDDA.

(A) " In the Hall cal-
" led Brymer."] *Brymer*, according to the strict etymology of the word, means a Hall very hot; as *Okolm* does a place inaccessible to cold. The miseries of the last day are to commence by a very long and severe winter. The windows and doors of hell stood open towards the north. We see plainly that all this must have been imagined and invented in a cold climate. The ancient Scandinavians were more frank and honest than some of their descendants; than the famous RUDBECK, for example; who seems to have been tempted to put off his own country for the seat of the Terrestrial Paradise *.

(B) " Torments the
" bodies who are sent in
" thither."] Before this stanza of the VOLUSPA, Bartholin has given another, † which deserves to be produced.

" THEN the Master, he who governs all things,
" issues forth with great power from his habitations
" on high, to render his divine judgments, and to
" pronounce his sentences. He terminates all diffe-
" rences, and establishes the sacred destinies, which
" will remain to eternity."

The description which the EDDA gives of the place of torment, bears a striking resemblance to what we meet with in the religious books of the ancient Persians.

" HELL (say they) is on the shore of a fœtid stink-
" ing river, whose waters are black as pitch, and cold
" as ice; in these float the souls of the damned. The
" smoak ascends in vast rolls from this dark gulf: and

---

* Vid. Keysl. p. 123. † Vid. Bartholin, p. 599.

" the

" the infide of it is full of Scorpions and Serpents."
Vid. Hyde de Relig. vet. Perf. p. 399, & 404.

(c) " After the death of the Gods."] In the new earth, which was to fucceed that which we inhabit, there were to be again fubaltern divinities to govern it; and men to people it. This, in general, is what the EDDA means to tell us: although the circumftances of the relation are darkly and allegorically delivered: yet not fo obfcurely; but that one eafily fees it was the idea of the northern philofophers, as well as of the ftoics, that the world was to be renovated, and fpring forth again more perfect and more beautiful. This is what is expreffed here with regard to the Sun and Moon. *Lif* fignifies life; which is a farther proof, that by the fable of thefe two human beings who are to furvive the deftruction of the world, thefe northern philofophers * meant to fay that there ftill exifted in the earth a vivifying principle and feed, proper to repair the lofs of the former inhabitants. It is certain that all thefe different forms of expreffion were underftood by thefe ancient people in their true fenfe; viz. only as figurative modes of fpeech, and ornaments of difcourfe; and therefore, we, who in reading their works, continually lofe fight of this circumftance, are in reality authors of many of thofe abfurdities, which we fancy we difcover in them.

(D) " Among the people by oral tradition."] This paffage may poffibly ftart a queftion, Whether the doctrines here difplayed were peculiar to the northern nations, or embraced by the other 'Go-'thic and' Celtic tribes? My opinion is, that the latter had adopted at leaft moft of the principal points: and that they all derived their religious tenets from the fame fource. It is very probable, as the Abbé Banier fenfibly obferves, " That

* *Les Celtes.* Fr. Orig.

"the northern Celtes, the anceſtors of the Gauls, borrowed their doctrines either from the Perſians or their neighbours, and that the Druids were formed upon the model of the Magi." (Mythol. expl. Tom. II. 4to. p. 628.) We are, it is true, but very moderately acquainted with what the Gauls, the Britons or the Germans thought on this head; but as the little we know of their opinions, coincides very exactly with the EDDA, we may ſafely ſuppoſe the ſame conformity in the other particulars of which we are ignorant. Let thoſe who doubt this, caſt their eyes over the following paſſages.

"Zamolxis" (a celebrated Druid of the Getæ and Scythians) "taught his contemporaries, that neither he nor they, nor the men who ſhould be born hereafter, were to periſh; but were on the contrary to repair, after quitting this life, to a place where they ſhould enjoy full abundance and plenty of every thing that was good." Herod. L. 4. § 95.

"If we may believe you," (ſays Lucan to the Druids) "the ſouls of men do not deſcend into the abode of darkneſs and ſilence, nor yet into the gloomy empire of Pluto: you ſay that the ſame ſpirit animates the body in another world, and that death is the paſſage to a long life." Luc. Lib. 1. v. 454.

"The Gauls" (ſays Cæſar) "are particularly aſſiduous to prove that ſouls periſh not." Cæſ. Lib. 6. c. 14.

Valerius Maximus, in a paſſage quoted above in my REMARKS on the 16th Fable*, comes ſtill nearer to the doctrine of the EDDA; for he tells us that the Celtes looked upon a quiet peaceable death as moſt wretched and diſhonourable, and that they leaped for joy at the approach of a battle, which would afford them oppor-

* Pag. 88.

tunities

tunities of dying with their swords in their hands.

"Among the ancient Irish," says Solinus, "when a woman is brought to bed of a son, she prays to the Gods to give him the grace to die in battle." This was to wish salvation to the child. (See Solin. c. 25. p. 252.)

These authorities may suffice *: they do not indeed say all that the EDDA does; but that makes this work so much the more valuable.

* I cannot help adding to the authorities of our Author, what Quintus Curtius relates of the Sogdians: a nation, who inhabited to the eastward of the Caspian Sea; not far from the country of ODIN and his companions. When some of that people were condemned to death by Alexander, on account of their revolt, "*Carmen, Lætantium more, canere, tripudiisque & lasciviori corporis motu, gaudium quoddam animi ostentare cœperunt.*"—When the king enquired the reason of their thus rejoicing, they answered——"*A tanto Rege, victore omnium gentium, MAJORIBUS SUIS REDDITOS, bonestam mortem, quam fortes viri* VOTO *quoque expeterent, Carminibus sui moris Lætitiaque celebrare.*" Curt. Lib. 7. cap. 8. Edit. Varior.   T.

THE END OF THE FIRST PART OF THE EDDA.

AN IDEA

OF THE

SECOND PART

OF THE

EDDA.

ALL the moſt important points of the 'northern *' Mythology have been laid open in the preceding Dialogue, which forms the Firſt Part of the EDDA. In the Second Part, the Author changing his ſtile, confines himſelf to the relation of ſeveral adventures which had happened to theſe Deities whom he hath been deſcribing to us. The ancient SCALDS or Poets, are the guides he follows; and his chief aim is to explain the epithets and ſynonymous expreſſions, which have been in a manner conſecrated in their language. The ſame taſte and mode of compoſition prevails every where through this Second Part as in the former: We have conſtantly Allegories, and

---

* *Celtique*, Fr.

Combats; Giants contending with the Gods; Loke perpetually deceiving them; Thor interpofing in their defence, &c. This is nearly the whole of the Second Part. It would tire our Reader's patience to infert it here intire, although it is three-fourths lefs than the former. I fhall perhaps ftand in need of his indulgence, while I barely aim at giving him a fuccinct idea of it.

"Æger, a Danifh nobleman, was defirous, in imitation of Gylfe, of going to Asgard, to vifit the Gods. The Deities expecting his coming, immediately mounted on their lofty feats, that they might receive him with the greater dignity: and the Goddeffes, who yielded to them in nothing, took their places along with them. Æger was fplendidly entertained. Odin had ranged all along the hall where they feafted, fwords of fuch an amazing brilliancy and polifh, that no other illuminations were wanted. All the walls were covered with glittering fhields. They continued drinking for a long time large draughts of the moft excellent mead. Brage, the God of Eloquence, fat next to Æger, and the Gods had committed their gueft to his care. The converfation that paffed between Æger and this Deity, is the fubject of this Second Part of the Edda. Brage begins with relating

lating an evil turn which LOKE had played the Gods. The Reader will remember that they prevented the effects of old age and decay by eating certain apples, entrusted to the care of IDUNA. Loke had, by a wile, conveyed away this Iduna, and concealed her in a wood, under the custody of a Giant. The Gods beginning to wax old and grey, detected the author of this theft, and with terrible threats, obliged him to make use of his utmost cunning to regain Iduna and her salutary apples back again for the Gods."

" This is one of the Fables." I shall present the Reader with another, concerning a Duel between the Giant RUGNER and the God THOR. " The Giant carried " a lance made all of whetstone. Thor " broke it in pieces by a blow with his " club, and made the splinters fly so far, " that all the subsequent whetstones found " in the world are parts of it; as indeed " they appear evidently broken off from " something by violence."

I must detain the Reader somewhat longer, with the account of the origin of Poetry. It is an allegory not altogether void of invention.

" The Gods of the north had formed a man much in the same manner as the Grecian Deities are said to have formed *Orion*.

This

This man was called *Kuaſer*. (Ears accuſtomed to the muſical Greek names muſt pardon our Gothic appellations.) He was ſo clever, that no queſtion could be propoſed which he was not able to reſolve: he traverſed the whole world teaching mankind wiſdom. But his merits exciting envy, two Dwarfs treacherouſly ſlew him; and receiving his blood into a veſſel, mixed it up with honey, and thence compoſed a liquor, which renders all thoſe that drink of it, Poets *. The Gods miſſing their ſon, enquired of the Dwarfs what was become of him. The Dwarfs, to extricate themſelves out of the difficulty, replied, That Kuaſer had died, ſuffocated with his knowlege, becauſe he could not meet with perſons to eaſe and diſembogue his mind to, by propoſing to him ſo many learned queſtions as was neceſſary to his relief. But their perfidy was afterward diſcovered by an unexpected accident. Theſe Dwarfs having drawn upon themſelves the reſentment of a certain Giant, he ſeized and expoſed them upon a rock ſurrounded on all ſides by the ſea. In this frightful ſituation, their only recourſe was to purchaſe their deliverance

---

* It is probable, that by the blood of this wiſe man blended with honey, was meant that union of reaſon or good ſenſe, with the ſweeter embelliſhments of ſentiment and language, ſo eſſential to the perfection of true Poetry.

at the price of that divine beverage. The Giant being satisfied with this ransom, carried it home, and delivered it to the custody of his daughter *Gunlöda:* hence, adds my author, Poetry is indifferently, in allusion to the same Fable, called " The blood of " Kuafer:" " The Beverage," or " The " ransom of the Dwarfs," &c.

" This valuable acquisition was eagerly sought after by the Gods, but very difficult to obtain, because it was concealed under rocks. ODIN was nevertheless determined to try for it, and he made the attempt in the following manner. * Transforming himself into a Worm, he glided through a crevise into the cavern where the Beverage was kept. Then resuming his natural shape, and gaining the heart of Gunloda, he prevailed on her to let him drink three draughts of the liquor entrusted to her care. But the crafty Deity, resolving to make the most of his advantage, pulled so deep, that at the last draught, he left none behind him in the vessel; and transforming himself into an eagle, flew away to Asgard, to deposit in safety the precious treasure he had obtained. The Giant, who was a Magician, instantly discovered the arti-

---

* In his first Edit. our Author had given here some farther circumstances of this Icelandic Tale; which in his second Impression (here followed) he dropt as unimportant and puerile.   T.

fice that had been practifed, and changing himfelf alfo into an Eagle, flew with all fpeed after Odin; who had almoſt reached the gates of Afgard. Then the Gods all ran out of their palaces to affiſt and fupport their maſter; and forefeeing that he would have much difficulty to fecure the liquor, without expofing himfelf to the danger of being taken, they immediately fet out all the veffels they could lay their hands on. In effect, Odin finding he could not efcape but by eafing himfelf of that burden which retarded his flight, inſtantly filled all the pitchers with this miraculous liquor: and from hence it hath been diſtributed among both Gods and men. But in the hurry and confufion in which the liquor was difcharged, the bulk of mankind were not aware that Odin only threw up part of it through his beak; the reſt was emitted from a more impure vent: And as it is only the former liquor that this God gives as a Beverage to the good Poets, to fuch as he would animate with a divine infpiration: fo it is only the latter fort that falls to the fhare of bad Rhymers; for as this flowed from its inferior fource in greateſt abundance, the Gods beſtow it in liberal draughts on all that will apply; this makes the crowd very great about the veffels, and this is the reafon why the world

is

is overwhelmed with such a redundance of wretched verses."

AFTER this remarkable fiction, there are many Fables in the EDDA which have little or no relation to Mythology. These are historical strokes, blended with fictions, which are neither important for their instruction, nor agreeable for their invention. I shall therefore proceed, without farther delay, to say something of the SCALDA, or " Poetical Dictionary," which I have before mentioned in the Introduction to this Volume.

We have already seen that it was compiled by SNORRO, for the use of such Icelanders as applied themselves to the profession of SCALD or Poet. As this Author wrote in the thirteenth century, he hath not only given the Epithets belonging to the ancient Poetry, but also such as were become necessary, in consequence of the new religion, and new sources of knowlege that had been introduced into the north. The work begins with the Names of the Twelve Gods, which SNORRO produces afresh, in order to range under each their several epithets and synonymous appellations. ODIN alone has one hundred and twenty-six; whence we may judge of the number of ancient Poems which had been written to celebrate this Deity. I shall present the Reader with a

few

few of thofe Epithets; felecting fuch as have not already occurred in the EDDA.

"ODIN, the Father of the Ages; the Supercilious; the Eagle; the Father of Verfes; the Whirlwind; the Incendiary; he who caufes the arrows to fhower down," &c.

THOR is defigned by twelve Epithets; the moft common is that of "The fon of Odin and the earth."

LOKE is ftiled, "The Father of the Great Serpent; the Father of Death; the Adverfary, the Accufer, the Deceiver of the Gods," &c.

FRIGGA is "The Queen of the Gods."

FREYA, "The Goddefs of Love; the *Norne* or Fairy who weeps Golden Tears; the Kind and Liberal Goddefs," &c.

After thefe Epithets of the Gods, follows an alphabetical lift of the Words moft commonly ufed in Poetry. Some of them are now unintelligible, fome appear infipid, and others are like thofe idle Epithets of the ancient Claffics, which follow a word as conftantly as the fhade does the body, and are introduced rather to fill up the meafure of the verfe, than to add to the fenfe. Some are neverthelefs worth knowing, were it only for their fingularity. For inftance, RIVERS are called by the SCALDS "the fweat of the earth;" and "the blood of the vallies." ARROWS are "the daugh-

"daughters of Misfortune;" "the hail-stones of helmets." The BATTLE-AX is "the hand of the Homicide, or Slaughterer:" The EYE, "the torch or flambeau of the countenance;" "the diamond of the head." The GRASS and HERBAGE, "the hair, and the fleece of the earth." HAIR, "the forest of the head:" and if it be white, "the snow of the brain." The EARTH is, "the vessel that floats on the ages;" "the basis, or foundation of the air;" "the daughter of the night." NIGHT, "the veil of discourse and cares." A COMBAT, "the crash of arms; the shower of darts; the clangor of swords; the bath of blood." The SEA is "the field of pirates:" A SHIP, "their skate;" and "the horse of the waves." ROCKS are "the bones of the earth." The WIND is "the tiger, the lyon, who darts himself upon the houses and vessels," &c. &c.

SNORRO's work, as published by Resenius, concludes with this collection of Epithets; but in the old MS. preserved at Upsal, and in some others, we find at the end of this Dictionary a small Treatise, by the same Author, on the Construction and Mechanism of the Gothic or Icelandic Metre. If we had a greater number of the ancient Celtic verses remaining *, this
work

* If by "Celtic Verses" here, our Author means those of the ancient Gauls in particular; I know not
that

work would be extremely valuable, since it would then facilitate the knowlege of a species of Poetry, which might serve to many useful purposes: but it has the misfortune to have become exceedingly obscure. However, as some persons of distinguished learning have undertaken to explain it, there is room to hope, that such curious Readers as are fond of researches of this kind, will shortly have nothing wanting to gratify their desires on this subject.

What we know of it at present is, that their art of Versification consisted in combining together a number of syllables, with a regular repetition of the same letter at the beginning or end of each verse, at once resembling the nature of our modern Versification with rhyme, and the taste for acrosticks. Were this inquiry to be traced very far back, I believe we should find the original or model of this sort of Mechanism, to have been taken from some eastern nation, either from the ancient Persians or

that there is one of these remaining: if he means those of the Celtic nations in general, then it may be observed, that not only the British, but the Irish and Erse languages are Celtic; and in these are innumerable quantities of ancient verses still extant: but, I fear, none of these would receive much illustration from the SCALDIC Rules. If he applies the word "Celtic" to the ancient verses of the Scalds themselves, then it may be remarked, that there is no want of them in the libraries of the north, or even in print. T.

the Hebrews. The Hebrew poetry abounded with acroſtics of various kinds. The ſame are found in all the ancient Odes of our Icelandic Scalds. It is equally probable, that the verſes of the BARDS, thoſe ancient Britiſh and Gallic Poets, were of the ſame kind: ſome few fragments which we have of the poetry of Gaul or Bas Bretagne, put this matter out of doubt. The fact is ſtill more certain with regard to ſuch verſes of the Anglo-Saxons as have been handed down to us.

REMARKS ON THE FOREGOING PASSAGE.

[Our ingenious Author appears to me to have here thrown together ſeveral things, in their nature very different, without ſufficient diſcrimination.

In the firſt place it may be remarked, that even if we ſhould admit that the LOGOGRYPHS of the Icelandic Scalds *, are compoſed in a taſte not very different from that of the Hebrew ACROSTICS; yet theſe Acroſtics ought by no means to be confounded with the ALLITERATIONS of the Runic or Scaldic Metre: for theſe are as natural to the Icelandic verſe, as Dactyl and

* See Vol. I. p. 404.—Wormij Literatura Runica, p. 183. 4to.

Spondee feet are to the Greek and Latin numbers *. So that I muſt beg leave to differ from my Author, in thinking the Alliterative Metre of the Scalds ſimilar either to the Taſte for Acroſtics, or our modern Rhyme. Not but the Scalds often uſed Rhyme in the ſame manner as the moderns, and that with very nice exactneſs †.

But granting that the Icelandic Scalds often compoſed little artificial poems, much in the taſte of the Hebrew Acroſtics, I fear it will be going too far, to fetch their Original from thoſe of the Hebrews: for it may be ſafely affirmed, That all nations (without deriving it from each other) have, in the infancy of taſte, run into all the ſpecies of Falſe Wit. The Chineſe, for example, deal in many little artificial forms of poetry, very much reſembling the Rondeaus and Madrigals, ſo current among the French and us in the laſt age ‡, and yet neither party will be ſuſpected of imitation. So again, ſome of the other eaſtern

---

* Vid. Vol. I. p. 401, 402. Note.

† See the Icelandic original of Egill's Ode, among the "Five Pieces "of Runic Poetry," 8vo, p. 92.——Vid. Vol. I. p. 399.

‡ See Specimens of Chineſe Poetry (the Rhymes of which are very artificially diſpoſed) at the end of the Tranſlation of a Chineſe novel: intitled, *Hau Kiou Choaan*, &c. 4 Vol. 12mo. 1761.

nations

nations have innumerable small poems, very mechanically disposed into the shapes of Ovals, Lozenges, and other mathematical figures *, exactly parallel to the Eggs, Wings and Axes of some of the Greek minor Poets; yet both sides may be acquitted from the suspicion of stealing this happy invention from each other. Upon the whole, therefore, I much doubt whether we ought to attribute the Icelandic attempts of this kind, either to a Persic or Hebrew origin: even though some of the first emigrations of the northern people may be allowed to come from the neighbourhood of Persia.

As to the Anglo-Saxon, and Icelandic poetry: these will be allowed to be in all respects congenial, because of the great affinity between the two languages, and between the nations who spoke them.

---

* The Reader may find many of these little mechanic Trifles translated into English, in an ancient ART OF ENGLISH POESIE, 1589, 4to. p. 77, 78. The writer (one Pultenham) says, These are in great request among the Sultans of Tartary, Persia and the Indies, (and even the Chinese) who often make presents to their ladies of poems arranged in these forms; the letters of which are composed of diamonds, rubies, &c.—This sort of gallantry is also practised in Turkey, as we learn from Lady Mary Wortley Mountague's LETTERS, Vol. III. Letter XL.

They were both Gothic Tribes, and used two not very different dialects of the same Gothic language. Accordingly we find a very strong resemblance in their versification, phraseology and poetic allusions, &c. the same being in a great measure common to both nations *.

But there is also a resemblance between the laws of versification adopted by the British Bards, and those observed by the Icelandic Scalds; at least so far as this; that the metre of them both is of the alliterative kind: and yet there does not appear to be the least affinity in the two languages, or in the origin of the two nations. But this resemblance of metre, I think, may in part be accounted for on general philosophical principles, arising from the nature of both languages †: and in part from that intercourse, which was unavoidably produced between both nations in the wars and piratical irruptions of the northern nations: whose Scalds, as we learn from Torfœus ‡, were respected and admired for their

---

* Compare the Anglo-Saxon Ode on Athelstan's Victory, preserved in the Saxon Chronicle, (Ann. DCCCCXXXVIII. beginning, Apelstan cyning, &c. Gibson. Edit. 1692. p. 112.) with any of the Scaldic poems. See also Reliques of Anc. Eng. Poetry, Vol. II. p. 268, 269. 2d Edit.

† See Vol. I. p. 402. the latter part of the Note.

‡ Præfat. ad Hist. Orcad. folio.

poetic talents, even in the courts of thofe princes whofe territories were moſt invaded by their Daniſh countrymen. This he exprefsly affirms of the Anglo-Saxon and Iriſh kings; and it is to the full as likely to have been the cafe with the Welſh princes, who often concurred with the Danes in diftreffing the Engliſh. I am led to think that the latter Welſh BARDS might poffibly have been excited to cultivate the alliterative verfification more ſtrictly, from the example of the Icelandic SCALDS, and their imitators the Anglo-Saxon Poets; becaufe the more ancient Britiſh Bards were nothing near fo exact and ſtrict in their alliterations, as thofe of the middle and latter ages: particularly after the Norman conqueſt of England, and even after king Edward the Iſt's conqueſt of Wales *: whereas fome centuries before this, the Icelandic metre had been brought

to

---

* A very learned and ingenious Britiſh Antiquary thus informs me, "Our profody depends "entirely on what you "call ALLITERATION, "and which our Gram- "marians term *Cynghan-* "*nedd,* i. e. *Concentus,* "*vel Symphonia Confo-* "*nantica.* This at firſt "was not very ſtrict : for "the Bards of the fixth "century ufed it very "fparingly, and were "not circumfcribed by "any rules. The Bards "from the [Norman] "conqueſt to the death "of Llewellyn our laſt "prince, were more ſtrict. "But from thence to "queen Elizabeth's time, "the rules of Alliteration were to be obferved "with great nicety; fo "that

to the higheſt pitch of alliterative exactneſs. This conjecture, however, that the Welſh Bards borrowed any thing from the Poets of any other country, will hardly be allowed me by the Britiſh Antiquaries, who, from a laudable partiality, are jealous of the honour of their countrymen * ; nor is it worth contending for : It is ſufficient to obſerve, that a ſpirited emulation between the BARDS and

"that a line not per-
"fectly alliterative, is
"condemned as much by
"our Grammarians as a
"falſe quantity by the
"Greeks and Romans.
"They had ſix or ſe-
"ven different kinds of
"this conſonantical har-
"mony, ſome of which
"were of a looſe nature,
"and were allowed in
"poetry, as well as the
"moſt ſtrict Alliteration,
"&c."

"The moſt ancient
"IRISH POEMS, were
"alſo ALLITERATIVE,
"according to Mr.
"LLWYD, of the Mu-
"ſæum; and as he was
"well verſed in all the
"branches of the Celti
"now extant, viz. The
"Britiſh, Iriſh, Armo-
"ric, Corniſh and
"Manks, no perſon was

"better qualified to judge
"in this matter."

* It would be unfair to conceal the objections of the ſame learned perſon, eſpecially as it would deprive the Reader of ſome very curious information concerning the ancient Celtic Poetry. "I can
"by no means think that
"our Bards have bor-
"rowed their ALLITE-
"RATION from the
"Scalds of the north:
"for there are traces of
"it in ſome very old
"pieces of the Druids
"ſtill extant, which I
"am perſuaded are older
"than the introduction
"of Chriſtianity ; and
"were compoſed long
"before we had any com-
"merce or intercourſe
"with any of the inha-
"bitants of Scandinavia,
"or

and the SCALDS, might excite each of them to improve their own native poetry, and to give it all that artificial polish, which they saw admired in the other language. Whoever would understand thoroughly the Poetry of both people, and compare their respective metre, may examine, for the Icelandic, WORMIUS's *Literatura Runica*; and for the British, JOHN DAVID RHYS's *Cambro-Britannicæ Cymraecæve Linguæ institutiones & rudimenta*, &c. Lond. 1592 *.]

T.

" or any branch of the Gothic race whatsoever: and I believe before the Roman Conquest. Cæsar says, The Druids learned a great number of verses by rote, in which no doubt a great deal of their Morality was couched, and their mystical doctrines about the Oak and the Misseltoe. These kind of Verses are, by the Britons, called *Englyn Milwr*, or THE WARRIOR's SONG, and consist of a triplet of seven syllables each verse, which are unirythm: For Rhyme is as old as poetry itself, in our language. It is very remarkable, that most of our old Proverbs are taken from the last verse of such a Triplet, and the other two seem almost nonsense; they mention the Oak, high Mountains, and Snow, with honour. Those are certainly remains of the Pagan Creed."

* See also some account of the Welsh Poetry in SELDEN's Remarks on DRAYTON's Poliolbion. ——And a remarkable passage in GIRALDUS CAMBRENSIS (Cambriæ Descriptio, p. 260, 261.) beginning thus, *Præ cunctis autem*, &c.

AN IDEA

OF THE

MORE ANCIENT

EDDA.

IT is now time to describe what remains of the former EDDA, compiled by SOEMUND, surnamed the LEARNED, more than an hundred years before that of Snorro. It was a collection of very ancient poems, which had for their subject some article of the Religion and Morality of Odin. The share that Sœmund had in them, was probably no more than that of first collecting and committing them to writing. This collection is at present considered as lost, excepting only three pieces, which I shall describe below: But some people have, not without good reason, imagined that this ancient EDDA, or at least the greatest part of it, is still preserved. It were to be

wished,

wished, that the possessors of such a treasure could be induced to esteem the communication of it to the world, the greatest advantage they can reap from it; and they are now urged, in the name of the public, to this generous action. Be that as it may, the admirers of the antiquities of the north have, in the fragments of this work, which may be seen and consulted, sufficient to reward their researches. The remainder is probably less interesting; and this may perhaps have been the cause of its being consigned to oblivion.

THE first of these pieces is that which I have so often quoted under the title of VOLUSPA; a word which signifies the Oracle, or the Prophesy of Vola. It is well known, that there were among the Celtic nations, women who foretold future events, uttered oracles, and maintained a strict commerce with the Divinity. Tacitus makes frequent mention of one of them, named Velleda, who was in high repute among the Bructeri, a people of Germany, and who was afterwards carried to Rome. There was one in Italy, whose name had a still nearer affinity to this of Vola, viz. that Sibyl, whom Horace (Epod. V.) calls *Ariminensis Folia*. VOLA or FOLIA might perhaps be a general name for all the women of this kind. As these names are evidently connected with

the

the idea of FOLLY or Madness, they would at least be due to those enthusiastick ravings and mad contortions with which such women delivered their pretended oracles. The word FOL bore the same meaning in the ancient Gothic, as it does in French, English, and in almost all the languages of the north; in all which it signifies either a Fool or a Madman *.

This Poem attributed to the Sibyl of the north, contains within the compass of two or three hundred lines, that whole system of Mythology, which we have seen disclosed in the EDDA; but this laconic brevity, and the obsoleteness of the language in which it is written, make it very difficult to be understood. This, however, does not prevent us from observing frequent instances of grandeur and sublimity, and many images extremely fine: then the general tenor of the work, the want of connection, and the confusion of the style, excite the idea of a very remote antiquity, no less than the matter and subject itself. Such were,

---

* FOOL, (*antiq.* Fol) *Stultus, delirus, fatuus, rationis expers.* Gallicè Fol. Islandicè 𝔉ol, *ferox, iracundus, fatuus infipiens.* 𝔉olſka, *Stultitia.* Ang. Folly: Gall. Folie. *Hinc forſan Ital.* Fola, *Ineptiæ,* *nugæ, quid vanum, fatuum fabulofum, &c. Inde verbum* Folare, *Ineptias, aut ftultas & inanes fabulas recitare, nugas venditare.* Hickes, in Junij Etymolog. a Lyc Edit. T.

doubt-

doubtless, the real Sibylline verses so long preserved at Rome, and so ill counterfeited afterwards. The Poem of the VOLUSPA is perhaps the only monument now remaining, capable of giving us a true idea of them.

I need not here quote any passages from this Poem: the text of the EDDA, is (as we have seen) quite full of them: and I have given pretty long extracts from it in my Remarks. It is sufficient briefly to observe, that the Prophetess having imposed silence on all intellectual beings, declares, that she is going to reveal the decrees of the Father of Nature, the actions and operations of the Gods, which no person ever knew before herself. She then begins with a description of the chaos; and proceeds to the formation of the world, and of that of its various species of inhabitants, Giants, Men and Dwarfs. She then explains the employments of the Fairies or Destinies; the functions of the Gods, their most remarkable adventures, their quarrels with Loke, and the vengeance that ensued. At last, she concludes with a long description of the final state of the universe, its dissolution and conflagration: the battle of the inferior Deities and the Evil Beings: the renovation of the world: the happy lot of the good, and the punishment of the wicked.

THAT

THAT Poem is followed by another no lefs deferving of regard. It made part of the EDDA of SOEMUND; and, in point of antiquity, does not yield to the VOLUSPA: this is called HAVAMAAL, or "The Sublime Difcourfe of Odin," and is attributed to that God himfelf, who is fuppofed to have given thefe precepts of wifdom to mankind. This piece is the only one of the kind now in the world. We have, directly from the 'ancient' * Scythians themfelves, no other monument on the fubject of their morality: whatever we know from any other quarter on this article, being imperfect, corrupted and uncertain. Thus this moral fyftem of Odin's may, in fome meafure, fupply the lofs of the maxims which Zamolxis, Dicenæus, and Anacharfis gave to their Scythian countrymen: maxims which thofe fages pretended to have derived from heaven, and which were frequently the envy of the Greek Philofophers.

The HAVAMAAL, or Sublime Difcourfe, is comprifed in about one hundred and twenty ftanzas. There are very few which are not good and fenfible; but as fome of them contain only common truths, and others, allufions which it would be tedious and difficult to explain, I fhall give only

* *Des Celtes & des Scythes.* Fr.

the following extracts, assuring the Reader anew, that he will find them translated with the most scrupulous exactness.

" * CONSIDER and examine well all
" your doors, before you venture to
" stir abroad: for he is exposed to conti-
" nual danger, whose enemies lie in am-
" bush concealed in his court.

" To the guest, who enters your dwel-
" ling with frozen knees, give the warmth
" of your fire: he who hath travelled over
" the mountains hath need of food, and
" well-dried garments.

" Offer water to him who sits down at
" your table: for he hath occasion to cleanse
" his hands: and entertain him honour-
" ably and kindly, if you would win from
" him friendly words, and a grateful re-
" turn.

* In translating the following maxims from the French, I occasionally consulted a MS copy of Resenius's Latin Version, and have in some few passages, where the French seemed not to be sufficiently explicit, been determined by the latter; from which I have also supplied a few omissions. But not being able to procure the original, I have, in all other instances, chosen to follow M. Mallet's Translation, though it differs extremely from that of Resenius: As presuming that M. Mallet had good authority for every deviation. See the Introduction to this Volume. T.

" He

"He who travelleth hath need of wisdom. One may do at home whatsoever one will; but he who is ignorant of good manners, will only draw contempt upon himself, when he comes to sit down with men well instructed.

"He who goes to a feast, where he is not expected, either speaks with a lowly voice or is silent: he listens with his ears, and is attentive with his eyes: by this he acquires knowlege and wisdom.

"Happy he, who draws upon himself the applause and benevolence of men! for whatever depends upon the will of others, is hazardous and uncertain.

"A man can carry with him no better provision for his journey than the strength of Understanding. In a foreign country, this will be of more use to him than treasures: and will introduce him to the table of strangers.

"There is nothing more useless to the sons of the age, than to drink too much ALE: the more the drunkard swallows, the less is his wisdom, till he loses his reason. The bird of oblivion sings before those who inebriate themselves, and steals away their souls.

"A coward thinks he shall live for ever,
"if he can but keep out of the reach of
"arms: but though he should escape every
"weapon, old age, that spares none, will
"give him no quarter.

"The gluttonous man, if he is not upon
"his guard, eats his own death: and the
"gluttony of a fool makes the wise man
"laugh.

"The flocks know when to return to
"the fold, and to quit the pasture: but
"the worthless and slothful know not how
"to restrain their gluttony.

"The lewd and dissolute man makes a
"mock of every thing: not considering
"how much he himself is the object of
"derision. No one ought to laugh at an-
"other, until he is free from faults him-
"self.

"A man void of sense, ponders all night
"long, and his mind wanders without
"ceasing: but when he is weary at the
"point of day, he is nothing wiser than
"he was over-night.

"He thinks he is profoundly knowing;
"being indeed most superficial and shal-
"low.

" low. But he knows not how to sing an
" answer, when men pose him with a dif-
" ficult question *.

" Many are thought to be knit in the
" tyes of sincere kindness: but when it
" comes to the proof, how much are they
" deceived. Slander is the common vice
" of the age. Even the host back-bites his
" guest.

" One's own home is the best home,
" though never so small †. Every thing
" one eats at home is sweet. He who
" lives at another man's table is often
" obliged to wrong his palate.

" I have never yet found a man so ge-
" nerous and munificent, as that to receive
" at his house was not to receive: nor any
" so free and liberal of his gifts, as to re-
" ject a present when it was returned to
" him.

---

* Alluding to the Ænigmas and Riddles which it was usual to propose as a trial of wit. See many of them in the *Hervarer Saga*. Both the riddle and answer, I believe, was usually sung in the manner of a little catch.

† This is like our English Proverb, " Home is " home, be it never so homely."

" Let friends pleasure each other reci-
" procally by presents of arms and habits.
" Those who give and those who receive,
" continue a long time friends, and often
" give feasts to each other.

" Love both your friends, and your
" friends friends: but do not favour the
" friend of your enemies.

" Peace, among the perfidious conti-
" nues, for five nights, to shine bright as
" a flame: but when the sixth night ap-
" proaches, the flame waxes dim, and is
" quite extinguished: then all their amity
" turns to hatred.

" When I was young I wandered about
" alone: I thought myself rich if I chanced
" to light upon a companion. A man
" gives pleasure to another man.

" Let not a man be over wise, neither
" let him be more curious than he ought.
" Let him not seek to know his destiny,
" if he would sleep secure and quiet.

" Rise early, if you would enrich your-
" self, or vanquish an enemy. The sleep-
" ing wolf gains not the prey; neither the
" drowsy man the victory.

" They

"They invite me up and down to feasts, if I have only need of a slight breakfast: my faithful friend is he who will give me one loaf when he has but two.

"Whilst we live, let us live well: for be a man never so rich, when he lights his fire, Death may perhaps enter his door, before it be burnt out.

"It is better to have a son late than never. One seldom sees sepulchral stones raised over the graves of the dead, by any other hands but those of their own offspring.

"Riches pass away like the twinkling of an eye: of all friends they are the most inconstant. Flocks perish; relations die; friends are not immortal; you will die yourself: but I know one thing alone that is out of the reach of fate: and that is the judgment which is passed upon the dead.

"Let not the wisest be imperious, but modest: for he will find by experience, that when he is among those that are powerful, he is not the most mighty.

"Praise

"Praise the fineness of the day, when it is ended; praise a woman, when you have known her; a sword, when you have proved it; a maiden, after she is married; the ice, when once you have crossed it *; and the liquor after it is drunk.

"Trust not to the words of a girl; neither to those which a woman utters; for their hearts have been made like the wheel that turns round; levity was put into their bosoms.

"Trust not to the ice of one day's freezing; neither to the Serpent who lies asleep; nor to the caresses of her you are going to marry; nor to a sword that is cracked or broken; nor to the son of a powerful man; nor to a field that is newly sown.

"Peace between malicious women is compared to a horse who is made to walk over the ice not properly shod; or to a vessel in a storm, without a rudder; or to a lame man who should attempt to follow the mountain-goats with a young foal, or yearling mule.

* This is not unlike the English Proverb, "Praise the Bridge that carries you safe over." T.

"He who would make himself beloved
"by a maiden, must entertain her with
"fine discourses, and offer her engaging
"presents: he must also incessantly praise
"her beauty. It requires good sense to be
"a skilful lover.

"There is no malady or sickness more
"severe, than not to be content with ones
"lot.

"The heart alone knows what passes
"within the heart: and that which be‑
"trays the soul is the soul itself.

"If you would bend your mistress to
"your passion, you must only go by night
"to see her. When a thing is known to
"a third person, it never succeeds.

"Seek not to seduce another's wife with
"the alluring charms of Runic incanta‑
"tions.

"Be humane and gentle to those you
"meet travelling in the mountains, or on
"the sea.

"He who hath a good supper in his tra‑
"velling wallet, rejoices himself at the
"approach of night.

"Ne‑

" Never discover your uneasiness to an
" evil person, for he will afford you no
" comfort.

" Know, that if you have a friend, you
" ought to visit him often. The road is
" grown over with grass, the bushes
" quickly spread over it, if it is not con-
" stantly travelled.

" Be not the first to break with your
" friend. Sorrow gnaws the heart of him
" who hath no one to advise with but him-
" self.

" Obsequiousness produces friends: but
" it is vile indeed to flatter ones own self.

" Have never three words of dispute
" with the wicked. The good will of-
" ten yield up a point, when the wicked
" is enraged and swollen with pride. Ne-
" vertheless, it is dangerous to be silent,
" when you are reproached with having
" the heart of a woman; for then you
" would be taken for a coward.

" I advise you, be circumspect, but not
" too much: be so, however, when you
" have drunk to excess; when you are near

" the

" the wife of another; and when you
" find yourself among robbers.

" Do not accustom yourself to mock-
" ing; neither laugh at your guest, or a
" stranger: they who remain at home,
" often know not who the stranger is that
" cometh to their gate.

" Where is there to be found a virtuous
" man without some failing? or one so
" wicked as to have no good quality?

" Laugh not at the gray-headed de-
" claimer, nor at thy aged grandsire.
" There often come forth from the wrin-
" kles of the skin, words full of wisdom.

" The fire drives away diseases: the oak
" expels the stranguary: straws dissolve in-
" chantments *: Runic characters destroy
" the effect of imprecations: the earth
" swallows up inundations; and death ex-
" tinguishes hatred and quarrels."

* Hence probably is derived the custom of laying two straws crosswise in the path where a witch is expected to come.

THESE Fragments of the Ancient EDDA are followed, in the Edition of Refenius, by a little Poem called, The RUNIC CHAPTER, or the MAGIC OF ODIN. I have before obferved, that the Conqueror, who ufurped this name, attributed to himfelf the invention of Letters; of which, they had not probably any idea in Scandinavia before his time. But although this noble art is fufficiently wonderful in itfelf, to attract the veneration of an ignorant people towards the teacher of it: yet Odin caufed it to be regarded as the ART of MAGIC by way of excellence, the art of working all forts of miracles: whether it was that this new piece of fallacy was fubfervient to his ambition, or whether he himfelf was barbarous enough to think there was fomething fupernatural in writing. He fpeaks, at leaft in the following Poem, like a man who would make it fo believed.

" DO you know (fays he) how to en-
" grave Runic characters? how to
" explain them? how to procure them?
" how to prove their virtue?" He then goes on to enumerate the wonders he could

per-

perform, either by means of thefe letters, or by the operations of poetry.

" * I am poffeffed of fongs: fuch as nei-
" ther the fpoufe of a king, nor any fon
" of man can repeat; one of them is called
" the HELPER: it will HELP thee at thy
" need, in ficknefs, grief and all adver-
" fities.

" I know a Song, which the fons of men
" ought to fing, if they would become
" fkilful phyficians.

" † I know a Song, by which I foften
" and inchant the arms of my enemies;
" and render their weapons of none effect.

" I know a Song, which I need only to
" fing when men have loaded me with
" bonds; for the moment I fing it, my
" chains fall in pieces, and I walk forth at
" liberty.

" I know a Song, ufeful to all mankind;
" for as foon as hatred inflames the fons of
" men, the moment I fing it they are ap-
" peafed.

* Barthol. p. 658.   † Ibid. p. 347.

" I

" I know a Song, of such virtue, that
" were I caught in a storm, I can hush
" the winds, and render the air perfectly
" calm."

One may remark upon this last prerogative of the verses known to Odin, that among all the 'Gothic and' Celtic nations, the Magicians claimed a power over the Winds and Tempests. Pomponius Mela tells us, that in an island on the coast of Bretagne (he probably means the Isle of SAINTS, opposite to Brest) there were priestesses, separated from the rest of the people, who were regarded as the Goddesses of Navigation, because they had the winds and tempests at their disposal. There are penal statutes in the Capitularies of Charlemagne, in the canons of several councils, and in the ancient laws of Norway, against such as raise storms and tempests; *Tempestarii* is the name there given them. There were formerly of these impostors on the coasts of Norway, as there are at present on those of Lapland, to whom fear and superstition were long tributary. Hence silly travellers have, with much gravity, given us ridiculous accounts of witches who sold wind to the sailors in those seas. It is no less true, that the very Norwegian fishermen

men would long since have forgotten that so foolish an opinion had ever existed, if foreign mariners, who were not disabused like them, did not often come to buy their wind of them, and pay them money for being the objects of their ridicule.

The Missionaries and first Bishops, were early in their endeavours to root out this pernicious weed from the soil where they wished to plant the Gospel. They attacked the Pagan religion with all sorts of weapons. As they were often so credulous as to believe the false miracles of Paganism, they were weak enough to oppose them with others, that were no whit better, except in the purity of the intention. In an old Icelandic Chronicle *, we meet with a bishop laying a storm with Holy-water, and some other ceremonies.—— But to proceed on with the discourse of Odin:

"When I see, says he, Magicians tra-
"velling through the air, I disconcert
"them by a single look, and force them
"to abandon their enterprize." He had before spoken of these aerial travellers.

"† If I see a man dead, and hanging
"aloft on a tree, I engrave Runic charac-

* K. Oloff Trygguason Saga, c. 33.
† Barthol. p. 641.

"ters

" ters so wonderful, that the man imme-
" diately descends and converses with
" me."

By the operation of these Characters, and at other times by Verses, Odin had frequently raised the dead. There is a very ancient Ode preserved to us by Bartholin *, wherein this Deity causes a Prophetess, whom he wanted to consult, to rise from her tomb. The beginning of this Ode may serve to give us an idea what kind of Magic Poetry it was, which 'the northern †' nations were heretofore possessed of.

" *ODIN, the sovereign of men arises: he saddles his horse* SLEIPNER; *he mounts, and is conveyed to the subterraneous abode of Hela* (i. e. Death.)

" *The* DOG *who guards the gates of* DEATH *meets him. His breast and his jaws are stained with blood; he opens his voracious mouth to bite, and barks a long time at the father of Magic.*

---

* Lib. III. cap. 2. p. 632.———The original in Bartholin consists of Fourteen Stanzas, of which M. Mallet has here produced only five. In the following Version, the Latin of Bartholin has been consulted.
T.

† *Tous les Peuples Celtes.* Fr. Orig.

" *Odin*

"*Odin pursues his way; his horse causes the infernal caverns to resound and tremble: at length he reaches the deep abode of* DEATH, *and stops near to the eastern gate, where stands the tomb of the Prophetess.*

"*He sings to her verses adapted to call up the dead. He looks towards the north; he engraves Runic characters on her tomb; he utters mysterious words; he demands an answer: until the Prophetess is constrained to arise, and thus utters the words of the dead.*

" WHO *is this unknown that dares dis-*
" *turb my repose, and drag me from my*
" *grave, wherein I have lien dead so long,*
" *all covered with snow, and moistened with*
" *the rains, &c.*"

The other prodigies, which Odin in the Runic Chapter boasts he has the power of performing, are not of less importance.

" * IF I will that a man should neither
" fall in battle, nor perish by the sword, I
" sprinkle him over with water at the instant
" of his birth." We may here recollect what I have said in the former Volume concerning the baptism of the people of the north, while they were yet Pagans †.

* Barthol. p. 348.   † Pag. 335.

" IF

"If I will, I can explain the nature of
"all the different species of Men, of Genii,
"and of Gods. None but the wife can
"know all their differences.

"* If I aspire to the love and the fa-
"vour of the chastest virgin, I can bend
"the mind of the snowy-armed maiden,
"and make her yield wholly to my de-
"sires.

"I know a secret, which I will never
"lose; it is to render myself always be-
"loved by my mistress.

"But I know one which I will never
"impart to any female, except my own
"sister, or to her whom I hold in my
"arms. Whatever is known only to one's
"self, is always of very great value."

After this, the Author concludes with exclamations on the beauty of the things he has been describing.

"NOW, says he, have I sung in my
"august abode, my sublime verses; which
"are both necessary to the sons of men,
"and useless to the sons of men. Blessed

* Barthol. p. 658.

"be

" be he who hath sung them! Blessed be
" he who hath understood them! May
" they profit him, who hath retained them!
" blessed be they, who have lent an ear to
" them!"

THE END OF THE EDDA.

ODES,

AND OTHER

ANCIENT POEMS.

I THOUGHT proper to subjoin to the EDDA the following pieces, selected out of that vast multitude of verses, which we find preserved in the ancient Chronicles.

These are such as appeared to me most expressive of the genius and manners of the ancient inhabitants of the north, and most proper to confirm what I had advanced in the preceding Volume; as also to shew that the Mythology contained in the EDDA, hath been that of all the northern Poets, and the religion of many nations drest out with fictions and allegories.

I shall first of all present the ODE which *Regner Lodbrog* composed in the torments preceding his death. This Ode was dictated by the Fanaticism of Glory, animated by that of Religion. Regner, who was a celebrated Warrior, Poet and Pirate, reigned in Denmark about the beginning of the ninth century: after a long series of maritime expeditions into the most distant countries, his fortune at length failed him in England. Taken prisoner in battle by his adversary Ella, who was king of a part of that island, he perished by the bite of serpents, with which they had filled the dungeon he was confined in. He left behind him several sons, who revenged this horrible death, as Regner himself had foretold in the following verses. There is some reason, however, to conjecture that this prince did not compose more than one or two stanzas of this Poem, and that the rest were added, after his death, by the Bard, whose function it was, according to the custom of those times, to add to the funeral splendor, by singing verses to the praise of the deceased. Be that as it may, this Ode is found in several Icelandic Chronicles, and its versification, language and stile, leave us no room to doubt of its antiquity. Wormius has given us the text in Runic Characters, accompanied with a Latin Version, and large notes in his Lituratura Runica. Vid. p. 197. It is also met with in M. Biorners's collection. Out of the twenty-nine strophes, of which it con-

consists, I have only chosen the following, as being what I thought the generality of my readers would peruse with most pleasure. I have not even always translated entire stanzas, but have sometimes reduced two stanzas into one, in order to spare the Reader such passages as appeared to me uninteresting and obscure *.

* Our elegant Author having taken great liberties in his Translation of this and the following ODES, in order to accommodate them to the taste of French Readers; it was once intended here, instead of copying the French, to have given extracts from the more literal Version of all these Poems formerly published, which hath been so often quoted in the Notes to this work: viz. The FIVE PIECES OF RUNIC POETRY, TRANSLATED FROM THE ICELANDIC LANGUAGE. 1763. 8vo. But an ingenious Friend having translated from the French this part of M. Mallet's Book, I have got leave to insert his Version, and shall take the liberty to refer the more curious Reader to the pamphlet above-mentioned; which the Translator professes he occasionally consulted in the following pages. There the ODES here abridged may be seen at large, confronted with the Icelandic Originals, and accompanied with two other ancient Pieces of Northern Poetry.   T.

EXTRACTS

FROM THE ODE OF

KING REGNER LODBROG.

* * * * * *

"WE fought with swords †, when, in my early youth, I went towards the east to prepare a bloody prey for the ravenous wolves: 'ample food for the yellow-footed eagle.' The whole

---

† WE FOUGHT WITH SWORDS. The Icelandic original *hiuggum* or *huiggum*, is a word of the same origin, as the Anglo-Saxon *heawan*. Germ. *houwen*. Low Dutch, *hauwen*, *houwen*. Engl. *to hew*. From the same root comes also our Rustic word *to hough*. The passage therefore of the text might perhaps have been rendered more exactly: "WE STRUCK, or CUT, or HACKED AND HEWED WITH SWORDS." Wormius has rendered it as in the text, *Pugnavimus ensibus*. But Bartholin seems to have come nearer to the exact idea in *Secuimus ensibus*. Our Author, M. Mallet, renders it *Nous nous sommes battus à coups d' Epees*. T.

" ocean

" ocean seemed as one wound: the ravens
" waded in the blood of the slain.

* * * * * *

" We fought with swords, in the day
" of that great fight, wherein I sent the
" inhabitants of Helsing to the Hall of
" Odin. Thence our ships carried us to
" Ifa *: there our steel-pointed launces,
" reeking with gore, divided the armour
" with a terrible clang: there our swords
" cleft the shields asunder.

* * * * * *

" We fought with swords, that day
" wherein I saw ten thousand of my foes
" rolling in the dust near a promontory of
" England. A dew of blood distilled from
" our swords. The arrows which flew in
" search of the helmets, bellowed through
" the air. The pleasure of that day was
" equal to that of clasping a fair virgin in
" my arms †.

" We

---

* Or the Vistula.

† I cannot help thinking, that the Reader will censure our ingenious Author, as not having here exerted his usual good taste in selecting, when he finds he has omitted such stanzas as the following, particularly the two last.

" We fought with swords, in the Northumbrian land. A furious storm descended on the shields:

* * * * * *

" We fought with swords, that day
" when I made to struggle in the twilight
" of death that young chief so proud of
many a lifeless body fell to the earth. It was about
the time of the morning, when the foe was compelled
to fly in the battle. There the sword sharply bit the
polished helmet. The pleasure of that day was like
kissing a young widow at the highest seat of the table."

* * * * *

" We fought with swords in the Flemings land:
the battle widely raged before king Freyr fell therein.
The blue steel all reeking with blood, fell at length
upon the golden mail. Many a virgin bewailed the
slaughter of that morning."

* * * * *

" We fought with swords; the spear resounded;
the banners reflected the sunshine upon the coats of
mail. I saw many a warrior fall in the morning:
many a hero in the contention of arms. Here the
sword reach betimes the heart of my son: it was Egill
deprived Agnar of life. He was a youth who never
knew what it was to fear."

* * * * *

" We fought with swords in the isles of the south.
There Herthiofe proved victorious: there died many
of my valiant warriors. In the shower of arms, Rogvaldur fell, I lost my son. In the play of arms came
the deadly spear: his lofty crest was dyed with gore.
THE BIRDS OF PREY BEWAILED HIS FALL: THEY
LOST HIM THAT PREPARED THEM BANQUETS."

Vid. Five Pieces of Run. Poet. p. 31, 32, 35, &c.

T.

" his

" his flowing locks ‡, he who spent his
" mornings among the young maidens;
" he who loved to converse with the hand-
" some widows. * * * * * * What is
" the happy portion of the brave, but to
" fall in the midst of a storm of arrows †?
" He who flies from wounds, drags a te-
" dious miserable life: the dastard feels no
" heart in his bosom.

" We fought with swords: a young man
" should march early to the conflict of
" arms: man should attack man or bravely
" resist him. In this hath always consisted
" the nobility of the warrior. He who
" aspires to the love of his mistress ought
" to be dauntless in the clash of swords.

" We fought with swords: but now I
" find for certain that men are drawn
" along by fate: there are few can evade
" the decrees of the Destinies. Could I
" have thought the conclusion of my life
" reserved for Ella, when almost expiring,
" I shed torrents of blood? When I thrust

---

‡ He means Harald, surnamed Harfagre, or Fair-
locks, king of Norway.   T.
† Literally, a hail-storm of darts. *Une grêle de
traits.*   T.

" forward my ships into the Scotish gulphs?
" When I gained such abundant spoil for
" the beasts of prey?

" We fought with swords: I am still
" full of joy, when I think that a banquet
" is preparing for me in the palace of the
" Gods. Soon, soon in the splendid abode
" of Odin, we shall drink BEER out of
" the sculls of our enemies. A brave man
" shrinks not at death. I shall utter no
" words expressive of fear as I enter the
" hall of Odin.

" We fought with swords. Ah! if my
" sons knew the sufferings of their fa-
" ther: if they knew that poisonous
" vipers tore his intrails to pieces! with
" what ardour would they wish to wage
" cruel war! For I gave a mother to my
" children, from whom they inherit a va-
" liant heart.

" We fought with swords: but now I
" touch upon my last moments. A serpent
" already gnaws my heart. Soon shall my
" sons black their swords in the blood of
" Ella: their rage is in flame: those va-
" liant youths will never rest till they have
" avenged their father.

" We

"We fought with swords, in fifty and one battles under my floating banniers. From my early youth I have learnt to dye the steel of my lance with blood; and thought I never could meet with a king more valiant than myself. But it is time to cease: Odin hath sent his Goddesses to conduct me to his palace. I am going to be placed on the highest seat, there to quaff goblets of BEER with the Gods. The hours of my life are rolled away. I will die laughing."

REMARKS on the preceding ODE.

I Will not anticipate the reflections that necessarily occur to the Reader on perusing this Poem; but will only observe, that it strongly confirms what I have advanced in the former part of this work, concerning the peculiar sentiments of the northern nations with regard to the fair sex. It has been commonly supposed, that we owe to the Laws of Chivalry, (i. e. to an institution so late as the eleventh century) that spirit of generosity, which formerly rendered the ladies the umpires of the glory and honour of the male sex; which made their favours the object and the reward of virtuous and gallant actions; which caused the care of serving, defending and pleasing them, to be considered as the sweetest and most noble of all duties; and which hath, even to this day, entailed on them a respect and deference, of which there is not the least idea in other climates. But it is certain, that long before the eleventh century, this manner of thinking had been familiar, and, as it were, naturalized among the Germans and Scandinavians. Let us call to mind what Tacitus says of the respect shewn by these nations to their women. The Romans by no means introduced sentiments of this kind into the countries they conquered. It was not from them that they were adopted in Spain, France, England, &c. Whence comes it then, that after the fall of the Roman Empire, we find this spirit of gallantry all of a sudden spread so wide? We see plainly that this spirit, so peculiar to the northern nations, could only be spread and diffused by themselves. Formed and cherished by their religious prejudices, by their passion for war, and the chastity natural to their women, at the same time intimately connected with their customs and manners, IT could not but follow them into all their settlements, and there would continue to maintain its influence for many ages. But afterwards, when the nations descended from them became more civilized and wealthy, the splendid and shewy effects, which this fine spirit of gallantry then produced, would easily dazzle the eyes of inquirers, and prevent them from discerning the origin of it among so rude a race of men as their Gothic ancestors: so that at present, when one would trace it up to its real source, we have strong prejudices to encounter and surmount.

IF there are many strokes of gallantry in the Ode of king REGNER, the genius of Chivalry itself will seem to speak in that composed by a Norwegian prince, named HARALD THE VALIANT, which is found in an old Icelandic Chronicle, called Knytlinga Saga. This piece is of much later date than the preceding: but it is yet sufficient to show, that these northern people had learned to combine the ideas of love and military valour, long before those very nations themselves, whose taste and manners they had afterwards so strong an inclination to adopt. Harald the Valiant lived about the middle of the eleventh century. He was one of the most illustrious adventurers of his time. He had traversed all the seas of the north, and carried his piratical incursions as far as the Mediterranean itself, and the coast of Africa. He was at length taken prisoner, and detained for some time at Constantinople. He complains in this Ode, that the glory he had acquired by so many exploits, had not been able to make any impression on Elissif *, the daughter of Jarislas, king of Russia.

* In the original, as given by Bartholin, it is ELIZABETH. T.

THE ODE OF
HARALD THE VALIANT.

"My ships have made the tour of Sicily: then were we all magnificent and splendid. My brown vessel, full of mariners, rapidly rowed to the utmost of my wishes. Wholly taken up with war, I thought my course would never slacken, and yet a Russian maiden scorns me.

"In my youth I fought with the people of Drontheim. Their troops exceeded ours in number. It was a terrible conflict: I left their young king dead in the field: and yet a Russian maiden scorns me.

"One day we were but sixteen in a vessel: a storm arose and swelled the sea: it filled the loaded ship, but we diligently cleared it out. Thence I formed
"hopes

" hopes of the happiest success: and yet a
" Russian maiden scorns me.

" I know how to perform eight exer-
" cises *: I fight valiantly; I sit firmly
" on horseback; I am inured to swim-
" ming; I know how to run along in
" scates; I dart the launce; and am skil-
" ful at the oar: and yet a Russian maiden
" scorns me.

" Can she deny, that young and lovely
" maiden, that on the day, when posted
" near a city in the southern land, I joined
" battle, that then I valiantly handled my
" arms, and left behind me lasting monu-
" ments of my exploits? and yet a Russian
" maiden scorns me.

" I was born in the high country of
" Norway, where the inhabitants handle
" their bows so well. But I preferred
" guiding my ships, the dread of peasants,
" among the rocks of the ocean: and far
" from the habitations of men, I have run
" through all the seas with my vessels:
" and yet a Russian maiden scorns me.

* See the Five Pieces of Runic Poetry, p. 80.

THE Ode which follows is of a different kind from the preceding, it is called, in the ancient Chronicles, the ELOGIUM OF HACON. This prince was son of the famous Harald, surnamed Harfagre, or Fair-Locks, the first king of all Norway. He was slain in the year 960, in a battle wherein eight of his brothers fell along with him. Eyvind, or Evinder, his cousin, a celebrated Scald, who was called THE CROSS OF POETS on account of his superior talents for verse, was present at this battle, and afterwards composed this Ode, to be sung at the funeral of his relation. It is Snorro himself, to whom we owe the EDDA, that hath preserved this Ode in his Chronicle of Norway.

THE ELOGIUM OF HACON.

AN ODE.

"THE Goddesses 'of Destiny' who
"preside over battles, come, sent
"forth by Odin. They go to chuse a-
"mong the princes of the illustrious race
"of Yngvon, him, 'who is to perish, and'
"go to dwell in the palace of the Gods *.

"Gon-

---

* Eight stanzas are here omitted, which the Reader may see at large in the FIVE PIECES OF RUN. POET. p. 63, & seq.—One of them presents a fine picture of a youthful Chieftain.

"The leader of the people had just before cast aside his armour; he had put off his coat of mail: he had thrown them down in the field a little before the beginning of the battle. He was playing with the sons of renowned men, when he was called forth to defend his kingdom. The gallant king now stood under his golden helmet." T.

N. B.

* * * * * * * *

" Gondula, 'one of these Goddesses,'
" leaned on the end of her lance, and thus
" bespake 'her companions:' the assem-
" bly of the Gods is going to be increased:
" 'the enemies of' Hacon * come to in-
" vite this prince with his numerous host,
" to enter the palace of Odin.

" Thus spake these beautiful nymphs of
" war: who were seated on their horses;
" who were covered with their shields and

N. B. The Translator has borrowed here and there a word or two from that Version, which he hath inclosed between two inverted commas ' ': he hath also distinguished by the same marks, some passages, which M. Mallet seems to have superadded to the original, without sufficient foundation. Let the curious Reader compare the two Versions.
T.

* Rather, " The Gods " invite Hacon." Our Author seems to have here departed from the original without necessity. The dying a violent death was so far from being considered as an evil, by the ancient Scandinavians, or as the act of an enemy; that the Gods could not do them a greater favour than to take that method of inviting them to their eternal abode. We have seen it established as a sacred truth in the EDDA, " Odin is called the Fa-
" ther of Battles, because
" he adopts for his chil-
" dren all those who are
" slain with their swords
" in their hands:" i. e. in battle. See FA LL. X. p. 61.
T.

" helmets,

" helmets, and appeared full of some great
" thought.

" Hacon heard their discourse: Why,
" said he to one of them? why hast thou
" thus disposed of the battle? Were we
" not worthy to have obtained from the
" Gods a more perfect victory? It is we,
" she replied, who have given it to thee:
" it is we who have put thine enemies to
" flight.

" Now, proceeded she, let us urge for-
" ward our horses across those green and
" verdant worlds, which are the residence
" of the Gods. Let us go tell Odin that
" the king is coming to visit him in his
" palace.

" When the father of the Gods hears
" this news, he says, Hermode and Brago,
" my sons, go to meet the king: A king
" admired by all men for his valour, now
" approacheth to our hall.

" At length king Hacon approaches, and,
" arriving from the battle, is still all be-
" sprinkled and running down with blood.
" At the sight of Odin he cries out, Ah!
" How severe and terrible doth this God
" appear to me!

" The

"The God Brago replies; Come thou, that waſt the terror of the moſt illuſtrious warriors: Come hither, and re-join thine eight brethren: the heroes who reſide here ſhall cultivate peace with thee. Go drink ALE therefore in the full circle of the Gods.

"But this brave king cries out: I will ſtill retain my arms: a hero ought carefully to preſerve his mail and helmet: it is dangerous to be a moment without the ſword* in one's hand.

"Then was fully ſeen how religiouſly this king had ſacrificed ever to the Gods: ſince the great celeſtial council and all the inferior Gods, received him among them with reſpectful ſalutations.

"Happy is the day on which that king is born, who thus gains to himſelf ſuch favour from the Gods. The age in which he hath lived ſhall remain among men in happy remembrance.

"The wolf Fenris ſhall burſt his fetters, and dart with rage upon his enemies, before ſo good a king ſhall again appear

* Or lance.

"upon the earth; which is now reduced
"to a defolate ftate of widowhood by his
"lofs.

"Riches perifh; relations die; the coun-
"tries are laid wafte; but king Hacon will
"dwell for ever with the Gods; while his
"people give themfelves up to forrow."

I Shall

I Shall only produce one piece more, but one much more confiderable than any of the preceding, and which, by the many little circumftantial ftrokes it abounds with, will give us a ftill deeper infight into the manners and genius of the times we wifh to know. It is extracted from a Collection of ancient hiftorical Monuments of the North, publifhed by Mr. E. J. BIORNER, a learned Swede, under the title of " *Nordifka* " *Kâmpedater,* &c." i. e. " The Exploits " of the northern Kings and Heroes, &c. " Stockholm, 1737." This Author publifhed the following piece from a manufcript preferved in the Archives of the College of Antiquities in Sweden, and accompanied it with a Swedifh and Latin Verfion. I have been as much affifted by the former, as I have been careful to keep at a diftance from the latter: for Mr. Biorner, who had faithfully followed his original in the one, hath employed fo many rhetorical flourifhes in the other, or, to fay the truth, a ftyle throughout fo puffy and inflated, that inftead of an ancient northern Scald, one would think one was hearing a boy newly come from ftudying his rhetoric. This loofe and faithlefs manner of tranflating, cannot, in my opinion, be too much

con-

condemned, especially in works of genuine antiquity; of which the principal merit consists in the simplicity and original spirit of the composition.

It would be a frivolous objection to urge, that, as this piece rather belongs to the antiquities of Sweden, than to those of Denmark, it therefore ought not to be inserted in the present work. Those who know the two nations, are not to learn that anciently the manners and customs of them both were so much the same, that the compositions of the one kingdom might easily be attributed to the other, without causing any material error or mistake. Besides, the Poem in question hath been claimed in their turn by the Danish Literati, as a production of their own country: and it hath even been printed nearly the same as it is given here, in a collection of ancient Danish Songs [*]. For my part, I am inclined to think that it was sung indifferently throughout all Scandinavia, and that each people placed the scene of action among themselves, in order to have the honour of those prodigious feats of valour, which are so largely described in it. Examples of

---

[*] See N. 20. in Centur. Cant. Danic. prior Part. prim. ab And. VELLEIO compil. & edit. Ann. 1695. cum cent. sec. a PET. SYVIO.

this

this kind are frequent enough in all remote ages.

With regard to the time when this Poem was compofed, if we may judge from the language of the original as we have it at prefent, it fhould feem to be of the thirteenth or fourteenth century: but it certainly muft be of a far more diftant period; fince the manners defcribed in it, and the Pagan religion, which is more than once alluded to, inconteftibly belong to times preceding the tenth century. It is therefore very probable, that the language and ftile of this Poem have been occafionally reformed and modernized, as often as was neceffary to render it intelligible. It's being fo general a favourite throughout the north, muft have invited more Poets than one to do the public this acceptable fervice. Mr. Biorner informs us, that he himfelf had heard it fung in his youth, with fome flight alterations, by the Peafants of Medelpadia and Angermania, Provinces which lie to the north of Stockholm. As to what he afferts farther, that the Heroes celebrated in it muft have lived in the third century, it is a point very difficult to maintain with any certainty.

The History of Charles and Grymer, Swedish Kings; and of Hialmar, the Son of Harec, King of Biarmland.

*THERE was a king named Charles, who commanded valiant warriors: in Sweden were his dominions; where he caused to reign repose and joy. Widely extended and populous was his country; and his army was composed of chosen youths. His queen, who was herself most beautiful, had borne him a lovely daughter, called Inguegerda; whose lively and graceful accomplishments daily encreasing,

---

* The English Translator could here only follow the French of M. Mallet, not being able to procure either the original or any other Version. He has, however, altered two of the names, which in French are written *Grym* and *Grund*, to Grymer and Grunder; as presuming they are in the original (according to the usual Icelandic idiom) *Grymr* and *Grundr*; the final r is, in translation, either dropt or retained at pleasure of the writer. T.

were

were no less the objects of admiration, than was the splendor of her birth and fortune. The breast of the king was replete with felicity.

The defence of the king's power and dominions were intrusted to the care of a valiant count (A), named ERIC. This warrior had past his life amidst the clash of swords and javelins, and had vanquished many a mighty Hero. His wife, a lady of illustrious birth, had brought him a son, named GRYMER; a youth early distinguished in the profession of arms; who well knew how to die his sword in the blood of his enemies, to run over the craggy mountains, to wrestle, play at chess, trace the motions of the stars, and to throw far from him heavy weights; in short, he was possessed of every accomplishment that could perfect and compleat the Hero. By the time he was twelve years old, no one durst contend with him, either with the sword, the bow, or at wrestling. He frequently shewed his skill in the chamber of the damsels, before the king's lovely daughter. Desirous of acquiring her regard, he displayed his dexterity in handling his weapons, and the knowlege he had attained in the sciences he had learned. At length he ventured to make this demand; " Wilt thou, O
" fair Princess, if I may obtain the king's
" con-

"consent, accept of me for a husband?" To which she prudently replied; "I must not make that choice myself; but go thou, and offer the same proposal to my father."

This gallant young man proceeded directly to the king, and respectfully addressing him, said, "O King! Give me in marriage thy rich and beautiful daughter." He answered, in a rage; "Thou hast learnt in some degree to handle thy arms; thou hast acquired some honourable distinctions; but hast thou ever gained a victory, or given a banquet to the savage beasts that delight in blood?" "Whither shall I go then, O King, said GRYMER, that I may dye my sword in crimson, and render myself worthy of this fair enchanting maiden?" "I know a man, replied the king, who has made himself terrible by the keenness of his sword: the strongest shields he cuts in pieces; he wins in combats the most splendid armour, and loads all his followers with riches. His name is HIALMAR: he is the son of HAREC, who governs Biarmland*. I know not a bra-

---

* This Province is thought to be that tract of country known at present by the names of Medelpadia, Angermania, &c. Others suppose it to have been to the east of the gulph of Bothnia. T.

"ver

"ver man, nor one who commands more
"gallant warriors. Go then, without de-
"lay, attack this Hero, and thus give a
"proof of thy valour. Affail him with
"undaunted refolution, and caufe him foon
"to bite the duft: then will I give thee
"the fair INGUEGERDA, all bedecked with
"gold, and with her, befide, great ftore
"of riches. Confider well the honour
"thou wilt acquire by fubduing fo illu-
"ftrious a chieftain as Hialmar. In the
"mean time, thy deftined bride fhall be
"kept fafe for thee till thy return, and
"they fhall take care to adorn her with
"fplendid attire." GRYMER inftantly returned to the fair INGUEGERDA, and with
looks full of love, refpectfully faluted her.
"What anfwer haft thou received," faid
fhe, "from the king? Tell me; it is what
"I am impatient to know." Before he
could find words to reply, his colour alter-
nately came and went. At length he uttered
this fhort fentence. "The king has di-
"rected me to the fearlefs Hialmar: nor
"can I obtain thee till I have deprived him
"of life." Then INGUEGERDA exclaimed,
with grief, "Alas! My father has devoted
"thee to death! But behold a fword that
"can penetrate through and embrue in
"blood the beft tempered armour. Handle
"it well in battle, and ftrike heavy blows."

GRYMER

Grymer viewed, with attention, the edge of this fabre, which he called, from an affurance of its efficacy, Trausta, (i. e. Comforter.) At the fame time his miftrefs prefented him with a fuit of armour; at the fight of which Grymer vowed never to yield or give way, when he was in fight of Hialmar. Then he went to his father; " The time is come, faid he, in the " which I may now acquire glory: Give " me, without delay, veffels and foldiers: " I cannot wait for them longer." " I " will entruft thee," replied his father, " with fifteen galleys, and one large and " fplendid fhip. Thou art permitted to " chufe thyfelf the moft excellent arms, " and to felect thofe warriors whom thou " moft regardeft."

An affembly was then immediately convoked; to which numbers reforted from the moft diftant parts of the country. Grymer felected a fine troop, all compofed of the braveft warriors. Each of them preffed to follow him with a noble ardour. Soon to the fhore of the fea marched this chofen and valiant band. They lanch their veffels, richly bedecked, into the wide ocean. Armed with cuiraffes of a fhining blue, they unfurl their fails; which inftantly catch the fpringing gale. The fhrowdes rattle; the white waves foam and dafh

against

against their prows. In the mean time GRYMER prepared himself for the rude shock of battle, and to spread a carnage wide around him. Persuaded that no warrior could stand before the force of his arrows, he exacted an oath of fidelity from his followers. These valiant Heroes steer their numerous vessels towards the shores of Gothland, eager to glut the hungry ravens, and to gorge the wolf with ample prey. The fleet now reaches the enemy's coasts: those fatal coasts where so many warriors were soon to perish.

Thus landed GRYMER on the shores of GOTHLAND; and thus did a beauteous maiden occasion the feast that was going to be prepared for the greedy wolf, and that all those proud and valiant heroes were about to risque their lives in battle. Looking around them, they perceived an extensive encampment, which stretched along a plain, and near it a fine army drawn up, and large fires blazing. No one doubted that this was the camp wherein HIALMAR commanded. So it proved; and that chieftain himself advancing, demanded of GRYMER's valiant soldiers; To whom belonged those vessels which he saw. Then GRYMER stepped forward, and told him his name; adding, that he had spent a whole summer to seek him. "May your arrival," replied

HIAL-

Hialmar, " be fortunate; and may health
" and honour attend you. I will inſtantly
" preſent you with gold, and the unmixed
" juice of the vine." " I cannot," ſaid
Grymer, " accept thy offers. I came
" hither with a mind reſolved on thy de-
" ſtruction. Prepare thyſelf for battle;
" and let us haſten to give a banquet to the
" beaſts of prey." Hialmar artfully replied, " Let me adviſe you better; let us
" unite in ſtrict brotherly confederacy *
" (B)." " Let us not be ſeparated day
" nor night. Let us not riſque the com-
" bat you propoſe: I have had ſufficient
" knowlege of ſuch encounters; and had
" much rather ſeek to eſpouſe from your
" country a beautiful damſel, and to bring
" her home hither." Grymer, full of
indignation, exclaimed; " Arm inſtantly,
" I ſay; nor let thy unmanly fear lock up
" thy ſword: let our bucklers claſh toge-
" ther, and be bruiſed with our blows."
" I have a ſiſter," proceeded Hialmar,
" who is moſt fair to look upon. I will
" beſtow the damſel upon you in marriage,
" and her portion ſhall be the principality
" of Biarmland; if you will for once de-
" ſiſt from this ſlaughter." " I will nei-
" ther," ſaid Grymer, " accept of thy

* *Confraternité.* Fr.

" ſiſter,

" sister, nor parly any longer. He must
" be a coward, who would shun the com-
" bat on such conditions: and, besides,
" that fair princess would soon be informed
" of it." HIALMAR, at length, all enraged, replied—" Come on: I have done
" enough to elude thy demands: since it
" must be so, let us die our swords in blood,
" and try their sharp points against our well-
" tempered shields." At that instant he
seized his white cuirass, his sword and
buckler, so resplendent, as never till then
was seen the like. GRYMER, on his part,
who was to begin the attack, stood ready
for the combat. Immediately, by a violent blow of his sabre, he strikes off the
border of HIALMAR's shield, and cuts off
one of his hands: but HIALMAR, little
affected by that loss, and far from asking
quarter, drives his sword with fury; he
strikes off the helmet and cuirass of GRY-
MER; he pierces him at once in the breast
and sides, and causes the blood to run in
such abundance, that his strength begins
to fail him. Yet HIALMAR complained
that his weapon had done too little execu-
tion; assured, that could he have grasped
it with both his hands, his adversary would
soon have bit the earth. Then GRYMER
raising his sabre with both his hands, let it
fall on the casque of HIALMAR, and he
him-

himself likewise dropt, enfeebled by the loss of blood that flowed in torrents from his gaping wounds.

Hialmar's warriors carefully interred the dead body of their chief, and buried his gold along with it (c). Grymer was conveyed on ship-board by his followers; who immediately set sail. Thus ended the combat between these two Heroes. By the time that Grymer drew near his own country, his wounds were enflamed, his strength was wasted away, and his life seemed to draw near to its end. On his arrival, the king and his daughter being informed of his danger, that princess chearfully undertook his cure; which having effected, they were united in marriage. A grand banquet was prepared to celebrate their nuptials in the royal hall, and all the courtiers, richly habited, were sumptuously entertained. Wine and Hydromel * flowed plentifully round, and as for Water it was not so much as thought of. During these nuptials, the joy was great and uninterrupted: the king distributed gold among his guests; and the great men of the realm returned to their homes loaded with presents. But above all, the beauteous bride of Grymer overwhelmed her Hero with all kinds of felicity.

* Or Mead.

We muſt now relate what paſſed in the interim. HIALMAR's warriors, aſtoniſhed to ſee their chief fall by the ſword of the valiant GRYMER, with grief-pierced hearts declared, they ſhould never find his equal. They departed home ſorrowful and dejected; but at the ſame time nouriſhed in their boſoms an implacable deſire of vengeance. They ſet ſail toward BIARMLAND; and the violence of the waves favouring their courſe, they ſoon beheld the caſtle of HAREC Hialmar's father. The ſight of this ſomewhat conſoled their grief. Inſtantly landing, they entered the palace, as the king was coming forth to meet them. This aged prince ſeeing his warriors pale and dejected, with downcaſt eyes, enquired if HIALMAR remained on ſhip-board, and whether he had gained the fair prize he ſought for? "Hialmar," ſaid they, " has
" not received ſlight wounds in the com-
" bat: he is diſpoiled of life: he hath not
" even ſeen his beautiful miſtreſs." The king, ſtruck with conſternation, poured forth a deep ſigh, and cried, " Certainly
" the death of HIALMAR is a moſt affect-
" ing loſs!—Let the Bugle Horn ſound to
" arms. I will go ravage Sweden. Let
" every man who bears a ſhield, launch his
" veſſel into the ſea: let us renew the war;
" let the helmets be broke in pieces, and
" let

"let all prepare for the clash of swords." The whole country was unpeopled by the assembling of the warriors; who ardently thirsted after battle, that by a speedy vengeance they might give comfort to 'the shade of' HIALMAR. The rendezvous being fixed, multitudes repaired thither from every quarter. The most distinguished warriors were covered with entire coats of mail, and their gilded arms cast a resplendent gleam around them.

HAREC having distributed to others suits of armour of the hardest steel, helmets and cuirasses, swords and darts and shields, put himself at the head of this resolute band; and led them forth to war. They immediately embarked, and full of courage, set sail, ranging their bucklers, which reflected rays of light, along the sides of their vessels. Their sails were composed of a fine stuff, bordered with blue and scarlet. HAREC exhorted them to revenge, and inspired them with intrepid resolution by his warlike discourses. The soldiers seconding his wishes, hoist and spread their sails with a generous emulation to outdo each other. The billows resound before the prows of the ships as they press forward; the wind redoubles its force; the sea foams and swells; and the white waves dash against the sides of the vessels. They scud along

as

as swift as the lightning; and the mermaids with difficulty follow them, in order to feast on the pitch with which their keels are besmeared. At length the Biarmian Heroes reach the Swedish coast: they cast anchor and moor in the bottom of the haven. Their cables are hove down, and lie floating from their sides. They soon gain the shore in their light shallops; and presently cover themselves with their helmets. HAREC again invites them to vengeance, and commands them to lay waste the land with fire and sword. His orders are obeyed; the ravage begins: the flames spread over the country, and the inhabitants lose at once their glory and their lives. Sweden becomes one continued stream of fire. Its Heroes are laid low. Nothing is heard but the resounding of the shrill clarion: nothing is seen but heads dissevered by the deep-cutting sword. At length count ERIC is apprised that war desolates the dominions of his king. That Hero instantly girds on his sword, to put a stop to these dreadful ravages. He collects together both the free-men and the slaves throughout the kingdom. Soon was this valiant troop in arms: this troop, among whom so many were destined to lose their lives. The two armies joined battle; the swords were blunted on the helmets and shields.

shields. The far-sounding trumpet animates the combatants; the darts pierce them thro', the sharp iron severs their limbs, so that almost all seem devoted to death.

A gallant warrior, named GRUNDER, was present at that engagement; whose sword was accustomed to break in pieces the best tempered buckler, and whose slaughter fattened the hungry wolves. He held the rank of Duke in HAREC's kingdom: full of ardour in the combat, whether he fought with the sword or lance, he had sent many a fair corpse to the regions of death. This valiant Hero threw himself into the thickest of the battle, and laying prostrate at his feet a multitude of warriors covered with sweat and blood, he devoted them a prey to the savage beasts. Count ERIC, enflamed with rage and vengeance, hastened to oppose the progress of this chief: but a shower of darts laid him in the dust, and forced his immediate followers to retire: the rest of his soldiers seeing him prostrate on the earth, cast their shields away, and saved themselves by a speedy flight. The conquerors shed rivers of blood among the vanquished, and raising the shout of joy dreadful to hear, hack with their swords the shields of their enemies. These hastily fly to the woods, leaving the field of battle spread over with the ghastly corps of their
com-

companions; being themselves irresolute and dismayed, having neither targets nor helmets left for their defence; while the victorious Biarmians, regardless either of glory or virtue, proceed to burn the houses every where scattered over the country.

King CHARLES is informed that his warriors are perished; that his chieftain ERIC himself is destroyed, and that his army are weltering in their blood. He is likewise told, that in HAREC's train there is a chieftain named GRUNDER, whose resplendent sword hath made a terrible carnage of his people. GRYMER heard also this relation, and throwing down his dagger, struck it with violence into the table; but the king, with his, pierced it through and through. All instantly fly to arms: every one prepares himself for battle. The trumpet sounds, each warrior is accoutered, and the women, sensibly alarmed, surrender up themselves to fear.

In the mean time the people flock around the king; crying, that a woful devastation was spread over Sweden, and that the flames, without distinction, devoured every dwelling. The king, at the hearing of this calamity, waxes red with fury, and orders the blue steel of their arms to be dyed in blood. At the loud clangor of the polished trumpets, the soldiers vow revenge for their loss. GRYMER, panting for battle, was dressed

dreſſed out in a coſtly cuiraſs: being thus in armour, he appeared ſtill more handſome than before; and his ſword reflected a dazzling luſtre. The whole army, impatient for the fight, began the onſet by flinging ſtones. HAREC's Soldiers, on their part, returned the attack, and ran eagerly to the combat. The wounds are impatient to be made with the points of the ſwords. Pikes and arrows fly with violence. GRUNDER cuts ſhort the thread of life of all who come in his way. GRYMER inflames the ardour of his people. CHARLES, an eye-witneſs of the encounter of theſe Heroes, deals deſtruction around him, and pays an abundant tribute to death. Every thing gives way to the reſiſtleſs craſh of his death-dealing blows: his glittering ſword pierces to the heart. Thus the warriors fall in crowds in the conflict. The vultures aſſemble to devour their prey: the young eagles ſcream around, and the carnivorous beaſts lie waiting for the dead. The high ſoaring hawks rejoice with ſhrill cries over their ſmoaking repaſts. Many wolves were likewiſe ſpectators of the action. GRUNDER was ever active in diſcompoſing his adverſaries, and his eager ſword ran down with blood. CHARLES beholds his people diſcomfited and hewn in pieces by this warrior. At length they meet, and with hearts boiling

ing with dreadful rage, they engage each other. Their ſtrokes are impetuouſly redoubled, till at length the king falls, covered with wounds; and his limbs float in his own blood. At that inſtant, the bright daughters of Deſtiny invite him to enter the palace of Odin.

Thus fell CHARLES, in ſight of the exulting and rapacious wolves: when GRYMER ran furiouſly through the oppoſing battalions, and uttered bitter cries amid the ſwords of his enemies; while GRUNDER vaunts to have ſnatched the victory out of the hands of his foes, and to have cut off the king and count ERIC with the ſword. Perceiving GRYMER, he exclaims, " Thou " alone remaineſt to enter the liſts with " me. Revenge the cauſe of thy friends: " come and let us fight in ſingle combat: " it is now thy turn to feel the keenneſs of " my ſword." Immediately their ſabres hang dreadful in the air, like dark and threatning clouds. GRYMER'S weapon falls like a thunder-bolt. Dreadful is the encounter: their ſwords furiouſly ſtrike; they are ſoon bathed in gore. At length GRUNDER is covered with wounds: he ſinks amidſt a deluge of blood. GRYMER gives a dreadful ſhout of triumph, and with his envenomed ſword, cleaves the caſque of his enemy, hews his armour in pieces, and pours the light in through his bosom. Then a shower of arrows is launched on both sides: the darts tear through whatever may oppose them: and the bodies of the warriors, or their steel-defended heads can no more resist the rapid sword, than a soft bank of yielding snow. The most illustrious of the chiefs are despoiled of their bracelets, and the blue-edged weapon shivers the helmets and the breast-plates of all. At length the Biarmians, worsted, retire to their ships; every one flies as fast as his strength will permit him. The vessels are instantly unmoored, and put to sea: those vessels which are destined to be the messengers of such sad tidings. Yet the bravest of their warriors retire but slowly, and seem by their gestures still desirous of insulting their conquerors.

HAREC was not seen to have fled among the crowd, nor had that gallant prince once turned his back during the combat. He was diligently sought for; when his companions presented themselves along with him to GRYMER, and thus addressed him. " Stay! behold in thy power this daunt-
" less Hero; who, weighed down with
" years, still maintains the fight with all
" the spirit and courage of youth.—Thy
" renown will be fallacious, if thou de-
" prive him of life; since he is a man
                                    " whose

"whose equal it will be difficult to find."
GRYMER cast a look on the king, nor was the animosity between these two warriors yet extinguished. HIALMAR's death was still regretted, although an ample vengeance had been taken. At length GRYMER thus bespake him. " The king, my father-in-
" law, hath lost his life; and thy son was
" become famous for his valour. Let our
" mutual losses be deemed equal; and let
" the death of GRUNDER atone and com-
" pensate for that of ERIC. For thee, O
" king, accept at my hands both life and
" peace. Thou hast signalized thyself in
" combats: keep henceforth thy mighty
" ships, and thy Biarmian kingdom."
Every one was pleased with this noble and generous sentence of GRYMER. The two Heroes entered into a strict and faithful alliance. The king, pleased to have preserved his life, immediately conducted his fleet to Biarniland. The warriors laid up their arms in peace: the wounded were brought home to be healed: and hilly monuments were raised for the slain (D). GRYMER reigned, honoured by his subjects, and beloved by the fair partner of his bed. He was magnificent, eloquent and affable: and all the inhabitants of those countries celebrated his praises.

REMARKS on the preceding PIECE.

(A) "A valiant count."] In all the states of Germany, that were subject to the monarchical form of government, besides the KING, who was hereditary, the nation chose to themselves a CHIEF or LEADER, who sometimes bore the title of COUNT, and sometimes that of DUKE *. The King was descended of one certain family; but the choice of the Chieftain was always conferred upon the bravest warrior. *Reges ex nobilitate, Duces ex virtute sumunt*, says Tacitus, De Mor. Germ. This passage, as Montesquieu hath clearly shown, is a clue that unravels the history of the middle ages. Under the first race of the Kings of France, the crown was hereditary, the office of Mayor of the Palace elective. This custom the Franks had brought with them from their original country.

(B) "Brotherly confederacy.—Fr. *Confraternité.*"] Here we plainly discover those Fraternities in Arms, which are so often mentioned in the history of Chivalry, in France, England, and elsewhere. Joinville is possibly the oldest Author who speaks of them in France, where they still subsisted in the time of Brantôme. M. de Ste. Palaye, in his excellent Memoirs of Chivalry, relates the terms and conditions of these associations. They differed in no respect from those in use in the north. Our most ancient Chronicles afford us examples of these Confraternities, and in general, every thing that constituted Chivalry was established in the north in those early ages, when they had not the least idea of it in the more southern nations.

(c) "Buried his gold

---

* *Islandicè*, IARL: whence our title EARL.   T.

"with

" with his body."] We have seen, in the former part of this work [*], that one of the chief funeral Ceremonies, consisted in depositing along with the defunct whatever had been most precious and dear to him during his life. Upon opening the old burial-places, various kinds of iron instruments are still found there; though, whatever our Poet may say, the little earnestness that is shown for searching into such recesses, is a sufficient proof that men seldom find any great quantity of gold concealed in them.

(D) " Hilly monu-
" ments .... for the
" slain."] This incontestably proves, that the events related in this Poem, are of very ancient date. From the first erection of churches in the north, it was strictly forbidden to bury in the open fields, as had been the custom in times of Paganism. It has been already observed [†], that these little sepulchral mounts are found every where in Scandinavia, and in the countries lying upon the Baltic. The Norvegians carried this custom with them into Normandy, where these little monumental Hillocks are often found, constructed like these of the north. The learned Montfaucon has given a full description of one that was discovered in the year 1685, in the Diocese of Evreux.

It were needless to extend these Remarks farther, the preceding Poem being of itself sufficiently characteristic of the manners of the times. In this, as in almost all other pieces of this Collection, may be perceived more force of imagination than could be expected from those ages of ignorance and ferocity; not to mention, from so rigorous a climate. It must however be added, that much of the beauty and force of these Poems is lost to us, who only read them in a prose Translation; who seldom, and not without much pains, can unfold the allegories with which their Authors a-

[*] See Vol. I. p. 341. Vol. II. p. 142.   [†] Vol. I. p. 222.

bound, and who enter neither into their syftem of Mythology, nor into the manners of the times wherein they were written.

What muft we conclude from all this? Can we doubt whether thefe Scandinavian Poets, fometimes lively and ingenious as they were, were the fame barbarians who fet fire to Rome, overturned the Empire, and ravaged Spain, France and England? Yet this muft be admitted, or we muft contradict the whole tenor of hiftory. Let us then grant, that the influence of the ruling paffion might fupply, in thofe Northern Climes, the abfence of the Sun, and that the imaginations of mankind may fubfift in full vigour and maturity, even during the infancy of reafon.

THE END OF M. MALLET'S SECOND VOLUME.

SUPPLEMENT.

ADVERTISEMENT.

WE have now seen the end of M. MALLET's *Introduction a l' Histoire de Dannemark*, and here the present Work might properly enough have been concluded: but as this Second Volume falls short in size of the preceding, the English Translator thought he should make a very acceptable present to the learned Reader, if he subjoined by way of SUPPLEMENT, the Latin Version of the EDDA by Mr. GORANSON, whom our Author has mentioned in the INTRODUCTION to this Volume. By comparing this Version with the preceding one from the French, the genuine literal sense of the original will the more compleatly be attained: And in illustrating so ancient and so peculiar a Composition, no kind of assistance will be found superfluous. It may be a farther recommendation of the following pages, that Mr. GORANSON's Latin Version, (which, however barbarous and unclassical, is yet esteemed literally exact) is in itself a great curiosity, as his own book will probably fall into the hands of very few Readers in this kingdom. This Latin Verſion was publiſhed a few years ago at the foot of a correct edition of the EDDA in 4to, accompanied with another tranſlation into the Swediſh language, and prefaced with a long Swediſh diſſertation, " De EDDÆ antiquitate, et indole, &c. ut et de antiquiſſimis et genuinis Skythis, Getis, Gothis, Atlantüs, Hyperboreis, Cimbris, Gallis, eorumque Satore Gomero."

If the preceding Verſion from M. MALLET ſhould be found in ſome places to differ pretty much from this of Mr. GORANSON, we probably muſt not attribute it wholly to the freedom, with which the former has ſometimes paraphraſed the original in order to accommodate it to the modern taſte, but in many inſtances to the different copies of the EDDA which they each of them reſpectively followed; and for this our Author has himſelf apologized in the INTRODUCTION. They alſo differ in their ſeveral diviſions of the work: but for this alſo M. MALLET has already accounted *. In the following Verſion Mr. GORANSON's own Diviſions are preſerved in the Text; but thoſe of M. MALLET are carefully noted in the Margin.   T.

* See above, pag. 24.

HYPERBOREORUM ATLANTIORUM

SEU

SUIOGOTORUM ET NORDMANORUM

E D D A,

Hoc eft, ATAVIA, feu Fons Gentilis illorum et Theologiæ et Philofophiæ, VERSIONE LATINA Donata, &c. Ad Manufcriptum, quod poffidet Bibliotheca Upfalenfis, antiquiffimum, correctiffimum, et quidem membranaceum, Goticum, in lucem prodit

Opera et Studio

JOHANNIS GORANSON,

Philof. Magiftri.

VOL. II. T.

BOK *theßi heiter* EDDA, *henna hever samsetta* SNORRI STURLO SON, &c.

LIBER hic vocatur EDDA, eam compofuit SNORRO STURLÆ FILIUS, eo modo, quo hic ordinatum eſt. Primum vero de Aſis et Ymio. Mox de Poeſi, et multarum rerum epithetis. Poſtremo Series Genealogica, quam Snorro confecit de Haquino Rege, et Duce Skula.

Pars Prima,

Seu

SNORRONIS STURLÆI

EDDA

PROPRIE SIC DICTA.

* OMNIPOTENS DEUS *creavit cœlum & terram & omnes res, quæ illa sequuntur: & postremo homines, ex quibus Generationes provenere, Adamum & Evam. Et dispergebantur familiæ per orbem deinceps. Sed cum exinde præterlapsa essent tempora, dissimilis evasit populus. Quidam erant boni; quidam vivebant secundum concupiscentiam*

* Vid. supra pag. 3. Not.

suam.

fuam. Propter hoc erat *fubmerfus aquis orbis, exceptis illis, qui cum Noacho in arca effent.* Poft hæc incolebatur iterum orbis *(mundus)* ab illis, *fed omnis multitudo negligebat tunc Deum. Quis vero poffet tunc narrare magna Dei opera, cum obliti effent* DEi *nominis?* Sed hoc erat per univerfum orbem, ut populus erraret. *Nihilo tamen minus dabat Deus hominibus terrena dona, opes & felicitatem, & fapientiam ad difcernendum terrenas res ac limites cœli terræque.* Hoc *admirabantur illi, quod terra ac animalia haberent eandem naturam in quibufdam, licet diffimiles effent.* Hoc eft unum, quod terra fit viridis in fummis montibus. Scaturitque ibi aqua, nec opus eft, ibi ut profundius fodiamus, quam in depreffioribus vallibus. *Ita etiam comparatum eft cum animalibus ac avibus, ut in illis fanguis clicitus, tam cito emanet in capite ac in pedibus.* Altera indoles hæc eft terræ, ut quolibet anno crefcat in illa gramen & flos, & eodem anno decidat. *Sic etiam animalibus, aut avibus contingit, ut eis crefcat pilus ac pennæ, & decidant quolibet anno.* Hæc eft tertia proprietas terræ, ut illa fit aperta & effoffa, tunc progerminat gramen in ipfo hoc pulvere, qui fupremus eft in terra. *Illi affimilarunt montes ac lapides dentibus offibufque.* Ita concludebant illi ex his, terram effe vegetam & habere vitam aliquo modo, cum illa aleret omne vivum, fuumque agnofceret

omne

omne, quod moriretur. Usque ad illam referebant genus suum. Videbant etiam, inæqualem esse cursum lunæ. Quædam (lunationes) longius progressæ, quam cæteræ. Hoc considerantes concludebant, aliquem hasce gubernare: eumq; divitem atq; præpotentem esse; etiam cogitabant, eum fuisse antequam lunationes, atque præesse lumini solis, rori terræ, & ventis, atque turbinibus. Non vero sciebant, ubi esset. Attamen credebant, cum esse omnium rerum gubernatorem. Utque hoc memoria tenerent, rebus omnibus nomina, etiam sibi, imposuerunt. Deinde superstitio dimanavit in varias partes orbis, in quas homines dispersi sunt; aut linguis discriminati sunt. Sed omnia judicabant illi more terreno (humano), quippe cum non haberent donum (aliquod) spirituale, atque credebant, omnia esse ex materia quadam creata, sive fabricata.

Quomodo divisa sit terra in tres partes.

Terra dividitur in tres partes. Harum una a meridie ad occidentem juxta mare mediterraneum extenditur, quæ Africa vocatur. Pars vero meridionalis adeo calida est, ut calore solis ardeat. Altera pars ab occidente septentrionem versus porrigitur, mari adjacens, Europa nuncupatur, seu Enea. Hujus septentrionalior pars adeo est frigoribus exposita, ut nec herbarum, nec incolarum sit patiens.

A feptentrione juxta orientem, meridiemque verfus fita regio, dicitur Afia. Hæc terræ habitabilis pars omnigeno ornamento, & divitiis auri, pretioforumque lapidum, fuperbit. Hic eft meditullium terræ. Et ficut heic omnia funt meliora, quam in cæteris locis; ita etiam homines ibi funt honoratiores, quam alibi, propter fapientiam, & fortitudinem, & pulcritudinem, & quæ funt reliqua. Ibi fita fuit urbs, quam Trojam vocamus. Trojanum vero imperium in duodecim minora divifum fuit regna, uni tamen capiti fubjecta. Ibi et jam duodecim linguæ fuere primariæ. Horum unus dictus fuit Memnon, cujus Conjunx erat filia Priami regis, Troja. Horum filius Tros, quem nos Thorem vocamus. Qui duodecim annos natus viribus polluit maturis. Tunc terrâ duodecim pelles urfinas fimul fuftulit. Hic de multis fimul pugilibus furiofis victoriam reportavit, nec non feris, draconibufq;. In feptentrione mulierem fatidicam invenit, nomine Sibillam, nobis vero Sif dictam. Profapiam eius nemo novit. Quorum filius vocatus fuit Lorida, ejus filius Vingitor, cujus filius fuit Vingener, c. f. Moda, c. f. Magnus, c. f. Sefsmeg; c. f. Bedvig; cujus f. Atra, nobis Anna: c. f. Iterman: c. f. Eremod; c. f. Skialdum, nobis Skold; c. f. Biaf, nobis Bear; c. f. Jat; c. f. Gudolfur; c. f. Finner; c. f. Frialaf. nobis Fridleif: c. f. Vodden, nobis Odinus.

De

De adventu Odini in Septentrionem.

Hic Odinus fuit perspicacissimus in rebus præsagiendis. Ejus conjux fuit Frigida, quam Friggam nominamus. Ille celeriter profectus in terram Borealem magno comitatu, & opibus. Et ubicunque venerant, magni æstimati sunt, Diisque similiores, quam hominibus sunt habiti. Hi venerunt in Saxoniam, ibique Odinus terram undicunque sibi subjecit. Ubi regni custodes reliquit tres suos filios. Vegdreg præfuit Saxoniæ Orientali: alter ejus filius, Beldeg vocatus, nobis Baldr, possidebat Vestphaliam, hoc regnum ita nominabatur. Tertius ejus filius, nomine Siggius, habuit filium Rerim, Patrem Volsungi; a quo Volsungi originem ducunt. Hi Franclandiæ præsiderunt. Ab hisce omnibus multæ nobilesque familiæ sunt ortæ. Inde profectus Odinus in Reid Gotiam, eandem suo subjecit imperio, ibique regem constituit filium suum Skoldium, Patrem Fridleifü, a quo Skoldungi provenere. Hæc vocatur jam Jotia, illis Reidgotia dicta.

Quomodo Odinus venerit in Svioniam, & dederit filiis suis regnum.

Hinc Odinus proficiscebatur in Suioniam, ubi erat rex, qui Gylsius nominabatur. Et cum hic audiret de Asiaticis viris, qui Asæ erant vocati

vocati ibat obviam eisdem, eosque invitabat in suum regnum. Sed hoc consequebatur itinera illorum, ubicunque morarentur in regionibus, ut esset ibi ubertas annonæ, & pax; & credebant homines, deos esse horum gubernatores. Cum hi magnæ auctoritatis viri superarent plerosque reliquos homines pulcritudine atque sapientia. Heic placuit Odino pulcra vallis, atque regionis bona conditio, unde etiam elegit sibi locum, urbi struendæ idoneum, quæ jam Sigtuna vocatur. Ordinavit ibi Gubernatores eodem modo ac Trojæ. Erant præfecti duodecim viri judiciis, lege regni faciendis. Deinde iter fecit Odinus versus septentrionem, usque ad mare, quod putavit cingere omnem terram, ibique regem constituit filium suum Semingum, quæ terra jam Norrigia vocatur. Et derivant Norrigiæ reges, ac Jarli, inde ab illo suum genus. Cum Odino profectus fuit Yngvius, qui ei in regno Svionum successit, cui etiam originem debent Ynglingi. Hi Asæ hic uxores ducebant, & fiebant hæ familiæ perplurimæ, in Saxonia, & Septentrione. Horum Lingua sola in usu fuit in hisce regionibus, & inde judicant homines, hos linguam attulisse in Septentrionem, in Norrigiam nempe, Daniam, Svioniam, & Saxoniam.

Hic incipit deceptio Gylfii, inde ab adveniu ejus ad Pantopatrem domi, Afgardiæ; de multifcientia ejus; deque Afarum illufione, & quæftionibus Gylfii.

GYLFIUS erat vir fapiens, & confiderabat hoc, quod omnis plebs laudaret illos, atque omnia evenerint, ad voluntatem illorum; five hoc naturæ illorum, five Divinæ virtuti effet adfcribendum. Afgardiam profectus affumfit formam fenilem. Sed Afæ erant perfpicaciores, (imo ut) præviderent iter ejus, eumque fafcinatione oculorum exciperent. Tunc cernebat ille altum palatium: Tecta ejus erant tecta aureis clypeis, ut tectum novum. Ita loquitur Diodolfius: *Tectum ex auro micante, Parietes ex lapide; Fundamina aulæ ex montibus, fecere Afæ fagaciores.* Gylfius confpicatus eft virum quendam in oftio Palatii, ludentem gladiolis, feptem fimul in aera vibratis. Hic illius quæfivit nomen, qui Ganglerus vocabatur, * Rifcos montes tranfvectus jam interrogavit,

---

* Iflandicè, *Al Rifils Stigum.*

qui

quis palatium poffideret. Hic refpondebat, eundem horum effe regem : & ego debeo comitari te ut illum videas. Ibi intuitus eft multa palatia, multofque homines, & multa pavimenta ; quidam bibebant, quidam ludebant. Tunc loquebatur Ganglerus, cum ei multa heic apparerent incredibilia : *Januæ omnes, antequam progeffus fueris, bene afpiciendæ, nam fciri nequit, ubinam inimici federint in fcamnis, tibi infidiaturi.* Tria confpicatus folia, alterum altero altius, & cuilibet virum infidentem. Jam nomen quæfivit regis illorum. Tunc ille refpondebat, qui eum intromifit : ille qui infimo fedet throno, eft rex nomine Har (Excelfus), cui proximus Iafn-Har (Excelfo æqualis), atqui fupremus, Tertius [*Thridi*] dicitur Har. Ille a Ganglero quæfivit, plurane effent ejus negotia. Sed cibus potufque fine pretio porrigitur. Ganglerus dicit, fe omnium primo effe interrogaturum, num eruditus & fapiens quidam adfit. Har (Excelfus) refpondit, eum non incolumem egreffurum, fi doctior effet. Atque tu progreffus ftabis interrogaturus : fedebit vero, qui refpondeat.

HISTORIA PRIMA.

De quæstionibus Gangleri.

GANGLERUS orsus est tunc suum sermonem. Quis est Supremus, seu Primus Deorum? Har respondet: Qui nostra lingua Pantopater dicitur. Sed Asgardiæ habebat ille XII nomina. * Pantopater; Vastator; Nictans; Neptunus; Multiscius; Sonans; Optator; Munificus; Depopulator; Ustulator; Felix. Tunc Gang. Ubi est hic Deus? Aut quid potest efficere? aut quid voluit ad gloriam suam manifestandam? Har resp. Ille vivit per omne ævum, ac gubernat omne regnum suum, & magnas partes & parvas. Tunc resp. Jafnhar (Excelso æqualis): ille fabricabat cœlum ac terram & aëra. Tunc loquebatur Tertius †: Hoc quod majus est, quam quod fabricabat hominem, & dabat ei spiritum,

---

* Islandicè, *Alfauthr. Herian. Nikadr. Nikuthr. Fiolner. Oski. Omi. Rifindi. Svithur. Svithrer. Vithrer. Salfkr.*

† Islandicè, *Thridi.*

qui

qui vivet; licet corpus evanuerit. Et tunc habitabunt omnes cum illo jufti, ac bene morati, ibi, quod Gimle, dicitur. Sed mali homines proficifcuntur in infernum. Ita dicit in Sibillæ [*Volufpæ*] vaticinio: *Initium erat temporis, Cum nihil effet, Neque arena nec mare, Nec fundamina fubter. Terra reperiebatur nullibi, Nec fuperne cœlum. Hiatus era perpetuus, Sed gramen nullibi.* Tunc refp. Jafnhar: Multos annos antequam terra erat creata, Niflheimium fuit paratum, ejufque in medio eft fons nomine Hvergelmer. Hinc profluunt amnes hifce celebrati nominibus; * Angor, Gaudii remora, Mortis habitatio, Celerrima perditio & vetufta, Vagina, Procella fæva, Vorago, Stridor & Ululatus. Late emanans; Vehementer fremens portas inferni alluit †. Tunc dicit Tertius [*Thridi*].

* Iflandicè, *Kvol. Gundro. Fiorni. Fimbulthul. Slithan. ok Hrithr. Sylgr. ok Ylgr. Vidleiptr. Gioll er næft Helgrindum.*

† Cum Divus ille Plato, quingentis circiter ante Natum mundi Sofpitatorem annis, iifdem, ac Edda, verbis vitæ futuræ mentionem injecerit, lubet eadem heic inferere. Ita vero ille in Axiocho T. III. f. 371. " Atque

OMNIUM
" fi alium fermonem quo-
" que audire velis, quem
" mihi Gobrias olim re-
" ferebat, vir cumprimis
" eruditus & Magi etiam
" nomine illuftris, ita ha-
" beto. Is Avum fuum
" & cognominem dicebat,
" in Xerxis memorabili
" illa in Græciam expe-
" ditione, in Delum mif-
" fum, ut infulam tuere-
" tur. Quæ quidem in-
" fula duorum Deorum
" natalibus

" natalibus celebris est.
" Ibi ex æneis quibusdam
" tabulis, quas ex Hyper-
" boreis montibus Opis
" & Hæcaerga detulissent,
" hæc se intellexisse com-
" memorabat: Quum vi-
" delicet animi & corporis
" facta esset solutio, ani-
" mum ad inconspicabi-
" lem quendam locum
" proficisci, subterraneum
" quidem illum; in quo
" Plutonis regia non mi-
" nor Jovis aula sit in ter-
" ra: Terram mundi uni-
" versi medium obtinere:
" Cœlum globosum esse,
" cujus dimidiam partem
" cœlestes, majorumque
" gentium dii tenerent:
" Alteram inferi, quorum
" alii fratres essent, alii
" eorum liberi. Vestibu-
" lum autem, quo aditus
" patet ad Plutoniam re-
" giam, claustris ferreis
" firmari, atque sepiri:
" Tum vero fluvium
" Acherontem occurrere;
" deinde Cocytum: Qui-
" bus trajectis, ad Mi-
" noem & Radamantum
" deduci oporteat, in eum
" locum, qui Campus Ve-
" ritatis appellatur. Ibi
" judices sedent, qui
" quam quisq; vitam vix-
" erit eorum, qui illuc

" veniunt, quibusque in
" studiis versatus sit, dum
" in corpore esset, quæ-
" stionem habent. At
" nullus ibi mendacio re-
" lictus est locus. Illos
" vero, qui boni dæmo-
" nis ductum auspicium-
" que sequuti vitam es-
" sent imitati Deorum,
" Beatorum, Piorumque
" sedes incolere. Ibi tem-
" pestates anni frugum
" omnis generis copia &
" ubertate abundare, fon-
" tes aquis limpidissimis
" scatere, herbis variis
" prata convestiri. Illic
" Philosophorum scholas
" esse, theatra Poetarum,
" & circulares choros,
" musicas auditiones, op-
" portune composita con-
" vivia, & dapes, quæ
" ultro ex ipso solo sup-
" peditantur, & immor-
" talem lætitiam, omni
" denique jucunditate
" perfusam vitam. Non
" enim vel iniquum fri-
" gus, vel intemperatum
" calorem ibi dominari,
" sed bene temperatum
" aërem diffundi, subtili-
" bus solis radiis illustra-
" tum. Ibi vero ipsis
" initiatis quendam esse
" principatum, & sacra
" diis recte fieri. Quo-
" rum

3

"rum autem vita per sce-
"lera traducta est, rap-
"tari a furiis ad Erebum
"& Chaos per Tartarum.
"Illic impiorum profliga-
"torum esse sedem desti-
"natam - - Ibi eos fe-
"rarum laniatu, & ignis
"flammis perpetuis, omni
"supplicio affectos, æter-
"nis pœnis cruciati-
"busq; vexari. Atq; hoc
"quidem ego a Gobria
"audivi."

HISTORIA SECUNDA.

Hic narratur de Muspellsheimio. & Surtio (Nigro).

OMNIUM primo erat Muspellshei-mium, quod ita nominatur. Hoc est lucidum, ac fervidum, atque impervium exteris viris. Niger dominatur ibi, & sedet in extremitate terræ. Ille tenet flamantem gladium manibus. Et in fine mundi est ille venturus, ac vincet omnes deos, atque comburet hoc universum (cum) igne. Ita dicitur in Vaticinio Sibillæ *; *Niger venit ab austro, Cum stratagematibus fallacibus. Splendet ex gladio Sol volubilis. Saxa & montes fragorem edunt; Sed dii perturbantur. Calcant viri viam mortis; Sed cœlum diffinditur.* Gang. perconctatus. Quomodo ordinatum fuit antequam familiæ, seu homines essent, populusque augeretur. Tunc Resp. Har.

* Islandicè, *Voluspa.*

HISTORIA TERTIA.

Hic narratur de creatione Ymii Gigantis.

AMNES illi, qui vocantur Elivagæ, funt ita procul progreffi ab fcaturigine fua, ut veneni volubilitas rigefceret, tanquam fcoria in fornace. Hoc fiebat glacies, ac fubftitit, nec manavit. Tunc fuperfufum fuit heic, & quicquid veneni induratum fuit, gelu obriguit, auctaque fuit pruina, altera fuper alteram, per totum Abyffum. Tunc Excelfo æqualis*; Abyffus, ad feptentrionem fpectans, oppletum eft mole, ac gravitate pruinæ, atque glaciei; fed intus, turbinibus, ac tempeftatibus. Auftralior vero pars elevebatur adverfus fulgetra, & fcintillas, quæ volarunt ex Mufpellfheimio. Tunc dicit Tertius †: Uti ex Niflheimio fpirabat frigidum, ac horridum: ita omnia, Mufpellfheimio oppofita, erant fervida, & lucida. Sed Abyffus erat levis, tanquam aura fine vento. Et cum fpiritus

* Ifl. *Jafn-Har*.   † Ifl. *Thridi*.

caloris

caloris occurreret pruinæ, liquefacta fuit, & destillavit. Et per POTENTIAM EJUS, QUI GUBERNABAT, fiebat homo, Ymius vocatus. Rimtussi (Pruinæ gigantes) vero vocarunt eum Oergelmium: Et ex illo propagatæ sunt eorum familiæ, uti hisce per hibetur. *Sunt fatidicæ omnes E Vittolfio; Spectra omnia E Vilmœdio; Gigantes omnes Ex Ymio progeniti.* Et iterum: *De Elivagis stillarunt veneni guttæ, eratq; ventus, unde fiebat gigas.* Ex quo familiæ provenere omnes. Tunc locutus est Ganglerus: Quomodo crescebant familiæ inde, seu, num creditis, eum Deum esse? Tunc regessit Jafnhar. Nequaquam credidimus nos, eum esse Deum. Malignus enim erat ille, & ejus progenies, quæ Rimtussi sunt. Et ille dormiens sudavit, & sub sinistra manu ejus crescebat mas, & fœmina. Et alter pes ejus procreavit filium cum altero, & inde familiæ venere. Tunc locutus est Ganglerus: ubi habitabat Ymerus, aut quid fuit alimentum ejus? Har respondet:

HISTORIA QUARTA [*].

De eo, quod creata sit vacca Oedumla.

PROXIMUM hoc erat, quod pruina stillavit, unde fiebat vacca Oedumla. Quatuor amnes lactei manabant ex uberibus ejus, illaque alebat Ymium. Vacca vero alebatur lingendo pruinosos lapides, salsugine obductos. Et prima quidem die, ea lingente, crines exiere humani: secunda die, Caput: Tertia vero, integer mas, nomine Buris celebratus; pater Boreæ, cujus conjunx Beizla, filia Bœldornis gigantis. Hisce tres fuere filii; Odinus, Vilius, Veus. " Et hoc nobis persuasum est, inquit
" Har, hunc Odinum, ac fratres ejus, esse
" gubernatores totius orbis atque terræ.
" Et hic ille est Dominus, quem, sine pari,
" magnum esse, novimus."

[*] Fab. III. apud Mallet, vid. p. 18.

HISTORIA QUINTA*.

Quomodo filii Boreæ crearent cœlum & terram.

BOREADES occiderunt Ymium, & tam multum sanguinis ex illo profluxit, ut hocce suffocarint omnes familias Rimtussorum, uno tantum excepto, una cum domesticis suis. Illum Gigantes nomine Oergelmeri insigniunt. Hic ascendens cymbam suam, conservatus est. Et hinc Rimtussorum familiæ.

Perplurimis annis, Antequam terra esset Creata iterum, tunc erat Bergelmer natus, Quod ego cumprimis memini, Sapientem gigantem Cymbæ fuisse impositum & conservatum. Iterum Gangl. Quid tunc negotii Boreadibus, quos Deos esse, credis? Har resp. Hoc non parvi est momenti: Hi enim ex Ymio, in medium abyssi translato, fecerunt Terram; ex sanguine Maria, & Aquam; Montes ex ossibus; Lapides ex dentibus. Et ex ossibus cavis, permixtis cum sanguine, ex vulneribus profluente, illum creaverunt

* Fab. IV. apud Mallet, vid. p. 22.

Lacum

Lacum seu Mare, quo terram circumligarunt. Deinde e cranio factum Cœlum circumcirca super terram posuerunt, quatuor divisum in plagas; cuilibet angulo sustinendo supposuere pygmæum, quorum nomina: Oriens: Occidens, Septentrio, Meridies. Deinceps assumtos ignes ex Muspellsheimio, & infra, & supra, per Abyssum collocarunt in cœlo, ut lucerent in terram. Hi locum certum fulgetris assignarunt omnibus. Hinc dierum exstitit distinctio, annorumque designatio. Ita dicitur. *Sol nesciebat, Ubi locum haberet, Luna nesciebat, Quid virium haberet. Stellæ nesciebant, Ubi locum haberent.* Tunc locutus est Gang. Magna hæc sunt facinora, magnaque fabrica. Har respondet: Rotunda est terra, & circumdata profundo mari: hujusque littora gigantibus inhabitanda dederunt. Sed intra littora, inque illo loco, qui a mari quaqua versum æque distabat, Urbem erexerunt contra incursiones gigantum, circum circa terram: Materiam autem huic moli struendæ suppeditarunt supercilia Ymii, nomine Midgardiæ imposito. Ex cerebro vero, in aërem projecto, Nubes fecerunt: uti hic narratur: *Ex Ymii carne erat Terra creata iterum. Sed ex sudore Maria: Montes ex ossibus: Prata graminosa ex crinibus: Sed ex capite Cælum: Verum ex superciliis fecere mansueti dii Midgardiam hominum filiis: Et ex cerebro erant duri animi (crudeles) Nubes.*

AMBU-

HISTORIA SEXTA.*

De Creatione Aſki & Emlæ.

AMBULANTES juxta littora Boreades invenere duas arbores, ex quibus duos creaverunt homines. Hiſce Primus Boreadum dedit animam, Secundus vitam; Tertius vero auditum & viſum. Vocatuſque fuit mas Aſkr, fœmina vero Emla. Unde prognatum fuit genus humanum, cui habitatio data erat ſub Midgardia. Deinde in medio regni Aſgardiam exſtruxere. Ubi habitabat Odinus, & illorum familiæ, quibus noſtræ originem debent. Adhuc Har: ibi ſita eſt urbs, nomine Hlidſkialf, & cum Pantopater heic ſupremo inſidet throno, oculis totum perluſtrat mundum, hominumque mores omnium. Conjunx ejus eſt Frigga, Fiorguni gigantis filia. Et ex hac proſapia familia Aſarum oriunda eſt, quæ Aſgardiam veterem ædificavit, eſtque divinum genus, cum ſit pater omnium Deorum. Terra erat filia ejus; horumque filius fuit Aſa Tor.

* FAB. V. apud Mallet, vid. p. 28.

HISTORIA SEPTIMA*.

De Nore Gigante.

NORUS gigas, primus fuit Jotunheimiæ incola. Filia ejus erat Nox; quæ nigra fuit. Hanc uxorem duxit Naglfara, quorum filius fuit Auder; Filia vero illorum Terra. Hujus maritus erat Dæglinger, quorum filius fuit Dag, (Dies) qui pulcritudine patrem suum æquavit. Tunc Pantopater assumtos Noctem & Diem in cœlum transtulit, deditque eis duos equos, duosque currus; & hi terram circumequitant. Nox insidet Rimfaxæ, qui terram irrorat guttulis, ex fræno stillantibus: Dies vehitur Skinfaxa, & splendet aura atque terra ex juba ejus †.

Mundilfara duos habuit liberos; filium nempe, nomine Manæ (Lunæ,) filiam vero, Solis, quæ uxor fuit Glorniris. Dii

---

* Fab. VI. apud Mallet, vid. p. 33.
† Rimfaxa, h. c. equus pruinosæ jubæ. Skinfaxa h. est, equus jubæ splendentis.

vero irati huic fummæ arrogantiæ, in tantis affumendis nominibus, hos trahendo currui Solis, quem ex igne de Mufpellſheimio volante creavere, junxerunt. Mane (Luna) duos rapuit liberos a terra, nomine Bil & Hiuka, difcedentes a fonte Bygvaro. Situla nominabatur Sæger: Vectis vero Simul. Patri illorum Vidfidris fuit nomen. Hi liberi Lunam comitantur, uti terricolis apparet. Tunc Gang. Celerrime currit Sol, veluti pertimefceret aliquid. Refp. Har: Prope adeft, qui ei inhiat: lupi duo nempe, Skoll & Hattius Hrodatvitnii filii. Tunc Gang. Quale eft genus luporum? Har refp. Gigantea quædam fœmina habitat ad orientem a Midgardia, in fylva Jarnvid nominata, & ita nominantur illæ giganteæ mulieres hic habitantes. Turpis & horrenda anus eft mater multorum gigantum, omniumque lupina forma indutorum. Hinc ortum eft monſtrum Managarmer, quod faturatur vita morti vicinorum hominum, & deglutit lunam, tincto cœlo fanguine; Tunc fplendor folis deficit, uti hifce narratur. *Verſus ortum habitat illa miſera in Jarnvide, & parit ibi Feneris filios: Ex quibus omnibus fit vaporis quædam exhalatio, Lunam devoratura, Gigantcis induta exuviis; Saturatur vita morti vicinorum hominum; Aſpergit deos (rubore ſanguinis) cruore: Niger fit ſol ſequenti æſtate: venti maligni erunt. Scifne hoc?*

GANG.

HISTORIA OCTAVA *.

GANG. Ubi iter a terra ad cœlum? Har ridens refpondet, hoc non fapienter effe interrogatum : Eftne hoc narratum, deos ponte junxiffe cœlum & terram, nomine Bifrœft celebrata ? Eam te vidiffe, oportet : fieri poteft, ut eum nomine Iridis infigniveris. Tribus conftat coloribus, & longe firmiffimus; factufque majori artificio, quam aliæ fabricæ. Licet vero firmiffimus fit, attamen frangitur, cum Mufpellii filii eum fuper equitant. Et tranatant equi illorum magnos amnes, deinde iter conficiunt. Tunc Gang. Non videtur mihi, deos fideliter hunc exftruxiffe, cum tamen, quicquid velint, facere valeant. Tunc Har: Non funt dii ob hanc fabricam vituperio digni. Bonus pons eft Bifrœft. Nulla vero pars in hoc mundo datur, quæ fibi confidere poteft, Mufpellfoniis exeuntibus vaftatum. Gang. pergit: Quid egit Pantopater, exftructa Afgardia? Har regeffit : In initio difpofuit gubernatores, fingulos fingulis infidentes foliis, juxta ejus mandatum lites hominum

* FAB. VII. apud Mallet, vid. p. 40.

dijudicaturos. Et confeffus judicum fuit in valle, nomine Idæ inclyta, in medio urbis. Primum illorum fuit opus, quod aulam exftruxerint, in qua duodecim illorum folia funt: excepto illo, quod poffidebat Pantopater. Hæc aula, artificiofiffima fua fabrica, omnes in terra domos vincit. Hic eft Gladheimium (Gaudii habitatio.) Aliam ædificarunt, in qua variæ variorum deorum fimulacra confpiciebantur; hæc Deabus fuit affignata; fuitque aula optima & pulcerrima. Hanc vocant homines Vinglod (Veneris & amicitiæ aula.) Proximum, fabricabant domum, in qua difpofuerunt fornacem; nec non malleum, & forcipem ac incudem, atque omnia reliqua inftrumenta. Deinde produxerunt metallum, lapides & lignum & perplurimum illius metalli, quod aurum vocatur; & omnem fuppellectilem, & phaleras equorum, ex auro fecere, unde HÆC ÆTAS AUREA falutatur: Antequam dilapidarentur hæ divitiæ a mulieribus de Jotunheimia oriundis. Tunc dii infidentes fedibus fuis regiis, in memoriam revocabant, unde Pygmæi ortum haberent, in pulvere nempe terræ, tanquam vermes in cadavere. Pygmæi primo erant creati, & vitam nacti in corpore Ymii, & tunc vermes erant; fed juffu deorum humanæ fcientiæ participes fiebent & habebant formam humanam, attamen intra terram habitabant &

in

in lapidibus. Modsognerus fuit primus illorum, & tum Dyrinus. Ita carminibus Sibillinis: *Tunc ibant. V. A. S. G. H. G. & ea de re hic consilium ineundum, Quis nanorum Principem rursus crearet, Ex ponte sanguineo Et luridis ossibus, Humana forma perplurimas, Fecere Nanos, in terra, uti illos Dyrinus docuit, eorumque recensens nomina:* Nyi, Nithi, Nordri, Suthri, Austri, Vestri, Althiofr, Dualin, Nani, Niningr, Dani, Bivor, Baur, Bambaur, Nori, Orr, Anar, Onni, Miothvitner, Viggr, ok Gandalfr, Vindalfer, Thorin, Fili, Kili, Fundin, Valithior, Thorin, Vitr, ok Litr, Nyrathr, Recker, Rathsvithr. Hi sunt nani atque, in saxis habitant: (Illi autem priores in pulvere:) Dramr, Dolgthuari, Har, Hugstar, Hleitholfr, Gloni, Dori, Ori, Dufr, Andvari, Heftifili.—Har dicit. Hi vero venerunt a Svarnis tumulo ad Oervangam, quod est in Juro campo, et inde venit Lofar. Sed hæc sunt nomina eorum: Skirver, Verver, Skatithr, Ai, Alfr, Yngvi, Eikinskialli, Falr, Frosti, Fidr, Ginar. Tunc quæsivit Ganglerus:

HISTORIA NONA *.

De sacris Deorum urbibus.

QUÆ est Deorum Metropolis, sive urbs sacra? Ad hæc Har: Sub fraxino Ygdrasili † dii quotidie sua exercent judicia. Tunc G. Quid de hoc loco dicendum est? reposuit Jafnhar: Fraxinus hæc est maxima & optima arborum omnium. Rami ejus per totum diffunduntur mundum cœloque imminent: Tribus innititur radicibus, perquam late patentibus: Harum una inter Asas; altera cum Rimtussis, ibi, quo olim erat abyssus: Tertia est super Nisheimio. Et sub hac radice est Hvergelmer fons. Nidhoger subtus radicem arrodit. Sed sub illa radice, quæ ad Rimtussos spectat, est inclytus fons Minois, in quo sapientia & prudentia absconduntur. Et appellatur ille Minos ‡, qui hunc possidet fontem: hic est abunde instructus scientia & sapientia, quippe qui fontis aquam ex cornu Gialliæ bibet.

* FAB. VIII. apud Mallet, vid. p. 49.
† Islandicè, *At aski Ygdrasils.*
‡ Isl. *Mimr.*

Aliquando venit Pantopater impetraturus unicum hauftum ex cornu; fed oculorum fuorum unum pignori prius daret. Uti in Carm. Sibill. perhibetur. *Omnino novi, Odine, Ubi oculum abdidifti; In liquido illo fonte Minois. Libat mulfum Minos Quolibet mane fuper pignore Pantopatris. Scifne hoc? nec ne?* Tertia radix fraxini fuper cœlum eminet: & fub hac radice eft Urdar Brun (fons præteriti temporis.) Hic diis locus eft judiciis faciendis. Quolibet die Afæ ad cœlum equitant per pontem Bifrœftam, qui et jam Afopons nuncupatur. Hæc funt nomina equorum Afarum: Sleipner eft optimus, octo gaudens pedibus, eum poffidet Odinus. II Gladerus; III Gyllir; IV Skeidbrimer; V Slintopper; VI Sinir; VII Gils; VIII Falofner; IX Gylltopper; X Letfeter. Eqvus Apollinis una cum ipfo crematus fuit. Torus autem ad locum, judiciis habendis confecratum, iturus, pedes proficifcitur, vadando amnes, nomine Kormt, Gormt, Kerlœger. Hos Torus vadando trajiciet fingulis diebus, quibus venit judicaturus ad fraxinum Ygdrafil; cum Afopons totus flamma exardet; aquæ autem facræ inundant. Tunc G. Num ardet ignis fuper Bifrœftam? Har refp. Quod in Iride confpicis rubrum, eft ignis ardens in cœlo. Tunc cyclopes calcaturi effent Bifrœftam, fi cuilibet iter pateret profecturo. Perplurimæ funt urbes in cœlo amœnæ, omnefque
divina

divina custodia munitæ. Ibi sita est urbs sub fraxino juxta fontem, & de hac aula prodeunt Virgines, ita nominatæ, Uder, Verdanda, Skuld. Hæ virgines hominum dispensant ætates. Has vocamus, Nornas, seu Parcas. Adhuc plures sunt Parcæ, singulos adeuntes infantes recens natos, ut ætatem creent. Hæ Divinæ sunt originis. Aliæ autem Alfarum progenies. Illæ vero Nanorum filiæ: uti hisce perhibetur. Diversas origine credo Parcas esse, Nec minus stirpis. Quædam Asarum filiæ; quædam Alfarum; quædam sunt filiæ Dvalini. Tunc locutus est Ganglerus; Si Parcæ hominum fatis imperant, tunc dispensant admodum inæqualiter. Quidam gaudent prosperis rebus & divitiis; quidam vero inopia rerum laudumque laborant: Quidam longævi sunt; quidam brevi vitam agunt. Har respondet: Bonæ Parcæ, quæ melioris sunt generis, bonæ quoque ætatis auctores sunt. Illi autem homines, quibus malum quoddam contingit, Parcis id adscribant malignis. Tum sermocinatus est ulterius Ganglerus; Quæ plura de fraxino sunt dicenda? Har: Plurima *;

AQUILA

* In Resenii Edit. hæc habemus. "Mytholo-
"gia XVII. Unde tanta
"existat diversitas, quod
"æstas calida sit, hyems
"frigida. Svasudur vo-
"catur qui pater est æsta-
"tis (delicatus & blan-
"dus:) ab ejus nomine
"Svasligt dicitur (quic-
"quid

"quid delicatum eft &
"gratum.) Sed pater
"hyemis interdum *Vind-*
"*lion* (ɔ: Venti Leo,)
"interdum etiam *Vind-*
"*fualur* (ɔ: frigidum fpi-
"rans) appellatur. Ille
"Vafadar (ɔ: frigidus &
"imbres paffus) filius eft:
"Erant autem homines
"illi crudelis & frigidi
"affectus, quorum inge-
"nium hyems imitatur.
"K. Gangl. Unde
"tantum difcrimen ori-
"tur, quod æftas calida,
"hyems vero frigida fit?
"Haar. Non ita quæ-
"reret fapiens, hæc nam
"funt in ore omnium:
"Verum fi ufque adeo
"es infipiens, ut ifta non
"audiveris, interpretabor
"benigne, quod femel,
"licet fatue quæras:
"quam carum rerum,
"quas fciri oportet, ultra
"ignarus maneas."

HISTORIA DECIMA.

De fraxino Ygdrafil.

AQUILA quædam ramis fraxini infidens multarum rerum eft gnara. Inter oculos ejus fedet Accipiter, qui Vederloefner vocatur. Sciurus, nomine Rottakofter, fraxinum afcendendo, & defcendendo difcurrit verba afportans invidiæ, inter aquilam & Nidhoggium. Quatuor vero cervi percurfitant ramos, arboris corticem devorantes, qui ita nominantur: Danin, Dvalin, Dyneger, Dyradror. Sed adeo multi ferpentes funt in Hvergelmio, apud Nidhoggium, ut enumerare nulla queat lingua; uti
hifce

hisce narratur. Fraxinus *Ygdrasil plura patitur, Quam ullus mortalium cogitatione assequi valeat.* Cervus depascitur inferius (rectius, cacumen,) Sed circa latera putrescit. Nidhoggius arrodit subtus. Et iterum : *Serpentes plures, Fraxino Ygdrasil subjacent, Quam cogitavit insipiens quidam.* Gonius & Monius, Sunt Gravitnis filii; Grabaker, & Grafvollduder, Osnerum & Svafnerum Credo assidue aliquid consumere. Præterea narratur, Parcas, ad Urdarum fontem habitantes, quotidie aquam de fonte haustam, una cum circumjacente luto fraxino superfundere, ne rami ejus putrescant, aut marcescant. Illa vero aqua adeo sancta est, ut omnia hâc tincta fiant candida instar membranulæ intra putamen ovi latitantis, Skiall vocatæ : uti hisce testatur Sibilla [Voluspa] : *Fraxinum novi stantem, Vocatam Ygdrasil, Proceram & sacram Albo luto. Hinc venit ros, Qui in valles cadit ; Stat super virente Urdar fonte.* Rorem hinc venientem vocant homines Mellis Rorem, & hinc apes pascuntur. Aves duæ nutriuntur in fonte Urdari, Cygni nominatæ, quibus originem debet hoc genus volucrum.

TUNC

HISTORIA UNDECIMA.*

TUNC locutus est Gangl. Perplurima tu potes enarrare: Quænam vero sunt plures urbes sacræ adhuc ad fontem Urdar? Har: Multæ sunt urbes ibi pulcerrimæ. Harum unam, Alfheimium dictam, incolunt Fauni lucidi. Nigri vero Fauni inferiora terræ viscera tenent, suntque aliis hominibus dissimiles visu, at magis factu. Lucidi solem claritate, at nigri picem nigredine, vincunt. Ibi sita est urbs, nomine Breidablik, quæ nulli pulcritudine est secunda. Nec non alia vocata Glitner, cujus parietes & omnia sunt auro micantia & rutilantia, ita etiam tectum est aureum. Ibi est urbs Himinborg, juxta terminum cœli sita, ad finem Bifrœstæ, ubi cœlum tangit. Ibi permagna urbs nomine Valascialf. Hanc ex puro argento ædificatam & tectam fecere dii. Ibi etiam est Hlidscialf, in hac aula; quod solium ita vocatur. Cum Pantopater

* FAB. IX. apud Mallet, p. 57.

sedet

sedet in summo throno totum circumspicit mundum. In australi parte orbis est urbs omnium ornatissima, solequelucidior, quæ Gimle appellatur. Hæc permanebit, coelo terraque pereuntibus; illiusque urbis incolæ sunt viri justi, in secula seculorum; testante Sib. *Curiam novi stare, Sole clariorem, Auro tectam, In Gimle, ubi debent virtuosi Homines habitare, Et per omne ævum gratia frui.* Tunc Gang. Quis custodit hanc urbem, cum nigra flamma exuret coelum ac terram? Har respondit: Ita dictum est, ad austrum alium esse mundum, hoc longe altiorem, Vidlæn dictum. Tertium vero hoc altiorem, nomine Oendlangeri, & in hoc coelo hanc esse urbem suspicamur, jam vero Faunis lucidis esse habitaculum solis.

HISTORIA DUODECIMA*.

Narratur hic de nominibus & regno Odini.

TUNC locutus Gang. Quinam sunt Asæ, in quos credundum est? Resp. Har: duodecim sunt Asæ Divinæ originis. Tunc loquebatur Jafnhar. Nec sunt Asy-

* Fab. X. apud Mallet, vid. p. 61.

niæ

niæ minus fanctæ, neque minoris potentiæ: Tunc dicit Tertius: Odinus eft Primus & Antiquiffimus Afarum. Ifle gubernat res omnes, & licet reliqui Dii fint potentes; attamen ei ferviunt omnes tanquam liberi patri fuo. Frigga vero uxor ejus etiam hominum fata præfcit, licet nulli revelet res futuras, ut perhibetur, Odinum Loconi adlocutum effe: *Infanum te, immo mente captum dico, quare excitas auram fatorum hominum? Friggam fcio fcire hoc cum ipfe ei revelem.* Odinus vocatur Pantopater, quoniam ipfe eft pater deorum omnium. Vocatur etiam Valfader, quia ejus optati filii funt, qui in acie occumbunt. Hifce Valhallam affignat, atque Vingolfam; tunc Monheroes falutantur. Ille vocatur etiam Hangadeus, Happadeus, Farmadeus; Et adhuc plura habet nomina, veniens ad Regem Geirraderum; vocatus fui inquit Grimr, ok Ganglri, Herian, Hialmbri, Theckr, Thrithri, Thuthruthr, Helblindi, Har, Sathur, Svipall, Sangetall, Herteitr, Hnikar, Bileygr, Baleygr, Bolverkr, Fiolner, Grimnr, Glapfvithr, Fiolfvithr, Sithhottr, Sithfkeggr, Sigfothr, Atrithr, Hnikuthr, Alfothr, Farmatyr, Ofki, Omi, Jafnhar, Biblindi, Gelldner, Harbarthr, Svithur, Svithrir, Jalker, Kialar, Vithur, Thror, Jalkr, Veratyr, Gantr.

Tunc Gang: Perquam plurima affignaverunt eidem nomina: & hoc mihi perfuafum

fum eft, multum requiri fcientiæ, ut diftincte noveris hæc nomina, & quænam cujuflibet fuere occafiones. Har refp. Ifta omnia rite commemoraffe, magna quidem eft eruditio. Sed ut brevius dicam: Pleraque nomina ei funt attributa hanc ob rem, quod variæ fint linguæ in mundo: Attamen omnibus populis placuit ejus nomina in fuam transferre linguam, ut eum fua adorent pro femetipfis. Verum quædam occafiones obvenere in itineribus ejus, quæque prifcis Hiftoricis infertæ funt. Tuque non potes viri eruditi nomen mereri, nifi has magni momenti narrationes enarrare valueris.

* Gang. Quænam funt reliquorum deorum feu Afarum nomina? Aut quid gloriofum patrarunt?

* Hic incipit FAB. XI. apud Mallet, p. 65.

HISTORIA DECIMA TERTIA.

Hic agitur de Toro ejufque regno.

TORUS eft præcipuus & primus illorum, vocatufque fuit Afo Torus, feu Oeko Torus. Is fortiffimus Afarum & omnium deorum, virorumque. Ejus regnum eft est Drudvanger, Aula vero Bilſkirner. In hoc aula quingenta ſunt pavimenta & quadraginta. Hæc domus est maxima omnium, hominibus cognitarum: ita in Grimneri ſermonibus, *Quingenta pavimenta & quadraginta, Talem credo Bilſkirnerem, cum curvis atriis, cujus tecta magnifica maximi filiorum natu non adeo accurate novi.* Torus duos habet hircos & currum: illorum nomina ſunt Tangnioſter & Tangriſner. Curru Torus vehitur Jotunheimiam aditurus, hircis trahentibus currum; ideo vocatur Oeko Torus. Tria illi etiam ſunt clenodia. Primum est Malleus Miolner, quem Rimtuſſi & Gigantes agnoſcant, in aura venientem. Nec mirum hoc est; nam illo multa confregit capita patrum cognatorumque illorum. Alterum clenodium ei est præſtantiſſimum, Cingulum Fortitudinis: Quo accinctus duplici divino perfunditur robore. Tertium clenodium ejus ſunt Manicæ Ferreæ, quibus, capulum mallei apprehenſurus, carere nequit. Nemo vero adeo eruditus est, qui ejus maximas res geſtas enumerare poſſit. Tibi vero plurima enarrare queo, ut dies deficiat prius, quam enarranda. Tunc Ganglerus: Scire cupio de pluribus ejus filiis.

* Har: Secundus, inquit, filius est Baldur (Apollo) ille Bonus, deque illo facile est

---

* Hic incipit FAB. XII. apud Mallet, vid. p. 70.

narratu. Ille optimus est, eumque omnes laudant. Hic pulcerrimus est visui, & ita splendens ut radios emittat. Et unica est herba adeo candida, quæ Apollinis supercilio comparetur; hæc omnium est candidissima herbarum. Et hinc ejus tibi æstimanda est pulcritudo & crinium & corporis. Ille Asarum & candidissimus, & pulcerrimus, atque eloquentissimus, ac maxime misericors. Sed hæc ejus naturæ conditio est, ut nemo ejus judicia irrita reddat. In illa habitat urbe, quæ Bredablikia vocatur, & antea commemorata est. Hæc in cœlo est, eamque nihil immundi ingrediatur. Uti hisce perhibetur: *Breidablikia vocatur, ubi Apollo Habet sua palatia undicunque. In ea regione, Qua ego collocatas esse scio columnas, quibus runæ, ad evocandos mortuos efficaces, sunt inscriptæ.* Tertius Asarum est Niordius, habitans Nontunæ, ibique ventorum dominus. Ille sedare valet mare, ventum & ignem. Is navigaturis invocandus est, ut & venaturis. Tantæ ei sunt divitiæ seu opes, ut cuicunque voluerit, potuerit dare regiones & opes. Eam ob rem ille invocandus est. Niordius non est Asarum origine, erat enim educatus in Vanaheimia. Vani vero eum obsidem diis tradiderunt, ejusque loco assumto Hæniro. Hinc pax deos inter & Vanas. Niordius uxorem habuit, nomine Skadæ, filiam Tiassii gigantis. Illa eandem, ac

pater

pater ejus, elegit habitationem; nempe in montibus quibufdam, nomine Tronheimiæ inclitis. Niordius autem juxta mare habitare voluit. Hinc inter illos conventum fuit, ut novem noctes in Tronheimia, tres vero Noatunæ, tranfigerent. Niordius autem de montibus Noatunam redux, ita cecinit. *Mihi ingrata funt montana, Diu dolui ibi, Licet novem tantum noctes: Lupi ululant; Mihi difplicuit cantus Cygnorum.* Tunc Skada: *Num quiete dormiam in toro Neptuni? Ob avium quærelas, Me excitantium, De fylva venientium Quolibet mane.* Tunc Skada montana petens habitavit in Tronheimia, & fæpenumero, affumtis ligneis foleis, atque arcu, exit feras venatura. Vocatur alias Ondurdea, feu Ondurdis. Uti hifce dicitur: *Tronheimia vocatur, Ubi habitat Tiaffius, Ille potentiffimus gigas. Jam vero ibi Skada habitat, Diferta Nympha deorum, In domibus antiquis Patris.*

HISTORIA DECIMA QUARTA.*

De Freyero.

NIORDIUS Noatunenfis deinde duos procreavit liberos; Frejerum nempe, deorum celeberrimum, atque dominatorem pluviæ folifque, ut & terra nafcentium. Ille vero pro annona & pace invocandus eft. Eft etjam pacis & divitiarum humanarum difpenfator. Liberorum ejus altero loco eft Freja, dearum celebratiffima. Ejus habitaculum in cœlo vocatur Folvanga. Eique pugnam adeunti dimidia pars cæforum cedit, reliqua vero Odino. Uti hifce commemoratur. *Folbvanga appellatur ubi Freja dominatur, In pretiofa & optima aula. Dimidiam cæforum eligit illa, Quotidie, Dimidiam vero partem Odinus.* Aula etiam ejus vocatur Seffvarna. Profectura vero Cattis fuis vehitur, fedens in curru. Illa adorantibus omnium celerrime opitulatur; Deque ejus nomine hic honoris titulus deductus eft,

* FAB. XIII. apud Mallet, vid. p. 76.

quod nempe Matronæ digniores Freyor feu Fruor vocitentur. Huic optime placent carmina amatoria, eaque amoris gratia adoranda eſt.

Tunc Ganglerus: Magni mihi videntur hi Aſæ, omnes; nec mirum, vos magnis gaudere viribus, cum Deos diſcernere poſſitis, atque ſciatis, quiſnam invocandus ſit de hac vel illa re; ſeu quales preces eſſe debeant. Sed funtne plures dii? Har:

HISTORIA DECIMA QUINTA*.

De Tyro.

ASARUM unus eſt Tyrus (etiam Tyſſus), reliquos audacia & inconſtantia animi ſuperans. Ille victorias diſpenſat. Is bellatoribus eſt invocandus. Tritum eſt proverbium, eum ſalutari Tyro fortem, qui reliquis virtute præſtat. Et hoc unum eſt indicium fortitudinis ejus atque audaciæ; quod, reliquis diis perſuadentibus lupo Feneri, ut ligaretur compede Gleipnero, jam vero renuenti, nec credenti fore, ut ſolveretur, Tyrus manum ſuam ori ejus inſertam

* Fab. XIV. apud Mallet, p. 79.

oppignoraffet. Afis vero eum folvere nolentibus, hic manum morfu præfcidit, in illo artu, qui jam Lupinus vocatur, unde Tyffus monochiros eft. Adeo fapiens eft, ut hinc refultaverit proverbium, Hic TYRI GAUDET SAPIENTIA. Pacificator vero hominum non creditur.

Bragius unus appellatur Afa, fapientia, ut & oris atque orationis gratia excellens. Hic Poëtarum non folum princeps, fed & parens; unde Poëfis Brager nominatur. Deque ejus nomine Bragemadur vocatur, & vir & fœmina, qui præ reliquis majori facundia gaudet. " Uxor Bragii appellatur Iduna, " quæ pyxidi fuæ inclufa, illa cuftodit poma, " quæ Dii fenefcentes guftando, rejuvenefcant " omnes," quod ad crepufculum Deorum durabit. Tunc Gang. Permultum, uti mihi quidem videtur, Idunæ cuftodiæ & fidei dii acceptum referant. Har ridens: Præfentiffimum, inquit, periculum aliquando hinc inftabat; quod tibi proponere poffem: fed reliquorum Deorum nomina eris auditurus.

* Heimdaler appellatur unus Afarum: hic eft Candidus Afa dictus: nec non Magnus & Sanctus. Eum pepererunt novem virgines, omnefque forores. Vocatus etiam fuit Hialmfkidius, & Gulltannius, quoniam dentes ejus de auro fuere. Ille habitat ibi,

* Hic incipit FAB. XV. apud Mallet, vid. p. 82.

quod

quod Himinsborgum vocatur, ad Bifrœftam. Hic Deorum cuftos, fedet juxta terminum cœli, impediturus, quo minus Gigantes pontem invadant. Ille minore, quam avis, indigens fomno, noctu æque ac interdiu, ultra centum gradus circumquaque perfpicit. Auditu percipit herbas crefcere e terra, & lanam in avibus, & omnia fonantia. Ei præterea eft tuba, Giallarhorn dicta, cujus vox per omnes auditur mundos. Uti hifce: *Himinborgum vocatur ubi Heimdaler habitat, Narratur eum facræ Deorum cuftodiæ imperare: Bibet in fecuris palatiis deorum mulfum.* Et adhuc in ipfius Heimdaleris Carmine: *Novem fum ego Virginum filius: Novem fum ego Sororum filius.*

Hœder etiam Afis adnumeratur, qui cœcus eft. Hic valde robuftus eft; fed & dii & homines optarent, ut nemini hic Afa effet nominandus. Nam ejus factorum memoria diu manet. Vidarus vocatur Taciturnus Ille Afa; cui admodum fpiffus eft cothurnus. Hic ad Torum fortitudine proxime accedit, unde etiam diis magno eft folatio in omnibus periculis. Atlas, qui & Valius, vocatur unus filiorum Odini & Rindaris. Hic virtute militari & arte fagittandi perplurimum eft pollens. Ullerus appellatur filius Sifiæ, Tori privignus. Qui etiam fagittarius promtus, tamque peritus currendi foleis ligneis, ut cum illo certare poffit nemo.

Formofus

Formosus est valde ut & heros : Unde hic monomachis est colendus. Forsetus nuncupatur filius Apollinis & Naunæ, Nesii filiæ. Is eam in cœlo habet aulam, quæ Glitner vocatur. Omnes vero ad eum causas deferentes discedunt reconciliati. Hic & diis & hominibus optimus est judicii locus. *Glitner appellatur aula, Quæ est auro fulta, Et argento fulta: Ibi vero Forsetus habitat, Plerisq; diebus; Et soporat cunctas causas.*

HISTORIA DECIMA SEXTA *.

Hic agitur de Locone.

IS etiam Asis adnumeratus fuit, quem nonnulli Asarum Calumniatorem, seu Deorum hominumque Delatorem, vocitant. Hic nominatur Loco, seu Loptius, filius Fœrbæti Gigantis. Mater ejus vocatur Lafeya, seu Nal. Fratres ejus sunt Bileiptius & Helblindius. Loco est formosus & venustus; ingenio malus, moribus varius, illâ scientiâ, quæ perfidia & fraus in rebus gerendis dicitur, omnes post sese relinquit.

* FAB. XVI. apud Mallet, vid. p. 85.

Asas

Afas fæpenumero in fumma præcipitavit pericula, & fæpius eofdem a periculis liberavit, technis & fraudibus fuis. Uxor ejus eft Siguna; filius vero Narius feu Narfius. Præterea plures habuit liberos. In Jotunheimia fuit gigantea quædam mulier, nomine Angerboda. Ex ea genuit Loco tres liberos, potius monftra; Primum erat Fenris Lupus. Alter Jormungarder, hoc eft Midgardiæ ferpens (Oceanus): Tertius eft Hela (infernum). Sed cum hi Loconis liberi in Jotunheimia educarentur, & dii oraculis edocti, fibi plurima ab hifce liberis finiftra redundatura: cum maternum genus peffimum effet omen; fed adhuc pejus paternum. Tunc Pantopater deos, ut hos fibi afportarent liberos, emifit. Quibus allatis, angvem in profundum projecit mare, quod totam alluit terram; Et crefcebat hic angvis adeo, ut circumcirca omnes extendatur terras, in medio jacens maris & ore caudam apprehendens. Hellæ vero in Niflheimium projectæ poteftatem dedit in novem mundos: ut habitacula diftribuat inter illos, qui ad eam fint venturi; hi funt omnes morbis aut fenio confecti. Illa ibi habet magna palatia diligenter adornata, magnifque munita cancellis. Ipfum ejus palatium Aliudner vocatur. (CONTINUA MISERIA): Menfa eft FAMES: ESURIES cultellus: PROREPENS MORS fervus: SPECTRUM ancilla:

PRÆ-

PRÆCIPITANS FRAUS cancellus: PATIEN-
TIA limen, seu introitus: DIUTURNUS
MARCOR & ÆGRITUDO lectus. HORREN-
DUS ULULATUS tentorium ejus. Ejus dimidia pars cærulea, reliqua vero humana
cute & colore cernitur, unde dignosci potest.

HISTORIA DECIMA SEPTIMA*.

De Lupo Fenere & Asis.

LUPUM domi nutrivere Asæ; Tyro
solo ei escam porrigere auso. Dii vero,
cognito, eum tam multum quotidie crescere,
& innuentibus vaticiniis, fore, ut illis no-
ceret, inito ergo consilio, factam compedem
fortissimam, vocatam Leding, lupo obtule-
runt; rogantes, ut hac vires suas experiretur.
Lupus vero hanc sibi ruptu non impossibilem
videns, permisit ut pro lubitu facerent uti
volebant. Sed quam primum artus disten-
deret, fracta compede, ex Lædingo fuit so-
lutus. Asæ ergo aliam fecere compedem,
duplo fortiorem, Dromam vocatam. Hanc
lupo tentandam voluerunt, dicentes eum

* FAB. XVII. apud Mallet, vid. p. 90.

tam

tam dura compede fracta, magnam fortitudinis reportare laudem. Lupus vero suspicatus fuit, hanc esse fortissimam; suas vero vires post fractam priorem acrevisse. Etiam meminit, " pericula esse adeunda celebri evasuro," ergo sese compediendum permisit. Quod cum Asæ peractum dicebant, lupus sese volutans, compedem terræ allidendo, & constringendo, extensis membris, frangebat compedem, ut particulæ in longinqvum dissiparentur. Et hoc modo ex Droma excussus fuit. Hinc proverbium, SOLVI EX LÆDINGO, ET EXCUTTI EX DROMA, De rebus vehementer urgendis. Postea pertimuerunt Asæ, ut lupus posset vinciri. Tunc Pantopater virum, nomine Skirnerum, in Svart Alfheimiam, ad Pygmæum quendam, qui nervum Gleipnerum conficeret, ablegavit. Hic nervus sex constabat rebus, strepitu nempe pedum felis, ex barba mulieris, radicibus montium, nervis ursinis, halitu piscium, & sputo avium. Licet vero antea has narrationes non sciveris; attamen vera invenias argumenta, me non fuisse mentitum: cum certo videris, mulieres barba, cursum felis strepitu, montes radicibus, carere. Et hoc mihi certo certius constat, omnia, quæ tibi retuli, esse verissima. Licet essent quædam res, quas experire nequires. Tunc Ganglerus: Hæc, quæ jam retulisti atque exempli loco attulisti verissima credo; sed qualis

qualis facta erat compes. Har, hoc, inquit, bene enarrare poffum. Erat illa glabra, & molliffima, inftar ligulæ ex ferico confectæ: attamen, adeo firma & fortis, uti jam eris auditurus. Afæ vero, hoc fibi adferentibus vinculum gratibus folutis, lupo fecum avocato in infulam lacus Amfvarneri Lyngvam, oftenfam ligulam ferici, fortiorem, quam craffities præ fe ferre videretur, effe dixerunt, rogantes ut difrumperet. Præterea alter altero ligulam tradidit tentantes finguli manibus rumpere, vinculo manente illæfo. Nihilo tamen minus fore, ut lupus rumperet. Tunc lupus refpondet: ita mihi videtur de hac vita, ut nullam promeream laudem difrumpendo adeo mollem ligulam. Si vero dolo confecta eft, aut arte, licet minima videatur, nunquam meos conftringet pedes. Tunc Afæ refpondent, futurum effe, ut quam facillime vinculum ferici adeo molle & tenue rumperet, cum celerrime confregerit fortiffima ferrea vincula. Si vero, ajunt, folvi nequiveris, Diis formidine effe non potes; quam ob rem ftatim te folvemus. Ad hæc lupus: fi me ita vinculis conftrinxeritis, intelligo, me a vobis fero folutum iri. Invitum ergo me hac ligula vincitis. Ne vero timiditatem mihi objiciatis; porrigite unus quifque veftrum manum fuam, ori meo inferendo in pignus, hoc fine dolo effe. Tunc Afæ mutuo fefe
adfpicientes,

adspicientes, geminum jam adesse periculum censuerunt. Nec ullus suam porrexit, Tyro excepto, qui dextram porrectam rictui ejus inseruit. Jam Asæ funem vinculi, Gelliæ nomine, per foramen saxi tractam imis terræ visceribus fixerunt, assumtum lapidem Dvite vocatum imponentes, ut profundiora peteret, cujus fundamen est saxum quoddam. Asæ, cognito jam, lupum satis compeditum, atque frustra renitentem, cum eo fortius constringeretur vinculum nec felicius artus distendentem, cum ligamen eo redderetur constrictius, in risum sunt soluti omnes, Tyro excepto, manum suam jam amittente. Lupus, rictu vehementer expanso, eos morsurus erat, vehementer sese volvens. Tunc rictui ejus immiserunt ensem quendam, capulo inferius, cuspide vero palatum, transfigente. Is truculenter ululando spumam emittit ex ore, unde amnis, nomine Vam (vitia). Hic jacebit ad Ragnarœk.

Gang. Pessimam Loco procreavit prolem; singulis vero hisce magnis, quare Dii lupum non interfecere, cum malum præberet omen? Har: Adeo magni fecerunt Dii sanctuaria sua & Asyla sua, ut eadem cruore lupino maculare noluerint, licet vaticinia indicarent, eum Odino fore exitio.

GANG.

HISTORIA DECIMA OCTAVA*.

De Asyniis.

GANG. dixit: Quænam sunt Asyniæ. Har: *Frigga*, ait, est Primaria, quæ aulam habet, nomine Fensaleris, longe ornatissimam. Secunda Dearum est *Saga*, habitans in Svartbeckio. *Oer* Asarum medicus est. *Gefion* alia vocatur, cui virgines post fata serviunt. *Fulla* illibata est virgo, cujus crines in humerum sunt demissi, capite vitta cincto aurea, eique pyxis Friggæ concredita est, ut & ejusdem calcei: nec Friggæ arcanorum est nescia. *Freyia* pulcritudine ad Friggam proxime accedens, nupsit viro nomine, Odero. Hæc adeo formosa fuit, ut de ejus nomine res prætiosissimæ Nossæ vocitentur. Oderum, in terras perquam dissitas profectum, lacrymans, quæsivit Freyia: Lacrymæ vero ejus sunt aurum obrizum. Perplurima ei sunt nomina; idque eam ab rem factum est, quod multa

---

* Fab. XVIII. apud Mallet, p. 96.

assumsit,

assumsit, apud varios populos Oderum investigatura. Vocatur vero *Mardœla, Hœna, Gefna, Syra*, &c. nec non *Vanadis*. Pretiosissimam habuit catenam auream. *Siofna*, amoris viros inter & fœminas est conciliatrix; unde amori de ejus nomine cessit titulus Siofna. *Lovam* *invocare & memores esse, perutile est, eique permissum est a Pantopatre, seu Frigga, copulare homines, antea prohibitos: de ejus nomine Lof † denominatur. *Vara* ad juramenta hominum & singulare negotium mares inter & fœminas attendit. Unde hæc negotia Varar ‡, (h. e. celanda, & cautissime tractanda.) Vara est admodum sapiens & perconctatrix adeo, ut nihil ei occultare queas. Est etiam proverbium; Mulier fit Vara. *Synia* est janitrix aulæ, occludens fores non intromittendis. Hæc in judiciis hisce præfecta causis est, quas negare volunt homines. Hinc proverbium: Synia negaturo adest. *Latona* § a Frigga ordinata est custos illorum hominum, quas Frigga a periculo liberatura occultat: Hinc communi sermone fertur, eum latere ||, qui occultatus fuerit. *Snotra* est sapiens & bene morata; & ex ejus nomine Snotra dicitur & mas & fœmina. *Gnam* in varias mundi partes Frigga suorum

* Isl. *Lofn, &c.*
† Anglice, Love.
‡ Ang. Wary.

§ Isl. *Hlin.*
|| Isl. *Leinir*, i. e. Latere.

negotiorum gratia ablegat. Hæc eum habet eqvum, qui & aërem & flammam percurrere valet. Factum est aliquando, ut Vana quidam eam equitantem per aera conspiciens dixerit. *Quis ibi volat? Quis ibi ambulat? Aut quis in aëre vehitur?* Hæc respondet: *Non ego volo, Attamen procedo, Tamen per aera vehor, insidens Hofvarpnero illo; quem Hattstryker ex Gardvora genuit.* Hujus Nymphæ nomen deinde translatum est ad omnia, quæ alte per aera ferri videntur, quæ eam ob rem GNÆVARI dicuntur. SOL & BIL quoque Asarum in numero sunt. Suntque adhuc plures, ministrantes in Valhalla, potum inferendo, mensæque & poculorum curam gerendo, quæ ita in Grimneri Rythmis: *Ristam & Mistam mihi volo cornua porrigant ; Skegoldam et Scogulam, &c.* Illæ pocula promant Monheroibus. Hæ vocantur Valkyriæ, quas Odinus prœliis interesse jubet, interficiendos electuras, victoriamque concessuras. *Guder* & *Rosta*, & Nornarum natu minima, *Skulld* vocata, quotidie equitant cædendos electuræ, & cædibus committendis imperaturæ. *Jord* mater Tori & *Rinda* mater Atlantis [*], deabus quoque adnumerantur.

[*] Islandicè, *Vala*.

GYMER

HISTORIA DECIMA NONA *.

Frejerus ducit Gerdam.

GYMER nominatus fuit vir quidam, cujus uxor erat Oerboda. Hic fuit monticolarum genere. His fuit filia, nomine Geradis *(Isl. Gerde)* mulierum formosissima omnium. Frejerus aliquando Lidaskialviam ascendens totum perlustrando orbem, cernit in septentrionaliori regni parte, villæ cujusdam ædificium magnificum, atque ab hoc mulierem egredientem, cujus crines ita rutilabant, ut & aer & aqua illuminarentur. Et ita ejus fastus, in sanctissimo ascendendo solio, punitus fuit, ut summa indignatione abierit, domumque redux dormire non potuerit. Adveniens vero Skirner, profectus inventæ Geradis amorem Frejero conciliavit; huic abituro Frejerus suum tradidit ensem, unde Belum, obviam sibi iturum, pugnis interficere deberet. Periculosius vero est, si sit inermis, cum conflictandum erit cum Muspellsoniis, vastatum exeuntibus. Tunc Ganglerus,

* Fab. XIX. apud Malle., p. 102.

HISTORIA VICESIMA*.

De cibo & potu Afarum.

QUID dat Odinus tam multis hominibus, si omnes in acie cæsi eum advenerint. Har: Permagna quidem ibi est multitudo hominum; attamen non justo plures æstimantur, veniente lupo. Nunquam tam multi fieri possunt, ut deficiat lardum apri, Særimneri. Quolibet die elixatus, accedente vespera integer conspicitur. Pauci vero hoc tibi enarrare possunt. Andrimner coquus, cacabus vero Eldrimner, vocatur. *Andrimner imponit Eldrimnero Særimnerum coquendum.* Pauci vero sciunt, quo *Monheroes vivant.* Tunc Gang. Num Odino eadem est mensa, ac Monheroibus? Har: Cibum, suæ impositum mensæ, inter duos distribuit Lupos, quos possidet, ita vocatos; Geri (bellator) et Freki. Nec ei opus est cibo: sed vinum illi & cibus & potus est: uti hisce testatur Sibilla [Voluspa]:

* FAB. XX. apud Mallet, vide p. 105.

Geronem

Geronem & Freconem faturat bellis affuetus atque celebris ille exercituum pater. Sed folo vino victoriofus Ille Odinus perpetuo vivit. Corvi duo humeris ejus infidentes fufurrant omnia illi in aures nova, quæcunque aut viderint, aut audiverint. Hi ita nominantur: Hugin, (animus) & Munin (memoria): Qui ab Odino emiffi, toto pererrato mundo, ad vefperam revertuntur; hinc nomen, Corvorum Deus, uti hifce dicitur. *Hugin & Munin quotidie Jormungandum fupervolant. Vereor, ut Hugin revertatur: Attamen magis expecto Munin.* Tunc Gang. Qualis Monheroibus potus, qui æque ac cibus fuppetat? Num aqua ibi eft potus? Har: Infipienter jam quæris, Pantopatrem nempe invitatis ad fe Regibus & Jarlis[*] aquam porrigere bibendam. Multi enim Valhallam advenientes, reputarent aquam hoc modo jufto carius emi, fi ibi uberius non daretur gaudium. Nempe, qui antea vulnera & cruciatus paffi funt, ufque ad mortem. Capra vero, nomine Heidrun, ftans Valhallæ, folia ramorum carpit arboris, Leradæ vocatæ. Ex ubere autem ejus tam multum manat lactis, ut hoc omnes capulæ impleantur, quæ adeo magnæ funt, ut Monheroibus fufficiant omnibus. Iterum Gangl. Artificiofa hæc eft capra; fed arborem illam, optimam effe, quam illa depafcitur, crediderim. Tunc Har: Plus de cervo Tak-

---

[*] i. e. Ducibus. Hing. Aa.l. Earls.

dyrno,

dyrno, ſtante Valhallæ, atque ramos hujus arboris depaſcente: de cornibus vero ejus adeo multum vaporis exhalat, ut hoc deſcendente in Hvergelmium, inde amnes, ita vocati oriantur; Sider, Vider, Sækin, Ækin, Svoll, Gundro, Fiorni, Fimbulthul, Gipul, Gioful, Gomol, Gerumul. Hi regionem Aſarum perfluunt. Præterea hi nominantur: Fyri, Vintholl, Holl, Grader, Gundro, Nautt, Reytt, Naunn, Hraumn, Vina, Veglun, Thiothnuma. Tunc Gangl. Magna domus Valhalla ſit, neceſſe eſt, & vix ac ne vix quidem introitus & exitus per fores tantæ pateat multitudini? Har: *Quingentas portas Et quadraginta, Valhallæ eſſe puto. Octingenta Monheroes, Exeunt per ſingulas portas, Proceſſuri Teſtibus ſtipati certatum.* Ganglerus, Magna, ait, Valhallæ eſt multitudo hominum: ſed quæ Monheroum recreatio, quando non poculis indulſerint? Har: Veſtibus induti inque aream egreſſi, nobili certamine, mutuiſque cædibus cadunt omnes. Hic eſt ludus illorum. Et ad meridiem, Valhallam omnes incolumes reverſi, convivantur uti hiſce indicat Sibilla*, *Omnes Monheroes in Odini urbe ſeſe mutuo cædunt. Quolibet die Cædem iligunt: Et equitant inde incolumes, Sedent magis læti, unus cum altero.* Gang. Unde oritur ventus? Hic eſt fortiſſimus, agitans magna maria, nec videri & cerni poteſt,

* Voluſpa.

unde

unde miraculo non caret ejus creatio? Har: In boreali mundi extremitate fedet gigas, nomine Hræfvelger, aquilæ indutus uxuviis; quo volatum intendente, oritur ventus fub alis ejus: uti hifce narratur, *Hræfvelger vocatur Gigas, qui boreali in cardine cœli fedet. Gigas in forma aquilæ; Ab alis ejus Ferunt ventum excitari, Super omnes homines.* Et iterum: *Fraxinus Ygdrafil Eft optima arborum; Skidbladner navium; Odinus Afarum; Sleipner equorum; Bifræft pontium; Bragius Poetarum; Habrocus accipitrum; Sed canum Garmnr.* Gang. Unde ortus Sleipner eqvus?

HISTORIA VICESIMA PRIMA*.

Quomodo Loco procreavit equum Sleipnerum cum Svadilfaro.

FABER quidam Afas adveniens, ad urbem illis ædificandam per tres annos fefe obtulit, eamque adeo munitam, ut tuta effet ab incurfionibus Gigantum. Mercedem vero laboris Frejam poftulavit, ut & lunam folemque. Dii vero, inito confilio,

* FAB. XXI. apud Mallet, vid. p. 112.

paciscuntur; si vero quid laboris prima die æstatis superesset, præmium amitteret; nullius vero opera ei uti liceret. Hic de auxilio equi sui Svadelfari tantum pactus fuit. Omnia vero hæc fiebant, dirigente & instigante Locone. Hic urbam ædificaturus, noctu per eqvum lapides attraxit. Asis mirum videbatur, eum tam magnos adferre montes; nec non equum plus, quam fabrum, conficere. Pacto autem multi interfuere testes: quippe cum gigas videretur non satis tutus inter Asas, si hic esset, Toro domum reverso. *Qui jam mari Baltico trajecto, hinc per amnes & fluvios ad Asiam progressus,* (quod priscis Austerveg audit) *bellum cum gigantibus gessit.* Urbs fuit munita & tam alta, ut perspicere non valeres. Tribus vero reliquis fabro diebus, Dii congregati solia sua ascendentes quæsiverunt, quisnam auctor esset, ut Freya in Jotunheimiam elocaretur? ut & aer perderetur, inducta cœlo caligine, sublatum solem & lunam dando gigantibus. Illos vero inter conventum fuit, Loconem hoc dedisse consilium. Dicebant, eum misera morte afficiendum esse, nisi rationem, qua faber mercedem amitteret, inveniret, adjicientes fore ut statim illum comprehenderent. Examinatus vero jurejurando promisit se effecturum, ut faber mercede frustraretur, quicquid tandem huic negotio impenderet. Fabro autem

lapidis

lapidis advehendi caufa, cum Svadilfaro, egreffuro, ex fylva profiliit equa quædam folitaria, equo adhinniens. Quam confpicatus equus, in furorem actus, rupto fune, eam adcurrit, jam in fylvam accelerantem, infequente fabro, eqvum affecuturo. Equa vero totam per noctem difcurrente, faber impeditus fuit, quominus, hac nocte, una cum die fequente, opus, uti antea, fuerit continuatum. Quo cognito, animo percellitur giganteo. Quo vifo, juramentis non parcentes Torum invocarunt: qui ftatim adveniens, vibrato in aera malleo, dataque mercede, occifum fabrum in Niflheimium detrufit. Loconi vero cum Svadilfaro res fuit, ut eqvuleum genuerit nomine Sleipnerum, octo habentem pedes. Hic eqvus eft optimus & apud Afas & apud homines. Ita in carmine Sibillæ [Volufp.] *(Tunc ibant omnes Dii ad fua folia, Et præfagientes Deæ, hoc confiderantes), Quis aërem dolo expofuiffet; Aut generi giganteo Oderi virginem elocaffet: Et violenter tractaffet juramenta. Omnia, hifce exceptis, funt poffibilia. Torus folus adeo promtus eft, ut ingruente periculo, adfit: Rariffime enim fedet tales audiens rumores.*

* Gang. Quid dictum eft de Skidbladnero, & num fit navium optima? Har: Op-

---

* Hic incipit Fab. XXII. apud Mallet, p 116.

tima

tima hæc eft, & fummo artificio confecta, Nagelfara autem eft navium maxima; hanc poffident Mufpellffonii. Nani quidam fecerunt Skidbladnerum & dederunt Frejero. Hæc adeo magna eft, ut par fit omnibus Afis, & quidem armatis ferendis. Velifque explicatis, ftatim ventum nancifcitur fecundum, quocunque fit abitura. Cum vero navigandum non fit, adeo multis conftat partibus, ut complicata, in pera includi poffit. Tunc Gang. Bona navis eft Skidbladner; multum vero artificii adhibitum fuit, antequam ita fuerit confecta. Ganglerus pergit ulterius:

HISTORIA VICESIMA SECUNDA [*].

De Afa Thoro.

NUMNE Torus inciderit in aliquem locum, quo robore & præftigiis fuperatus fit. Har refpondet: Pauciffimi enarrare valeant, quicquam ei occurriffe nimis arduum. Licet vero quædam res ei fuiffent fuperatu impoffibiles, attamen has, allatis

[*] FAB. XXIII. apud Mallet, p. 117.

exemplis,

exemplis, narrare non debemus, cum omnibus credendum eft, eum potentiffimum effe omnium. Gang. Videor mihi jam in eam incidiffe quæftionem, cui explicandæ fufficiat nemo. Refpondet Jafnhar: Audivimus ea, quæ nobis incredibilia videntur: Prope autem fedet ille, qui hujus rei non eft nefcius. Eique fidem adhibere debes, quippe qui jam primum falfa non erit relaturus, qui antea nunquam mentitus. Tunc Gangl. Jam diligentiffime aufcultabo refponfis de hifce rebus. Har:

HISTORIA VICESIMA TERTIA.

Hic incipit Hiftoria Tori & Loconis Utgardiæ.

INITIUM hiftoriæ hæc eft, quod Oeko Torus profectus fuerit hircis fuis una cum Locone: qui, inftante vefpera, ad rufticum quendam diverfi funt. Torus affumtos hircos mactans excoriavit & cacabo impofuit. Caprifque coctis cœnaturus confedit, ruricolam, ejufque liberos, ad cœnam invitans. Filius hofpitis appellabatur Telephus, filia vero Rafca*. Tunc Torus, expanfis

* Ifland. " Thialfi . . . Raufca."

hirco-

hircorum pellibus ut ossa injicerent liberi, mandavit. Telephus vero, cultello fregit crus, medullam nacturus. Torus, transacta hic nocte, mane surgens, vestibus indutus, assumtum Miolnerum vibravit, pelles consecraturus. Statim surgentium hircorum unus posteriore pede claudicabat. Torus, hoc viso, dixit, rusticum, seu domesticos ejus non prudenter tractasse ossa; adjiciens, crus hirci esse fractum. Rusticus, Toro supercilia demittente, trepidavit; & quantum ex visu colligi potuit, credidit fore, ut solo intuitu necaretur. Hic apprehenso capulo mallei manus tam firmiter applicuit, ut condyli albescerent. Ruricola, & domestici ejus pacem supplices petivere, mulcta oblata, si vellet. Torus vero, magno illorum perspecto metu, deposita ira, recepit liberos hospitis, Telephum nempe & Roscam, qui deinde ei servierunt. Relictis hic hircis, in Jotunheimiam profectus fuit usque ad mare, quod tranatans in terram ascendit, comitantibus Telepho, Rasca & Locone. Haud itaque multum progressis patens patuit campus. Totam per diem ambulabant. Telephus, hominum celerrimus, Tori portavit manticam. Cibi penuria laborabant. Ingruente vero vespera, de loco quietis circumspicientes, invenere in tenebris domum cujusdam gigantis, cujus ostium aeque late, ac domus, patuit. Illis
hic

hic noctem tranfigentibus, factum est media nocte, ut terra ingenti quodam motu sursum & deorsum ferreretur, domusque tremesceret. Tunc Torus surgens, vocavit commilitones, qui una cum eo sibi jam prospicientes invenere dextrorsum cameram quandam huic domui contiguam, quam intrarunt. Toro in ostio sedente, reliqui interiora petebant, metu perculsi. Torus vero, apprehenso mallei manubrio, sese defendere decrevit. Hic jam magnum audiverunt strepitum. Adveniente autem luce matutina, Torus egressus vidit virum quendam in sylva requiescentem, haud procul a se. Hic non mediocris staturæ vehementer stertuit. Torus jam intellexerit, qui sonus esset, quem noctu audierint. Toro sese jam cingulo fortitudinis accingenti accrescente robore, expergefactus est hic vir. Quo viso, Torus perterritus malleum vibrare non ausus est, sed nomen ejus quæsivit, qui sese Skrymnerum nominavit: Mihi vero, inquit, non est opus, ut quæram, num tu sis Asotorus: & numne tu chirotecam meam abstulisti? Quam nunc manum extendens assumsit. Torus jam deprehendit, hanc fuisse domum giganteam, in qua pernoctaverint; domunculam vero, pollicis fuisse vaginam. Skrymnero interroganti, annon reliqui una cum ipso proficiscerentur, consentit Torus. Skrymnerus assumtam explicuit crumenam, cibum capturus.

capturus. Torus vero ejufque focii alio in loco. Deinde Skymnerus peras conjungendas voluit, eafdemque affumtas humeris fuis impofuit, iter magnis paffibus ingrediens. Ad vefperam vero locum quietis fub quercu quadam elegit: Skrymnerus Toro indicans fefe cubiturum effe fub quercu atque dormiturum, illis vero, affumta pera, cibum effe fumendum. Skrymnerus vero obdormiens altiffime ftertuit. Torus autem manticam foluturus, nullum explicare potuit nodum; quod incredibile eft dictu. Quo vifo, affumtum malleum capiti Skrymneri allifit: Qui expergefactus fcifcitatus fuit; quænam frons feu folium in caput ejus caderet; feu quid hoc effet. Torus fub alia quercu dormiendum effe, dixit. Media vero nocte Torus, audito rhoncho Skrymneri, arrepto malleo, caput ejus verticem nempe percuffit, idque adeo, ut malleus in caput demerferit. Skrymnerus evigilans quæfit, annon granum quoddam in caput fuum delaberetur: Tuque Tore, quare vigilas? Qui, fefe jam fomno correptum iri, dixit. Jam vero Torus, ei tertium infligere vulnus deftinans, vibrato intenfis viribus malleo, genam furfum fpectantem ita percuffit, ut ad capulum demerferit malleus. Erigens fe Skrymnerus palpata gena, dixit: Quid? num aves quædam, infident fuper me arbori. Præfentire enim videbar, plumam meum in

caput

caput decidere. Quærit etiam: Quare tu vigilas Tore? adesse jam credo Tempus surgendi, vestesq; induendi. Vobis jam non multum super est viæ ad urbem, quæ Utgarda dicitur. Audivi vero, vos susurrasse inter vos, me vobis magnæ staturæ virum videri: ibi autem vobis cernere licebit viros, me majores. Vobis vero ego auctor sum, ne vosmetipsos extollatis. Tales enim homunciones ægre ibi feruntur: aut, quod consultius est, revertimini. Ad aulam vero vobis anhelaturis, orientem versus eundum est. Ego vero ad septentrionem deflectam. Assumtum igitur viaticum dorso suo imponens in sylvam divertitur. Nec relatum accepimus, Asas ei valedixisse. Ille Midgardiam * progressi urbem conspiciunt, in campo quodam sitam, quam visu superaturis capita ad cervices & humeros retroflectenda fuerunt. Porta urbis erat cratibus occlusa, quas Torus aperire non valuit: sed inter clatra irrepserunt. Magnam jam conspicati regiam, intrarunt, & viros heic proceræ staturæ cernunt. Ad solium accedentes Utgardiæ Loconem salutant; qui sero adspiciens iisdem irrisit loquendo: Longum esset de longo itinere interrogare veras narrationes, cum Ocko Torus parvulus quidam puerulus

* Juxta Resenianos codices, ad *Midtry*, Medium diei.

factus est. Major vero revera sis, necesse est, quam mihi appares. Quibus vero artibus excercendis estis assveti commilitones? Nemo enim nostrum est, qui artem aliquam non callet. Loco dicit, nulli hac in aula in cibo sumendo se esse cessurum. Respondet Utgardiæ Loco: hoc etiam artis est, præstito promisso tuo, quod experiendum. Hic ergo viro cuidam, scamno insidenti, nomine Logo, accersito præcepit certamen cum Locone inire. Tunc linter quædam, carne repleta, illata fuit, & in pavimento collocata. Ad alterum finem lintris Loco, ad alterum vero Logus, confedit, uterque, cibum quam celerrime consumendo, in medio lintris subsistentes. Loco jam omnem de ossibus consumsit carnem, at Logus & carnem & ossa & lintrem; unde etiam victor discessit.

* Tunc interrogat Utgardiæ Loco, cui ludo assvetus esset juvenis iste. Telephus respondit se soleis ligneis currendo cum quolibet aulicorum ejus esse certaturum. Ille vero hoc bonam esse artem pronunciat, mandans, ut optime semet præpararet, si hanc excerceret victurus. Egressus ergo multumque progressus accersivit puerum quendam, nomine Hugonis, eique præcepit, primum cum Telepho percurrere stadium. Hugo vero illi adeo antevertit,

---

* Hic incipit FAB. XXIV. apud Mallet, p. 125.

ut

ut juxta metam reverfus eidem obviaverit. Tunc Utgardiæ Loco locutus eft: Magis tibi feftinandum eft, attamen huc advenerunt viri non tardiores. Tunc aliam propofitam metam adveniens Hugo celerrime revertitur, quum adhuc Telepho baliftæ jactus reftaret. Tunc locutus eft Utgardiæ Loco: Optime mihi Telephus videtur currere; eum vero ludendo vincere athletam non crediderim. Tertium vero illis percurrentibus ftadium, experiamur, quis victor fit. Jam vero, Hugone metam contingente, Telephus ad medium ftadii nondum pervenit. Jam fatis hoc experti omnes.

* Tunc Utgardiæ Loco, Quam, inquit, tu Tore, calles artem? Et num tu illis tantum præftas, ac de te relatum accepimus, tuifque facinoribus? Qui refpondet, fe potiffimum bibendo effe certaturum cum aliquo aulicorum ejus. Loco Utgardiæ refpondet: Hoc fiat. Palatium ergo ingreffus, juffit adferri cornu expiatorium, ex quo aulici bibere confveverant. Hoc Toro porrecto, Bene, inquit, bibere videtur, qui unico hauftu exhauferit. Quidam vero duabus vicibus evacuant. Nemo vero adeo eft miferabilis, qui non ter bibendo exinaniverint. Toro videtur hoc cornu non quidem magnum, attamen perquam longum. Vehementer fitiens, cornu ori applicato, ftrenue fibi ingurgitat merum, fæpius fuper

* Fab. XXV. apud Mallet, p. 126.

cornu caput suum non inclinaturus. Remotum autem ab ore cornu intuens, reperiit paulo minus eidem quam antea, inesse. Tunc Utg. Loco. Bene potatum est, non vero adeo multum. Fidem nunquam adhibuissem relaturis, Aso-Torum plus bibere non posse. Altera vice Tibi bibendum est. Torus nihil respondet; sed cornu ori applicatum exhaurire destinavit. Certat jam bibendo quantum valuit. Sed adhuc cernit, minimam cornu extremitatem exaltari non posse. Cornu intuenti apparet, minus quam prima vice exhaustum. Jam vero sine periculo effusionis ferri potuit. Tunc Utgardiæ Loco: Quid, inquit, jam valet Torus? vis jam Tore a talibus abstinere haustibus, & tamen supremus censeri? ita mihi videtur, ut tertia vice bibas, qui haustus tibi maximus est destinatus. Heic vero non tantus haberis vir, quantum Asæ te vocant, si aliis in rebus te præstantiorem non præstiteris. Tunc Torus, ira accensus, cornu ori admoto, quam maxime valuit, bibens certavit. Jam cornu inspiciens cernit, tandem merum paulullum desedisse. Quo cognito, cornu recipiendum porrigit, ultra non bibiturus. Jam Utgardiæ Loco locutus: Facile est visu, potentiam tuam non esse magnam: sed visne ulterius ludere? Torus periculum ulterius esse faciendum, respondit. Mirum vero mihi videretur, si domi essem cum Asis, & tales potiones ibi parvæ

parvæ haberentur. Qualem vero ludum proponitis? Utgard. Loco. Juvenum ludus eft, ut cattum meum de terra elevent. Ita vero cum Afo-Toro loqui non poffem, nifi vidiffem, eum minoris effe virtutis, quam fama mihi vulgaverit. Tunc cattum coloris cinerei fuper pavimentum Palatii profilientem, valde magnum, Torus adgrediens, manu medio ventri felis fuppofita, elevaturus eft. Felis vero incurvans dorfum, & quantum Torus manum fuftulit, felis alterum pedum fuorum elevavit. Tunc Utgard. Loco. Ita evenit, ut cogitavi; felis enim grandis eft, tu vero brevis et parvus. Torus refpondet: Cum parvus fim, accedat huc quilibet veftrum, mecum ut luctetur; et jam quidem cum iratus fum. Utg. Loco. circumfpiciens regeffit: Video hic neminem, qui non ducat fe parum laudis mereri tecum luctando. Advocate igitur anum iftam, quæ me enutrivit, quacum eris luctaturus. Illa enim majores proftravit juvenes, & ut mihi videtur, te non debiliores. De ifta pugna nihil aliud relatum accepimus, quam, quo fortius Torus eam fuerit aggreffus, eo immobilior fteterit. Jam vero, anu excogitante ftratagemata, Torus pedes figere non potuit, facto vero impetu vehementiffimo, Toroque in genua proftrato, finem fieri, voluit Utg. Loco, dicens, Plures Toro non effe ad certamen provocandos.

* Transacta hic nocte, mane Asæ sese ad iter ingrediendum accingunt. Ille [Utg. Loc.] hos per plateam comitatus, interrogat, quænam via Toro ingredienda esset. Torus vero, dicit fore, ut hi homines eum parvulum vocarent virum. Utg. Loco. Jam tibi, urbe egresso, verum dicamus. Nunquam illam fuisses ingressus, si scivissem te viribus adeo prodigiosis pollere uti revera polles. Fascinatio vero oculorum facta fuit primo in sylva, egoque antea tibi obviam factus sum. Teque peram viatoriam soluturo, hæc constricta erat magno ferro. Unde aperiens, via non inventa, malleo me ter percussisti, & licet primus ictus esset levissimus, attamen tantus ut omnino superatus fuissem, si fuisset inflictus. Ast quod videbas in palatio meo rupem quandam, in cujus cacumine tres quadratæ erant valles; una profundissima; hæc fuerunt vestigia mallei tui. Rupem enim ictui opposui. Loco cum Animo, cui nec ille, neque ullus alius antevertere valet. Maxime vero mirum fuit, quando de cornu bibebas, cujus altera extremitas mari adhæret, unde sinuum origo. Posthac elevasti Angvem Midgardiæ, felem sublaturus. Te vero alterum pedum ejus elevante, nos omnes valde perterriti fuimus. Deinde cum Senectute luctatus, existimasti tibi cum anu negotium esse. Eam nemo in genua prostravit. Vos vero me sæpius domi nolite

* Fab. XXVI. apud Mallet, p. 129.

convenire. Tunc Torus, elevato malleo, nullum videt, neque Utgardiæ Loconem, nec urbem.

HISTORIA VICESIMA QUARTA *.

Quomodo profectus fuerit Torus ad extrahendum anguem Midgardiæ.

HIS peractis, Torus domum festinanter reversus, anguem Midgardiæ inventurus, gigantem quendam, nomine Eymeri, adiit. Mane vero, gigas abitum parans, piscandi ergo, Toro comitaturo respondit, talem pumilionem sibi nulli esse auxilio. Frigescas, necesse est, me tam diu, tamque procul a littore, sedente, ac mihi mos fuerit. Torus, ei valde iratus, dixit hoc non esse verum, interrogans, quidnam hamo ad inescandum suspenderetur. Ei hoc acquirendum, dixit Eymer. Hinc Torus, capite uni bovum Eymeri, nomine Himinrioderi, extorto, ad scalmos desidens, fortissime, uti Eymeri videbatur, remigavit. Hic, cognito, perventum esse ad solitum piscandi locum, subsistendum esse, dixit. Toro, se ulterius esse remigaturum, dicenti respondit Eymer, periculum instare a Midgardiæ angue. Toro autem ulterius remigaturo, contristatus fuit Eymer. Torus filum

* Fab. XXVII. apud Mallet, p. 134.

filum piscatorium explicuit, imposito capite hamo, quem profundum petentem devoravit anguis. Qui, transfixo palato, ambos Tori pugnos interscalmio duriter impegit. Hinc Torus, viribus perfusus divinis, tam firmis stetit talis ut, ambo pedes carinam penetrarent, in profundo subsistentes, anguemq; ad latus navis attraheret. Horribilius vero spectaculum vidit nemo, quam quum Torus anguem intuitus, hic vero sursum prospectans venenum spiravit. Gigas metu pallescens, viso angue, undisque in cymbam inundantibus, Toroque malleum apprehendente, arrepto cultello, filum Tori juxta interscalmium praecidit. Anguem vero ad profundum redeuntem malleo percussurus erat Torus; Giganti autem, inflicta, ut caderet, alapa, caput amputavit. In terram vero vadavit. Tunc Gang. Magna haec fuit victoria. Har respondet.

HISTORIA VICESIMA QUINTA *.

De morte Apollinis, atque itinere Mercurii ad infernum.

MAJORIS momenti fuit somnium Apollinis, de ingruente periculo, [Balderi] quod Asis retulit. Frigga pacem & immunitatem ei adprecata est, ne ei esset nocu-

* FAB. XXVIII. apud Mallet, vide p. 138.

mento

mento ignis, aut ferrum, aut aqua, aut metallum, aut faxa, aut arbor; nec morbus, neque animalia, avefve venonofique ferpentes. Quo facto, hic fuit Apollinis ludus, ut eum in concionis medio ftantem, quidam jaculando, quidam cædendo, quidam lapidando, peterent: ei vero nihil nocuit. Quod fpectaculum Ioconi admodum difplicuit. Fenfalam ergo adiit Friggam conventurus, affumta forma anili. Friggæ perconctatæ, quid in conventu agerent, refpondet, omnes in Apollinem jacula mittere, fine ulla ejus læfione. Frigga ait, nec arma, neque ligna Apollini effe mortifera. Juramenta enim ab omnibus accepi. Tunc anus: Num omnia juraverunt, fe Apollini honorem deferre? Refpondet Frigga, arbufculam quandam ad latus occidentale Valhallæ crefcere, nomine Miftiltein, vifamque fibi nimis teneram, quæ juramento obftringeretur. Muliere difparente, Loco ad Miftiltein abiens, eadem radicitus eruta, forum adiit. Hœderus vero in extremitate coronæ fubftitit, cum cœcus effet. Tunc Loco eum alloquens dixit: Quare tu in Apollinem nihil mittis? Hic refpondet: Cum cœcus fim, accedit, quod etiam fim inermis. Loco: Fac tu uti reliqui, cumque adgredere. Ad eum ego te adducam. Mitte in illum hunc baculum. Hœderus affumto Miftilteine Apollinem transfixit. Et hoc fuit infeliciffimum jaculum & inter homines &

inter Afas. Jam alter alterum adfpicit, omnefque facti atrocitate perterriti fuerunt. Nemo vero vindictam fumere potuit, in afylis nempe. Omnes fummopere lugebant, maxime vero Odinus. Hic fine modo fletus fuit. Tunc Frigga dixit, omnes fuos amores demerituro ad infernum effe equitandum Apollinis redimendi caufa. Hermannus, Odini filius, profectus fuit Sleipnero vectus. Navi Ringhornæ Apollo impofitus fuit, quam adduci voluerunt Afæ, cum exftructa pyra. Fieri autem non potuit, antequam advenit Hyrekena, lupis vecta, utens ferpentibus pro habenis. Quatuor Odinus Pugiles, qui furore corripi folerent, equos cuftodire juffit. Hi autem habenas moderare non valuerunt. Illa navem protraxit, primoque attractu ignis fumavit ex lignis fubjectis. Toro autem eandem percuttere volenti obftitere reliqui Afæ. Funus jam Apollinis pyræ impofitum fuit, quo cognito, Nanna, Nefii filia, dolore crepuit. Torus rogum Miolnero confecravit, Nanumque Liten pedibus pyræ admovit. Hic aderant omnes Afæ. Frejer cutru vectus, quem trahebat fus Gallborftius, feu Sligrutannius. Hemdalius Gulltoppio vehebatur. Frejæ vero currum trahebant feles ejus. Hic etiam fuerunt Rimtyffi omnes. Odinus rogo annulum Drypnerum injecit, una cum equo & phaleris.

Her-

* Hermannus per decem noctes equitando pervenit ad amnem Gialliam, adque pontem, auro oneratum. Hujus cuſtos erat Modguder, quæ dixit: Ante lucem Apollo hic prætervectus, una cum quinque millibus: Tu vero ſolus non minorem excitas ſonum. Tunc portam inferni advectus fratrem ſuum conſpiciens, quod ſibi mandatum fuerit, aperuit. Hæc vero ſola erat & unica, conditio, ſub qua demitteretur, ſi res omnes & animatæ & inanimatæ, una cum Aſis, eum deplorarent. Alias in inferno detineretur. Apollo tradidit ei annulum Drypnerum; Nanna vero tranſmiſit cingulum ſuum Friggæ. Fullæ vero annulum ſuum. Tunc Hermannus iterum Aſgardiam adiens hæc narravit.

Tunc Aſæ mandarunt, ut res omnes lacrimis Apollinem ab inferno redimerent. Homines nempe, animantia, terra, & lapides. Arbores, & omnia metalla, Apollinem deplorarunt, uti ſine dubio vidiſti, has res lacrimari omnes tempore frigoris & caloris. Ferunt, Aſas inveniſſe giganteam quandam mulierem in ſaxo quodam, cui nomen Dœka: hac, ut reliqua omnia, juſſa ploratu ſuo Apollinem ab inferno liberare, reſpondet, *Dœkæ plorandum eſt ſiccis lacrimis Apollinis funus: Licet fleant viva ſeu mortua. Retineat infernus quod habet.* Hoc experimentum Loconis fuit.

* FAB. XXIX. apud Mallet, p. 149.

* Quo cognito, Dii Loconi irati fuerunt. Hic vero in monte quodam habitavit, ejusque domui quatuor fuere oftia, ut in omnes plagas circumfpicere poffet. Interdiu vero erat in Eranangeri amnis praecipitio, affumtis falmonis exuviis. Memor fuit, fore, ut Afae fibi infiderentur. Hinc affumtum lineum in feneftratas colligavit plagas, perinde ac rete eft confectum. Tunc Afas advenientes cernit. Odinus eum a Lidafcalvia confpicatus fuit. Loco, reti in ignem projecto, in amnem fefe praecipitavit. Kvafer omnium primo ingreffus, quippe qui fapientiffimus erat, hoc ad pifcandum admodum utile judicavit: Et juxta formam cineris adufti rete aliud confecerunt. Ad cataractam euntes, Torus unum finem folus tenuit, reliqui autem Afae alterum. Loconem vero inter duos lapides delitefcentem caffes praetereunt. Iterum trahentes, adeo rete onerant, ut fubtus elabi nequiret. Tunc Loco, rete fugiens, & ad pontum perveniens, reverfus rete tranfilivit, in cataractam reverfurus. Afae, cognito curfu ejus, in duos diftribuuntur ordines. Torus vadando rete fequitur, & omnes ad ipfum mare ducunt. Loco vero, cognito periculo praefentiffimo, fi in mare reverteretur, rete tranfiliit. Torus autem eum manu apprehendit. Ille vero cum lubricus effet, hujus dextra figi nequivit priufquam ad pinnam

* Fab. XXX. apud Mallet, p. 154.

caudae.

caudæ. Quamobrem falmo hac fui parte tenuiſſimus.

* Loco jam captus atque fine ulla commiſeratione in antrum quoddam traductus. Treſque aſſumtas petras erigentes perforarunt. Loconis etiam filios, Valum nempe & Narium, adduxere, illum transformarunt in lupum. Quo facto Valus Narium dilaceravit. Jam Afæ hujus aſſumtis viſceribus, Loconem ſuper tres acuminatas petras colligarunt, quarum una humeris ſuppoſita fuit, altera lumbis, tertia vero poplitibus; factaque ſunt hæc ligamina ferrea. Skada aſpidem ſuper ejus appendit faciem; Siguna vero pelvim veneni ſtillis exceptis plenam evacuante, venenum in faciem ejus decidit. Hic Loco adeo horret & ringitur, ut terra moveatur. Hic jacebit uſque ad Ragnarœk (Deorum tenebras).

HISTORIA VICESIMA SEXTA †.

De Fimbulvetur & Ragnarœk.

QUID de Fimbulvetur narrare potes? ait Gang. Har: Tunc ex omnibus cœli plagis nix irruet. Tunc vehemens erit frigus atque ventus. Solis nullus eſt uſus. Hæc hyems conſtat tribus hyemibus ſimul,

* Fab. XXXI. apud Mallet, p. 157.
† Fab. XXXII. apud Mallet, p. 159.

nulla

nulla interveniente æstate. Præcedunt autem tres aliæ hyemes, & tunc totum per orbem erunt bella, fraterque alter alterum interficiet, avaritia ductus. Nec patris, nec filii rationem habebunt interfectores : ita dicitur. *Fratres mutuo conflictentur, seque mutuo necent. Tunc consobrini consanguinitatis obliti erunt. Permolestum tunc erit in mundo Multum adulterium : Ætas barbata; ætas ensea. Clypei secantur. Ætas ventosa; Luporum ætas : Usquedum mundus corruat.* Tunc unus alteri non parcet. Lupus solem devorabit; quod hominibus magnum adfert damnum. Tunc alter lupus lunam devorat. Stellæ de cœlo cadunt. Terra tremescit. Montes, & arbores, radicitus evelluntur. Vincula & ligamina rumpuntur. Tunc Feneris lupus solvitur. Tunc æquora in continentem exundant, angue Midgardiano in Jotunheimiam festinante. Tunc navis Naglfara solvitur, quæ fabricata est mortuorum hominum ungvibus. Propterea admittendum non est, ut quis ungvibus non præcisis moriatur, cum hac ratione magna suppeditetur materia navi Naglfaræ, quam sero confectam optarent & Dii & homines. In hac vero maris exuberantia Naglfara undis innatare incipit. Hujus gubernator est Hrymer. Feneris lupus expanso rictu procedit, inferiore maxilla terram, superiore vero cœlum, tangente. Latius adhuc os diduceret, si daretur spatium. Midgardiæ anguis venenum

nenum fpirat, & fuper eum cœlum diffinditur. Et in hoc fragore Mufpellfonii exeunt equis vecti. Primus equitat Surter. Hunc ignis ardens & præcedit & infequitur. Gladius ejus folem fplendore imitatur. His vero equitantibus, frangitur Bifroefta. Hi in campum Vigiridem, fequentibus Lupo Fenere, & angue Midgardiæ vehuntur. Hic adeft Loco, comite Hrymero. Loconem omnes genii infernales comitantur. Mufpellffonii fuum proprium ducunt agmen, admodum corrufcans. Campus Vigiridis eft centum gradus quaquaverfum. Heimdaler cornu Giallinum vehementiffime inflat, Deos excitaturus omnes, ad judicium convocandos. Odinus equitat ad fontem Minois *, hunc confulturus. Tunc Fraxinus Ygdrafil tremefcit; nec ulla res, five in coelo, five in terra, jam timoris eft expers. Afæ armantur, in campum prodituri, una cum Monheroibus univerfis. Odinus omnium primus vehitur, capite aurea caffide confpicuo, lupo Feneri obviaturus. Torus cum angve Midgardiano pugnat. Frejerus cum Surtio conflictatus cadit, optimo deftitutus gladio. Canis Garmer, ad Gniparam lucum alligatus, jam folvitur, cumque Tyro congreditur, amboque cadunt. Torus angvem Midgardiæ occidens, novem faltem greffus venenum ferpentinum præteriens, cadit. Odinum lupus devorat, &

---

* Forfan, 'Frontem Minois.' *Ifl. Minis-brunz.* T.

hæc

hæc est mors illius. Tunc Vidarus accurrens, altero pede inferiorem bestiæ premit maxillam. Huic ille est calceus, qui per longum temporis intervallum confectus fuit, collectis particulis ex calceis, pedicis & calcaneo, aptandis. Hæ ergo particulæ abjiciendæ funt, si Asis consulendum voluerimus. Altera manu superiorem lupi maxillam apprehendens tantopere os lupi dilatat, ut lupus moriatur. Loco & Heimdaler mutuo certamine occumbunt. Tunc Surtius ignem toti injicit terræ, totum exurens mundum, uti his testatur Sybilla [Volufpa]: *Altum inflat Heimdaler Cornu fublevatum: Loquitur Odinus cum capite Mimis: Concutitur Ygdrasil Fraxinus erecta, Personat frugifera arbor. Asæ foro celebrando occupantur. Quid apud Asas? Quid apud Asinias? Ingemifcunt Nani, Ante fores faxeas, Montium incolendorum gnari. Nostifne adhuc? nec ne? Sol obscuratur; Terra mari immergitur. Cadunt de cœlo splendentes stellæ. Ascendit vapor una cum igne. Dominatur vehemens calor, Etiam in ipso cœlo.*

* Gangl. Quid tunc futurum est, exusto cœlo, mortuisque & diis & hominibus omnibus? Har: Quonam in mundo tunc habitabimus? Tunc pergit Tertius Har: Multæ funt mansiones bonæ; & multæ malæ & miseræ. Optimum diversorium in Gimle cum Surtio; & generosissimus potus

* Fab. XXXIII. apud Mallet, p. 164.

sup-

suppeditatur in Brimle, seu in ista aula, quæ Sindri vocatur. Ibi habitant boni viri et justi. In Nastrandis magna est aula, verum pessima. Ostium septentrionem versus spectat. Hæc tota serpentibus constructa est; capita vero serpentina per foramina intus pendent, & veneni adeo multum exsibilant, ut magnus hinc evadat amnis, in quo vadandum est perjuris & homicidis, uti hisce perhibetur: *Aulam novi stare, Procul a sole, In Næstrandis Versus Boream spectant fores. Veneni guttæ stillant per fenestras. Hæc aula facta est ex spinis serpentinis. Hic vadabunt Trans rapidos amnes Homines perjuri, Et sicarii. Sed in Hvergelmio Est pessima conditio; Ibi enim Nidhoggius* (Diabolus) *excarnificat Cadavera mortuorum.* Tunc Gang. Annon adhuc vivent quidam Deorum? Respondet Har: Terra ex mari emergit, admodum viridis, & ornata agris, sine satione frugiferis. Vidar & Atlas * vivunt, nec nigra flamma quicquam damni eis intulit. Hi habitabunt in campo Idæ †, ubi antea erat Asgardia. Huc adveniunt Tori filii, Magnus & Modius, (Mannus), habentes Miolnerum. Huc accedunt Apollo ‡ & Hauderus ab inferis, sermocinando alter alteri, in memoriam res suas ipsorum gestas revocans. De angue Midgardiæ, & lupo Fenere multa commemorant. Tunc aureas, quas Asæ possederant, crepidas ibi in gra-

* In. *Vali.* † In. *Eythu.* ‡ In. *Balldr.*

nine inveniunt; uti hic dicitur: *Vidar &
Atlas Incolent asyla Deorum, Extincta nigra
flamma: Mannus & Magnus Miolnerum habebunt, Vignis filii ad judicium athleticum. Sed
in cadavere Minois latent Nymphæ, graſſante
nigra flamma. Lif & Lifdræſer, ibi in carne
Ymii ſeſe occultant, Et rore matutino nutriuntur per omne ævum.* Sol filiam genuit,
fibi fplendore non cedentem, paterna * cal-
caturam veftigia. *Unicam filiam Genuit rubicundiſſimus ille rex Antequam eum Feneris
devoraverit, Quæ curſura eſt, Mortuis diis,
Viam maternam, hæc virgo.*

Jam cum Ganglerus hæc audiret narrata,
magnus fit ftrepitus, jamque in planitie
quadam conftitutus fuit. Afæ vero, cum
has narrationes audiviffent, antiquorum Afarum nomina fibi tribuerunt, ut, præterlapfo
magno temporis intervallo, nemo dubitaret
hos, qui jam vixiffent, Afas pro antiquiffi-
mis illis Afis, jam commemoratis, reputare.
Unde evenit, ut Auko Tor vocaretur Afa
Tor.

* *Potius,* ' materna.'

FINIS AUSCULTATIONIS GYLFII.

FINIS · EDDÆ.

ADDITIONAL NOTES to Volume I.

Page 13. *line* 6. " Finns or Laplanders *."

* NOTE. Our Author speaks of these, as if they were but one; whereas they are two distinct people.

Page 18. *line* 9. " a language quite different from " theirs *."

* NOTE. It is now said that the Language of the Greenlanders is nearly the same with that of the American Savages in Newfoundland, and on the coast of Hudson's Bay. To prove which assertion, it is related, that a few years ago a Moravian missionary, who had long resided among the Greenlanders, went by the favour of Commodore Palifer to Newfoundland; that he there met with a tribe of Indians, who, at first sight, were shy and reserved, but hearing him address them very intelligibly in a dialect of their own tongue, cried out in a sort of transport, " Our " friend is come!" These Moravians or Hernhuters have, by most disinterested labour and wonderful perseverance, converted to Christianity and civil life great numbers of Greenland savages. See CRANTZ's " Account of Greenland," in 2 vols. 8vo.

Page 105. *line* 19. " scum and ice *."

* NOTE. This part of the Icelandic Cosmogony probably owes its existence to the appearance of the surface of Iceland, which, according to the accounts of Geographers, bears evident marks of fire, and seems to consist chiefly of matter thrown out by Volcanoes.

Page 129. *line* 15. " worship *."

* NOTE. Our Author has here fallen into a small inadvertency; for surely the ancient Worship in
VOL. II.   A a   TEMPLES,

TEMPLES is not proved by the Altars found scattered in the WOODS and MOUNTAINS.

Page 204. *line* 26. " jeering his enemies *."

* NOTE. We have an instance of the same unconquerable spirit, but of much later date, in our own island; which I shall quote from a very curious book lately published. Jevan ap Robert ap Meredith (a Welsh Gentleman in the fifteenth century) having taken two of his countrymen who had been concerned in a murder, " commanded one of his men " to strike off their heads, which the fellow doing " faintly, the OFFENDER told him, that if HE had " HIS neck under his sword, he would make his " sword take better edge than he did: soe resolute " were they in those dayes, and in contempt of " death; whereupon Jevan ap Robert, in a rage, " stepping to them, strucke of their heads." See the history of the Gwedir family, by Sir John Wynne. Lond. 1770. 12mo. p. 107.

Page 296. *line penult.* " a North-east Passage to the " Indies *."

* NOTE. I fear our Author has attributed too much knowledge to our great King ALFRED, and speaks of his attempt with modern ideas. I do not recollect that, in the Anglo-Saxon Relation, there is any mention made of the East-Indies; of which K. Alfred possibly knew nothing: he wanted to have the northern coasts of Europe and Asia explored, probably without knowing where such a voyage might lead to.

Page 309. *Additions to* NOTE (*).

To render the accounts of these excessive entertainments credible, it should be considered, that the ancient Scandinavians had probably large flocks, which were plentifully killed upon these occasions; then the northern seas abound with fish: and their banquets were probably distinguished rather by the quantity of gross simple food, than by the rarity of the viands, or the nice art in preparing them.

Page 367. *addition to the small* NOTE (*).

Vid. *Prefat.* (*à Dom. Joh. Ihre script.*) *in Librum cui Titulus*, " *Differtatione Philologicâ Ulphilas Illuftra-* " *tus, Authore Ericus Sotberg. Anno* 1752. *Holmiæ.* 4*to.*"

Vid. " *Differtatio Academica, de Lingua Codicis Ar-* " *gentei : a Nathaniele Thenftadt. Anno* 1754. *Upfa-* " *liæ* 4*to.*"

" *Differtatio Hiftorico-Philologica de Ulphila feu Ver-* " *fione IV. Evangeliftarum Gothica. Georg. Fredericus* " *Eupelius.* 1693. *Witteburgæ.*"

CORRIGENDA in Vol. I.

Pref. pag. v. *line* 10. *dele* now.
    viii. *note* ‡. *l.* 5. *read.* " **Cantabrigiæ.**"
    xix. *l.* 30. *for* inventive hands, *r.* fruitful invention.
    xxiii. *l.* 6. *r.* it is furprifing that.
    xxvii. *l.* 5. *r.* ULPHILAS.

Page 4. *l.* 23. *for* other fruits of the earth, *read* other productions and advantages.
    11. *l.* 10. *for* n the coafts, *r.* on the coafts.
    17. *l.* 21. *read* " 40 Danifh Miles."
    21. *l. ult. & alibi, for* epoque, *r.* epoch.
    25. *l.* 13. *r.* with fo many.
    80. *l.* 22. *r.* intrepid themfelves.
    ibid. l. 23. *for* derived, *r.* drew.
    81. *l.* 19. *for* features, *r.* traits.
    90. *l.* 2, 3. *r.* his name and worfhip. All that
    91. *note* †. *for* 1748. *r.* 1743. *and fubjoin* T.
    97. *l. laft but* 3. *r.* I fhall only point out.
    101. *l.* 19. *r.* Fulla or Fylla.
    109. *l.* 5. *for* liberty, *r.* freedom.
    ibid. l. 12. *for* in, *r.* into.
    111. *l.* 14. *r.* they are unalterable.
    112. *note* (*) *fubjoin* T.
    117. *ult. dele* here.
    139. *l.* 6. *r.* TEUTAT.
    155. *l.* 19. *r* Harold Harfagre.
    165. *laft line but* 4. *for* a troop, *r.* troops.
    168. *l.* 3. *r.* conq left by Odin.
    192. *note* †. *l.* 8. *for* in proofs, *r.* in proof.
    ibid. l. ult. r. Sun.
    194. *l.* 2 *for* object, *r.* oppofe.
    ibid. l. 7. *for* from, *r.* under.
    197. *l.* 8. *r.* of their childhood.
    ibid. l. 20. *r.* which was fignified by their receiving.
    232. *laft line but* 8. *r.* fields.
    242. *l.* 8. *r.* have the proofs.

Pag. 247. *l.* 19. *for* profeſſions, *r.* traffic.
252. *l.* 13. *for* income, *r.* ſubſiſtence.
261. *l.* 3. *for* derived, *r.* deduced.
291. *l.* 1. *for* manufactory. *r.* factory.
296. *l.* 11. *for* lately was, *r.* was lately.
297. *note*, *l.* 10. *r.* a Norwegian who had been ſent by him into the Northern Seas, to make diſcoveries. The narrative
334. *l.* 10. *r.* in the fifth Century.
354. *l.* 9. *r.* if indeed theſe are not.
357. *note* (*) *l.* 15. *r.* In this, JANUARY
370. *note* (*) *l.* 13. *for* Nander, *r.* Nauder.
381. *l.* 7. *for* have, *r.* hath.
409. *l.* 8. *r.* obſerving other nations.
ibid. *l.* 12, 13. *r.* combats - - - divides - - - triumphs.
410. *note* (*) *l.* 3. *r.* on this ſubject.

CORRIGENDA in Vol. II.

Introd. pag. vi. *note*, *line* 7. *read* Pelloutier.
    ibid. col. 2. *l.* 7. *from the bottom*, *r.* derive their deſcent both from.
    xxxi. *l.* 6. *r.* a pretty thick quarto volume.

Pag. 37. *Cancel the ſmall note* (*).
127. *to the note ſubjoin* T.
134. *l.* 2. *for* Journey, *r.* Voyage.
160. *l.* 13. *r.* render it totally.
195. *note*, *l.* 8. *r.* Puttenham.
196. *to note* (*) *ſubjoin* T.
198, 199. *to the three notes ſubjoin* T.
198. *note*, *col.* 1. *4th line from the bottom*, *r.* Celtic.
209, 215. *to the notes ſubjoin* T.
233. *l.* 2 *for* banniers, *r.* banners.
240. *dele* T *from the note.*
297. *l.* 15. *r.* atque in ſaxis.
299. *l.* 13. *for* et jam, *r.* etiam.
320. *l.* 16. *r.* pretioſiſſimæ.
342. *laſt line but three*, *r.* Apollinis [ſc. Balderi], de ingruente periculo.

FINIS.

www.ingramcontent.com/pod-product-compliance
Lightning Source LLC
Chambersburg PA
CBHW051246300426
44114CB00011B/909